Khap Panchayat, Women and Honour Killing

Khap Panchayat, Women and Honour Killing

Dr Deepa Awasthi

KALPAZ

ISBN: 978-93-5128-207-5

Price: ₹ 990

First Published, 2016

Published by

Kalpaz Publications
C-30, Satyawati Nagar,
Delhi – 110052
E-mail: kalpaz@hotmail.com
Ph.: 9212142040

Printed at: G. Print Process, Delhi

Cataloging in Publication Data—DK
Courtesy: D.K. Agencies (P) Ltd. <docinfo@dkagencies.com>

Khap panchayat, women and honour killing / [editor], Dr. Deepa Awasthi.
pages cm
Includes bibliographical references.
ISBN 9789351282075 (hardback)

1. Panchayat—India. 2. Caste—India. 3. Honour killings—India. 4. Sex discrimination against women—India. 5. Male domination (Social structure)—India. I. Awasthi, Deepa, editor.

HV6250.4.W65K43 2016 DDC 362.880820954 23

Contents

Section–C

Kahp Panchayats, Honour Crimes and Laws

Section–D

Khap Panchayats and other Non-State Agencies

Dedicated to

This Edited book is dedicated to all women, couples and their family members who faced the barbarism of khap panchayats and such type of other self originated illegal social institutions functioning with similar type of close minded feudal approach based on ideology of patriarchy and male dominance.

Acknowledgements

It is my immense pleasure to acknowledge all the learned authors who have contributed their valuable articles and research papers written by them with utmost pain, efforts and investment of time. Without their sincere, fearless and devoted thinking towards the subject of 'Khap Panchayat' - one of the most burning social issue in India and other developing countries, it would have been almost impossible to come up with desired result. I am also obliged to the distinguished panel of reviewers who invested their precious time and hard work in evaluating the contributions from various authors and further guiding them to make their writings focused, clear and appropriate for this edited book. I am also thankful to all my friends, teachers from University of Lucknow and family members who helped and encouraged me from time to time to remain stick to the mission of publishing this book on one of the most discussed and utmost important issue. Last but not the least, I thank to God and all who helped me directly or indirectly at every step and provided me the emotional support to compile this edited book.

—Dr Deepa Awasthi
(Editor)

Author's Introduction

Dr Deepa Awasthi

Ph.D - Education, Department of Education, University of Lucknow, U.P.

Editor of the book and Contributor of articles titled Barbaric Acts of Khap Panchayat-who is responsible? Complete Control over Women: The illegal Intentions of Khap Panchayat; Co-relating the Existence of Khap with skewed Sex Ratio in Haryana; Media Standing Tall Against Feudal Khap Panchayats.

Dr. Deepa Awasthi, Editor of this book is Doctorate in Education and Post Graduate in Education, Sociology and Economics. She has qualified UGC – JRF in Education and Sociology as well and has equal command on both the subjects. She has participated and presented her research papers in more than 50 national and international seminars and conferences. She has also edited a book on sociological issue titled "Eve Teasing: A Social Epidemic" and an Edited book series titled "Girl Education in India – Still Miles to Cover" in three volumes. Her publication work also involves 12 chapters in edited books, three research papers in form of conference and seminar proceedings and 17 research paper and articles in various journals of national and international repute. Her keen interest areas include the sociological issues related to women and various issues related to field of Education.

Vidya Vati

Lecturer [English] in Directorate of Education, NCT of Delhi

Contributor of article titled Past and Present of Khap Panchayats: Social and Cultural Perspective

Author is lecturer [English] in Directorate of Education, NCT of Delhi. For her performance in the field of teaching, she has been honoured with Indira Award and State Teacher Award by Delhi Government, and received a couple of other honours from NGOs and local politicians. She has participated in a number of seminars organised by SCERT and NCERT. Her review of a book 'Srijan' was published in NCERT journal. She has participated and presented her papers in three international conferences. She got prize of best speaker/presenter in her group in conferences. She takes great interest in issues related to women, culture, history, environment and language teaching. Her articles/research papers have been published in various edited books. Before joining the Directorate she worked in Ministry of Commerce, Government of India. She was also selected in Rajasthan Administrative Services.

Dr Mehnaz Najmi

Programme Chair/HOD in Political Science Department at School of Humanities and Social Sciences, Galgotias University, Grater Noida, UP.

Contributor of article titled Socio-political Role of Khap Panchayat in India

Author is a Programme Chair/HOD in Political Science Department at School of Humanities and Social Sciences, Galgotias University, Greater Noida, UP. She is Ph.D in Political Science from Jamia Millia Islamia, New Delhi, M.A. in Political Science from Jawaharlal Nehru University, New Delhi and B.A. (Hon) Political Science from Daulat Ram College, Delhi University. She has also qualified UGC - NET. She has more than seven years of experience in research and teaching. She has participated and presented papers in various national/ International seminars and conferences. Her special areas of interest are Indian politics, poverty, slum studies, woman in political process and minority affairs.

Goldy Gupta

Assistant Professor, K. L. College of Education, Dohki, Rewari, Haryana

Contributor of article titled Affirmative Aspects of Khap Panchayat

Author is an Assistant Professor at K. L. College of Education, Dohki (Rewari). She is post graduate in Mathematics and Education. She also did M. Phil. Education. Her topic of research in M. Phil. was related to personal values of secondary teachers. She also qualified UGC-NET in Education. She has been teaching at College of Education for more than eight years. She has participated in various seminars and workshops related to education. Her publication work involves one chapter in an edited book. She is also in charge of organising in-service Training Camps for Mathematics Secondary Teachers. Her special areas of interest are social issues and Mathematics teaching.

Palwinder Kaur

Senior Research Fellow in Department of Education, Punjabi University, Patiala, Punjab

Contributor of article titled Threatening Khap Panchayats

Author is a Senior Research Fellow in Department of Education, Punjabi University, Patiala. She is post graduate in Education and Political Science and also been awarded UGC- JRF in Education and UGC-NET in Political Science. She did Master of Philosophy (M.Phil.) in Political Science. She also worked as lecturer in Education in Guru Teghbahadur College of Education. She has participated and presented the papers in 13 national/international seminars and conferences. Four articles written by her on various issues have been published as seminar/conference proceedings and in national/international journals. Till now, she has contributed one chapter in distance education departmental notes, Punjabi University, Patiala. She had also worked as field investigator in state of nation survey, 2008 - 2009 conducted by *Lokniti* and sponsored by CNN-IBN and The Indian Express. Till now she has contributed one chapter in edited book titled Eve teasing- A Social Epidemic.

Dr Rashmi Singh

Assistant Professor, Department of B.Ed. Maharana Pratap Government P.G College, Hardoi, Uttar Pradesh.

Contributor of article titled Khap Panchayats and their Discriminatory Practices against Women

Author is Assistant Professor, Department of B.Ed. in Maharana Pratap Government P.G. College, Hardoi, Uttar Pradesh. She is Ph. D. (*Education*), M.Ed. and M.Sc. (*Chemistry*). She has also qualified UGC-JRF (*Education*). Her achievements involve P.C. Bonerjee Award for "Best Research Production of the Year – 2013" for her Doctorate thesis, Smt. Kailashwati Memorial Gold Medal – 2006 for being "Best Woman Student" obtaining the Highest Percentage of Marks in M.Ed. and "Master Kanhaiya Lal Smt. Sunder Devi Memorial Gold Medal – 2005" for obtaining the highest percentage of marks in B.Ed. Till now she has attended a number of seminars and conferences on various issues and various articles/research papers contributed by her, have been published in national and international journals, seminar and conference proceedings and edited books.

Dr Meenakshi Dwivedi

UGC Post-Doc Research Scholar, Department of Education, University of Lucknow, U.P.

Contributor of article titled Equally Unequal: Gender Discrimination in Khap Panchayats

Author is a UGC Post-doc Research Scholar in Department of Education, University of Lucknow, working on the Project for the Education of students suffering from Autistic Syndrome Disorder. She has completed her doctoral thesis on Pains and Gains of Visually Impaired Students Studying in Mainstream Higher Education. She is post graduate in Education, Mathematics and Physics. She has also worked as Assistant Professor (B.Ed) for Seven years. She has participated and presented the papers in 14 national/international seminars and conferences including 102nd Indian Science Congress. More than 13 research papers and articles written by her on various issues have been published in reputed national/international journals. She has also contributed one chapter for an edited book. The teaching and research work of the author is focused on Special Education, Psychology and Mathematics.

Sharabani Mazumdar

Lecturer, Department of Education, Institute for Education, Kolhan University, Jharkhand

Contributor of article titled Khap Panchayat and Discrimination against Women

Sharabani Mazumdar is an aspiring writer and avid reader. She made several trips around different parts of Bihar, Jharkhand and West Bengal during her studies. In this period, she came across different people and their cultures that ignited her passion for acquisition of knowledge of people and their customs. She holds a master degree in English from Indira Gandhi National Open University and Master in Education from Kolhan University. She taught English in Jamshedpur Women's College for one and a half year and currently working as a Lecturer in a B.Ed College, 'Institute of Education' where she is teaching Psychology and Educational Technology. She is an ardent lover of music, painter, good cook and loves travelling. In her spare time, she loves to spend time with nature, friends and family.

Zainab Farhat

Research Scholar, Department of Public Policy, Law and Governance, Central University of Rajasthan

Contributor of article titled Nothing Honourable in Honour Killings: A Study of Khap Panchayats, Honour Killings and the response of Indian Judiciary

Zainab Farhat is Research Scholar and currently pursuing her Ph.D from the Department of Public Policy, Law and Governance, Central University of Rajasthan. As an awardee of Maulana Azad National fellowship, her areas of interest are Minority Studies, Social Exclusion and Governance.

Dr Nagendra Ambedkar Sole

Dean, School of Social Sciences, Central University of Rajasthan

Co-contributor of article titled-Nothing Honourable in Honour Killings: A Study of Khap Panchayats, Honour Killing and the Response of Indian Judiciary

Dr Nagendra Ambedkar Sole is in the Department of Public Policy, Law and Governance and Dean School of Social Sciences, Central University of Rajasthan. He was Formerly Director and Regional Director of Vardhman Mahaveer Open University Kota, and IGNOU respectively and has served as members in various bodies like Academic Council, Finance Committee, Research Council and Board of Management. One of his articles is suggested reading of Department of Public and International Affairs, George Mason University, U.S.A. He has published seven books and 21 articles in reputed Journals and has successfully completed four projects. He has presented papers and chaired sessions of a number of National and International seminars and Conferences. He has 30 years of experience and is also serving as national Vice President of New Public Administration society.

Dr Amit Kashyap

Research Associate, Himachal Pradesh University, Shimla, Himachal Pradesh

Contributor of articles titled A Critical Jurisprudential Appraisal of Law and Justice in Crime of Honour Killings and Role of Khap Panchayats in India and Khap Panchayats: Killing for Honour or for the Ego

Dr Amit Kashyap is Doctorate in Law, with 10 years teaching experience. At present he is working as Research Associate at Himachal Pradesh University, Shimla. He is Post graduate Diploma in Journalism and Computers, Certificate courses in Human Rights and Computers. He is First UGC JRF/SRF in General (Male) Category in Department of Laws, Himachal Pradesh University, Shimla. His keen interest involves Socio-political development of India and Issues related to women and child. He has attended and presented papers in various national and international seminars and conferences. He has published more than 40 articles and research papers in various journals.

Shashi Bala Kashyap

Assistant Professor, SCD Govt. College, Ludhiana, Punjab

Co-contributor of article titled A critical Jurisprudential Appraisal of Law and Justice in Crime of Honour killing and Role of Khap Panchayats in India

Shashi Bala Kashyap is pursuing her Doctorate in Botany, with 14 years teaching experience. At present she is working as Assistant Professor at SCD Govt. College, Ludhiana. She is M.Ed. in Education. Her keen interest involves Socio-political development of India and Issues related to women and child. She has attended and presented papers in various national and international seminars and conferences. She has published more than 25 articles and research papers in various journals.

Sandesh Yadav

Research Scholar, Department of Geography, Jamia Millia Islamia, Delhi

Contributor of article titled Administrative Crisis in Dealing with the Honour Crimes and Khap Panchayats as Agencies of Honour Crimes

Sandesh Yadav is a Research Scholar in Department of Geography, Jamia Millia Islamia, Delhi, and pursuing his Ph.D. on topic "The Impact of Land Cover and Land Use on Urban Environment: A Case Study of NCT of Delhi." He is NET in Geography. His keen interest areas include Urban issues, Environmental and Ecological issues and Gender issues. His publications include 17 research papers in peer reviewed journals and four research papers in International journals. He has contributed five chapters in the edited books on Gender issues and urban geography. He has attended 16 national/international conferences/seminars. He also attended "Research Methodology Workshop" organised by Giri Institute of Development Studies (GIDS), Lucknow, Uttar Pradesh and the "Census Data Dissemination Workshop" organised by the University of Allahabad, Uttar Pradesh.

Dr Amitaraj Gargey

Principal, Daleep Walase Arts, Science and Commerce College, Pune, Maharashtra.

Co-contributor of article titled Khap Panchayats: Killing for Honour or for the Ego

Dr Amitaraj Gargey is Doctorate in English, with 18 years teaching experience. At present she is working as Principal at Daleep Walase Arts, Science and Commerce College, Pune. She is M.Phil. in Education, Diploma in German, and Certificate Course in Computers. Her keen interest involves Socio-political development of India and Issues related to women and child. She has attended and presented papers in various national and international seminars and conferences. She has published more than 18 articles and research papers in various journals.

Dr Nutan Sharma

Assistant Professor, Sri Sai College of Education, Badhani - Pathankot, Punjab

Contributor of article titled Khap Panchayats and Honour Killings

Dr Nutan Sharma is Assistant Professor in Sri Sai College of Education Badhani-Pathankot, Punjab, with more than 10 years teaching experience. He is NET in education and Post Graduate in Mathematics. His keen interest area includes Value Education, Philosophy, Teacher Education, Teaching of Mathematics and Women Empowerment. He has attended more than 23 national and international seminars and conferences. He has published more than 25 research papers in national and international journals. He has guided more than 20 students at Master level.

Professor Haseena Hashia

Senior Professor, Department of Geography, Jamia Millia Islamia, Delhi

Co-contributor of article titled Khap Panchayats as Agencies of Honour Crimes

Professor Haseena Hashia is a renowned Senior Professor in

Department of Geography, Jamia Millia Islamia, Delhi. She is serving the department for the last 21 years and till date 11 scholars have been awarded Ph.D under her supervision. She contributed 40 research papers in national and international journals and five books related to gender issues in the State of Jammu and Kashmir and the NCT of Delhi. She is well known at the international level and attended international conferences held at Baghdad, USA, Indonesia, Malaysia, Iran and Switzerland. She is an adept researcher in Gender issues and the Environmental issues.

Ruchi Dhyani

Senior Research Scholar, Punjabi University, Patiala, Punjab

Contributor of article titled Role of Khap Panchayats in Promoting Honour Killing

Ruchi Dhyani is a Research Scholar in Department of Education and Community Service of Punjabi University. She is Post graduate in Education, Commerce and Economics. Apart from this she has also completed PGDCA. She is UGC-JRF in Education. She worked as lecturer in Education in Punjab College of Education. She participated and presented 14 papers in national, international seminars and conferences. She also contributed one chapter in edited book on Eve teasing. Her four research papers have been published in reputed international journals.

Manvi Manisha Tigga

Post Graduate Teacher, Government School, Simuldanga, Jamshedpur

Contributor of article titled Khap Panchayat as Parallel Judicial System

Author is a voracious reader, a passionate writer and a born story teller. She has completed her Masters in English from the University of Delhi and Masters in Education from Kolhan University. She has worked for 'SRISHTI' publication as a translator for some time, before taking teaching as a profession. She has taught in school as well as college. She has also attended and presented several papers in national seminars. She has worked as Assistant Professor in

Jamshedpur Women's College, Jamshedpur. In her copious free time, she enjoys listening to music, reading, writing and arranging displaced things.

Preeti

Ph.D. Scholar, Department of Geography, Kurukshetra University, Haryana

Contributor of article titled Khap Panchayat, Inter Caste and Inter Religious Love Marriages

Preeti is research scholar in Department of Geography, Kurukshetra University, Haryana. She is pursuing her Doctorate on the topic "Violence against Women in Public and Private Spaces in Haryana." She has her Masters from Delhi School of Economics, University of Delhi. She has interest in issues related to women specifically violence, status, empowerment and development issues.

Introduction

In recent years khap panchayats have emerged as threat to civilisation through their unconstitutional and unlawful dictates imposing various restrictions on girls and youths. Law abiding citizens of country were shocked when media exposed the barbaric and inhuman ways of implementing those dictates. Apex Court of India has also declared them illegal and termed them as 'Kangaroo courts.' Although khap panchayats are particularly functional in few states of Northern India, mainly in Haryana and Western Uttar Pradesh, Rajasthan, Rural belt of Delhi etc. but its ideology based on patriarchy and male dominance is popular all over the country, cases of honour killing are listened in Tamil Nadu and tribal regions of Odisha, West Bengal and Bihar also.

This edited book entitled **'Khap Panchayat, Women and Honour Killing'** is written with the intention to provide complete information about origin, constitution, ideology, functioning, legality and its impact on society. This book contains 20 chapters written by various eminent scholars of their field. Book is divided into four sections –

(A) Understanding the Khap Panchayats

(B) Khap Panchayats and Discrimination against Women

(C) Khap Panchayats, Honour Crime and Laws

(D) Khap and other Non State Agencies

First section (A) of the book titled '**Understanding the Khap Panchayats'** comprises of five chapters giving complete detail about origin, existence, constitution, regional expansion and functioning of khap panchayats. It also deals with the positive and negative aspects of khaps. Second section (B) titled **'Khap Panchayats and Discrimination against Women'** include five chapters discussing the gender discriminatory role of khap panchayats in areas governed by khaps. This section especially focuses on the impact of discriminatory practices promoted by khap panchayats and its impact on their personal development especially by imposing various types of restrictions and bans on young girls. Third section (C) titled **'Khap Panchayats, Honour Crime and Laws'** include seven chapters dealing with the role of khap panchayats in promoting various types of honour crimes including honour killings. Section details the existing legal provisions available to address the illegal acts of khap panchayat. It establishes the need of special laws and provisions specially enacted to counter the menance of khap panchayats. Fourth section (D) termed as **'Khap and other Non State Agencies'** include three chapters focused towards three different issues related to khap panchayats.

Next part of the introduction details about the summary of every chapter one by one in ascending order with the purpose of providing glimpses and idea of contents included in these chapters.

In the first chapter of the book entitled **'Past and Present of Khap Panchayats: Social and Cultural Perspective'** author *Vidya Vati* has highlighted the origin of khap panchayats in India especially in northern India. According to her, usually people are mistaken as khap panchayats are caste panchayat. It is normal in India that different castes like Brahmin, Vaishya, Balmiki and others unite together to form institutions like Brahmin Sabha, Vaishya samaj, Balmiki samaj etc. but khap panchayat are clan or gotra based groups within the caste, especially in Jat community and named these khaps on the name of gotra. Initially this gotra system was popular among Brahmins; they used to name their gotra on the name of ancient Rishis. Following them on similar pattern Jats also developed their gotra system with even more strict rules and regulations. She also focuses on the origin of Jats and tries to link it with the existence of khap system by quoting number of famous historians. Author has also detailed about the existence of khap like institution in other part of country. In the last of the chapter she has mentioned various factors that provide strength to these khap panchayats.

Dr Mehnaz Najmi in her chapter titled '**Socio-political Role of Khap Panchayat in India'** states that existence of khap comes from the concept of extreme belongingness on the basis of blood, birth, proximity and choice. Khap represents the feeling of community and affiliation in northern India, basically cluster or union of villages based on clan as binding force. Although union of such type of villages exist all over the country with other names but the term khap is especially used in few states like Haryana, Western Uttar Pradesh, and Rajasthan. Inter- caste and inter-religious marriages are completely banned in khap governed areas, even marriages in same gotra (clan) or within same village whether belonging to similar or different gotra is also not permissible. In areas ruled by khaps young girls are threatened, abused or killed on regular basis. She also finds that usually khap rules and laws are relaxed for boys but girls are never allowed to surpass them at any cost. Even in case of arrange marriage they find that bride and bridegroom belong to same gotra or same village they interfere on the basis of *bhaichara* (brotherhood). She also views that political leaders of almost all political parties directly or indirectly support them or remain silent, as they fear of losing their vote bank in that particular region. She further mentions that even these khap like institutions do not have any legal sanctity but they make their all possible efforts to be sure that dictates passed by them are implemented word by word. According to author khap has emerged as a result of political vacuum in the region, they are more prominent in areas where political representative do not have substantial political hold. For ending the evil of khap she suggests that youth of India has to come forward to bring necessary social changes. Positive role of judiciary, strict legislation, will of political parties, leadership of social activists, NGOs, pressure of masses and other democratic forces can handle the social nuisance created by khap panchayat but a joint effort is needed.

In the third chapter of the book titled **'Barbaric Acts of Khap Panchayat – Who is Responsible?'** author *Dr Deepa Awasthi* focuses on the various barbaric acts of khap panchayats i.e. killing the couples who opt for sagotra, inter-caste and inter-religious marriages, raping the female family members of accused, compelling the victim to drink urine, publiclly beating, naked parade etc. and illegal verdicts like banning the girls to wear jeans and other tight outfits or banning the use of mobile phones, banning use of D.J., strictly prohibiting sagotra marriages etc. Their negative attitude towards youth especially girls who deny to obey the old ideology of khap is shocking in twenty first century. According to her, inspite of continuous demand of banning the khaps responsible for spreading anarchy in society they exists. Lack of will power in police and administration, ill intentions of political parties and political leaders, negligence of state and central government has provided them strength to stand so firmly. She has appreciated the role of media, judiciary and civil society in creating a negative environment against khap panchayat. Author has detailed the reason for strict involvement of khap panchayats in marriage related issues. She has also evaluated the role of various government and non- government agencies responsible for nourishing khaps. A number of useful suggestions have been given to control the khap panchayats. According to her, beside various legal and administrative initiatives collective effort is needed to aware the common man living in khap ruled areas.

In the next chapter titled **'Affirmative Aspects of Khap Panchayat'** author ***Goldy Gupta*** details that with passage of time Indian society has developed as agrarian society where every village has its own self-sufficient economy and well established self-developed judicial system for redressing the disputes. According to her, in rural areas khap panchayat works similar to Indian families. In family most of the time elderly person or head of the family uses his or her discretion to resolve the issue, their decision is final. Nobody in the family has the right to question his/her decision. In the similar ways elderly, experienced people of clan, caste and community call the meeting where both the parties involved in dispute come together to resolve the issue. According to author, distrust in system due to growing corruption, delay in judicial process, weak Panchayati raj system, inclination of khaps towards socio-economic reforms, ideology of preserving tradition and culture are the few reasons for continuous dominance of khap panchayat, inspite of strong criticism from media, judiciary and civil society. Author finds that media usually discuss the negative aspects of khap, hardly any news reflecting the positive initiatives taken by khap towards social reformation are given importance because media don't find anything sensational in that. Promotion of girl education, movement to stop female foeticide, infanticide, promoting the girls to take up employment and sports and adoption of girl child if parents are unable to bear responsibility are the important aspects often overlooked by the people in society who always see khap related issues with the black spectacles on their eyes. Author wants everybody to recognise khaps for movements like 'Beti Bachao, Selfie Banao' and 'Beti Pao, Dharm Kamao' campaign. Even the Satrol Khap the biggest khap in Haryana has allowed the inter-caste marriages. According to her banning khap panchayat is not appropriate solution, bringing the desired changes from time to time will be the better initiation to build happier society.

Fifth chapter of the book titled **'Threatening Khap Panchayats'** author ***Palwinder Kaur*** focuses on the evolution of khap panchayats in particular region of North India. She has explained the constitution of khaps in detail. She has also highlighted the functioning of khap panchayats with respect to its self-acquired legislative, adjudicative and executive powers. Author also states that although khaps have negative image in the eyes of modern India due to its uncivilised dictates but this do not represents the true picture because khaps also have a history of resolving the social issues like dowry harassment, widow marriages, marriages of poor girls etc. She feels the need of modernisation of khaps so that they can guard their culture and traditions with the help of means acceptable to civilised society. She also suggests that education and media are the tools which can counter the anti-effects of khap panchayat on society.

Dr Rashmi Singh in her chapter titled **'Khap Panchayats and their Discriminative Practices against Women'** states that khap panchayat are collective patriarchal bodies which functions not only as self-governed administrative and judicial bodies following their own rules and regulations but also have political influence in region. She further expresses that inspite of various disputes and criticism khap has dominance in mass and full support of people who are its members. According to author, issues of women rights, gender equality and gender sensitivity do not exist in the territories ruled by khaps. She further mentioned that female foeticide, honour killing, compromised marriages, child marriages, and restrictions on clothing and mobility of girls, denial to property rights are few gender discriminatory practices acquired by khap. Her study suggests that real motive of khap panchayat is to control sexuality for ensuring that property remains within patriarchal caste domain, the property remains the root cause for discrimination against women. Khap members believe that if women are given their due status in society their progress will be threat to their unlimited power. She further suggests that joint effort of politicians, civil society, police, academicians, media personnel and judiciary together can bring revolution to counter the discriminatory practices of khap panchayats. Before concluding the chapter she has made useful suggestions for law and policy-makers do deal with the evil of khap and such type of other institutions.

In the next chapter of the book titled **'Equally Unequal: Gender Discrimination in Khap Panchayats'** author ***Dr Meenakshi Dwivedi*** views that India has male dominant society from centuries and khap panchayats represents similar psychology and ideology of Indian society. Women have always faced the gender based discrimination resulting into poverty, illiteracy, lack of employment opportunities, and low level of awareness. Social customs, practices and beliefs are few common factors responsible for prevailing gender discrimination in society. According to author still huge population in India lives in villages where khap and such type of other institutions existed since ancient times. Basic problem with these institutions is that they denied evolving with passage of time and wanting to remain adheres to century's old ideology. Issues related to dress code for women, inter-caste and inter-religious marriages, marriages within same gotra or same village, honour killing, early marriages of girls, negative attitude on girl education and banning the use of mobile phones makes the situation vulnerable for women in khap governed areas. She further suggests that with more social development and increase in education level the strength of khap panchayats and hard line ideology of caste system is expected to get weaker day by day.

In the next chapter titled **'Complete Control over Women: The Illegal Intentions of Khap Panchayats'** author ***Dr Deepa Awasthi*** states that khap are centuries old institutions used to function on democratic pattern for regulating the social and personal life of individuals including men and women but with advent of civilisation these powers were taken by states. Unfortunately, these institutions were not abolished completely from society; they changed their functioning and restructured their roles. She further mentions that hardly any individual has courage to stand against mighty khaps and few extraordinary people who tried the same are either history today or living in isolation with fake identity. According to her in recent years they have emerged as most prominent agencies promoting violence against women especially young girls who opt to marry a boy of their wish. Most ironical about these khap panchayats is that they are active in region which is considered as developed region of Northern India with high per capita income. She further says that usually khap supporters argue that khap panchayats work on democratic pattern but in reality they are purely undemocratic because without involving almost half of the population of country, no institution can claim to be democratic. She has listed a number of issues on which khap panchayats have interfered unconstitutionally and been criticised due to their inhuman dictates. According to author, youth of India especially girls are no more ready to accept interference of khap panchayats and their ideologies in their life.

Dr Deepa Awasthi in her chapter entitled **'Co-relating the Existence of Khap with Skewed Sex Ratio in Haryana'** states that overall sex ratio of India is much lower as compared to number of other developed and developing countries. Although various government and non-government agencies are making the huge efforts for improving the situation but the results achieved till now are not appreciating. She has compared the sex ratio of khap affected states i.e. Punjab, Haryana, Uttar Pradesh, Rajasthan and Delhi, most of them situated in northern region with other non-affected states. She finds that existence of khap and expansion of its ideology based on male dominance and patriarchy, unfavourable fearful environment created by khap panchayat is directly linked with the declining sex ratio in khap affected region. In her study she has specially taken the case of

Haryana state, which is the centre point of khap politics. She found that none of the districts of Haryana have overall sex ratio or child sex ratio equivalent or near to national average. According to her continuously decline in child sex ratio suggests that crime of female foeticide and infanticide with the help of sex selective technique is still prevailing in Haryana. She also proves that even urbanisation and extensive economic progress of Haryana do not have any positive impact on sex ratio of state.

Sharabani Mazumdar in her chapter titled **'Khap Panchayat and Discrimination against Women'** mentioned that khap panchayat gain their power from deep-rooted traditional caste system and land ownership rights. Her study finds that some of sociological thinkers suggest that first time khap word was used in fourteenth century in Rajasthan during Rajput rulers. She states that social boycotts, monetary fines, honour killings, forcing the victim to commit suicide, gang rapes, compelling to drink urine, naked parade, publicly beating, shaving the head, dipping the nose in urine or rubbing the nose in dust, forcefully compelling individual to touch others feet are the few unlawful dictates given by khap panchayat to create fear in the mind of people especially among youth who neglect or tend to neglect rules and regulations of khap. She has quoted the poll survey of Thomas Reuters conducted in 2011, which suggest that India is fourth dangerous country for women on this earth. She has listed the number of reasons for dominance of khaps inspite of being illegal. She recommends that the darkness created by khap panchayat can only be removed through education and awareness.

Eleventh chapter of the book titled **'Nothing Honourable in Honour Killings: A Study of Khap Panchayats, Honour Killings and the Response of Indian Judiciary'** author *Zainab Farhat and Dr Nagendra Ambedkar Sole* states that honour killing is the extreme symptom of discrimination against women. People who support and promote such type of acts consider woman as their property and relate it with the concept of shame to family. In their study authors find that honour killing prevails in number of countries especially in third world countries in some or the other form. Most of the time police become helpless as family members acts very secretly and make their best collective effort to hide the truth. They mentioned that although Constitution of India is committed to provide full protection to every citizen against all type of violence but when comes the issue of protecting women from the evil of khap panchayat the ground reality is very much different and shameful. Authors have expressed that bill drafted by National Women Commission titled 'Prevention of Crime in the Name of Honour and Tradition Bill' seems to be very effective as it contains various prohibitive and penal measures. With the help of various landmark judgements authors have tried to prove the proactive role of judiciary against khap panchayats. In the last, some useful suggestions have been made in chapter to curb the impact of khaps on society especially on women and youth.

Dr Amit Kashyap and Shashi Bala Kashyap in their chapter titled **'A Critical Jurisprudential Appraisal of Law and Justice in Crime of Honour Killings and Role of Khap Panchayats in India'** have focused on origin, constitution and working of khaps and khap panchayats. They have classified the khaps into three categories – first the khap with single caste and single Gotra, second the khap with single caste and multiple Gotra and the third one the khap with multiple caste and multiple Gotra. Apart from this authors have detailed the modus operandi of khap panchayats explaining how khaps implement their verdicts and dictums by creating fear in the mind of innocent people. They stick to century's old illogical methods of testing the accused, i.e. compelling the accused to pick up the coin from boiling oil, forcing the accused to move seven steps with red hot iron in hand with seven 'pipal' leaves in hand and forcing the individual to fry 'puris' in boiling oil with bare hands to prove his/her innocence are the few examples reflecting the barbarism common in khap governed areas. Chapter also views that honour killing, female foeticide, forced marriages, prevention of sagotra, inter-caste and inter-religious marriages are the main challenges before civilised society in khap governed states. They have also mentioned few judgments by the Apex Court criticising the khap panchayat and such type of other social institutions functioning on similar ideology in various parts of the country. Authors have also focused on the legislative initiatives taken by Government of India to prohibit the unlawful activities of khap panchayat especially Prohibition of Unlawful Assembly (Interference with Matrimonial Alliances) Bill, 2011 and The Endangerment of Life and Liberty (Protection, Prosecution and Measures) Bill, 2011. Authors have concluded the chapter with few useful suggestions.

Sandesh Yadav in his chapter titled **'Administrative Crisis in Dealing with the Honour Crimes'** states that there is continuous increase in crimes on the name of honour, they could vary from very light nature, i.e. abusing the female by own family members and relatives to very severe nature i.e. brutal killing, rape or naked parade etc. He has divided the honour crimes in three main categories – Emotional, physical and sexual. Although every government authority is well aware that these honour crimes promoted by khap panchayats violate the fundamental rights of victim and still there exists no special legal provision or instrument to deal with cases of honour crimes. Even judges believe that honour crimes are different and much severe in nature as compared to other routine crimes. In absence of special provisions they have to apply best possible legal provision available under the umbrella of existing laws. Continuous debate on this issue and demand of special provisions has compelled the Government of India to draft a special bill to address honour crimes known as The Prevention of Crime in the Name of Honour and Tradition Bill, 2010. Apart from this government has also drafted Indian Penal Code and Other Laws (Amendments) Bill, 2010. Author has detailed the special provisions mentioned in these bills which will give an upper hand to authorities especially police and judiciary to deal with individual or group of individuals accused of honour crimes. Beside this Government of India has proposed the amendments in Indian Evidence Act 1872, under which accused of honour crimes will be burdened of proving their innocence, while till now it was responsibility of state to prove the crime of accused. Unfortunately even after passing more than five years these bills are lying on the table of house. Due to politicisation of issues related to women and lack of good intentions, theses bills could not be converted into Acts. Author believes that enactment of these proposals will certainly be proved as the mile stone in stopping the honour crimes against women.

In the fourteenth chapter of the book titled **'Khap Panchayats: Killing for Honour or for the Ego'** authors ***Dr Amit Kashyap, Shashi Bala Kashyap and Dr Amita Raj Gargey*** state that although everybody in country has the right to life, liberty and security without any limitation of race, caste, religion, clan, community and nationality under which every individual has right to marry or have a family of their own choice yet young men and women who opt for inter-caste or inter-religious marriages are threatened by violence. Court has already made it clear that if parents and family members are not ready to accept such type of marriages, maximum they can cut off the social relations with their son or daughter, they can't threat or instigate the acts of violence. Authors view that incidences of honour killing occurs in almost all parts of the world but in India they are observed as closely connected with khap panchayats. Authors find that refusal to enter arrange marriage, or choosing to marry by his or her own choice, engaging in extra marital affairs considered as immoral in society, marrying within same gotra/same village/in different caste or different religions are the major contributory factors, may result into honour killing. Authors further state that honour killing is gravest disregard for universal human rights and fundamental rights. Although laws of the country are powerful enough to deal with such institutions and many times judiciary have proved the same but when there come the issue of enforcement of laws, inefficient functioning of police and unwillingness of political leadership to deal strictly with khaps makes the situation vulnerable. Authors have detailed the merits and demerits of Prohibition of Unlawful Assembly (Interference with Matrimonial Alliances) Bill, 2011 drafted by Law Commission of India is still waiting to become Act. Authors find that this proposed Act (if passed) guarantees every possibility to deal with illegal acts of khap panchayats. Before concluding authors have made few useful suggestions to stop the honour killing and other illegal dictates of khaps.

Next chapter of the book **'Khap Panchayats and Honour Killings'** author ***Nutan Sharma*** states that khap existed in India since medieval era even in India under British rule. These type of institutions suited to British colonisers as they always desired that small social and religious issues must be settled at village level rather than overburdening the courts. Although they were irrelevant to democratic set up of India after independence but unfortunately they even continued and grown into power with passage of time. He further views that honour killing is not the problem of mortality but it is related to domination power and hatred against women. Today this problem is not limited to boundaries of any particular country or state. This social evil exist in all parts of the world, more prominent in Middle, South and East Asian countries. Author has defined the honour killing as taking the life for saving the honour by family members or relatives or both collectively victimising him/her for bringing disgrace or dishonour to family, clan, caste, community or religion. Existence of khap panchayats is biggest threat to 'right to life' without which every right is meaningless. Author further mentions that Indian society is changing continuously so there is always tiff between ancient traditional practices followed by elder generation and youth of India want to live with liberal and modern mindset.

Sandesh Yadav and Professor Haseena Hashia in their chapter titled **'Khap Panchayats as Agencies of Honour Crimes'** have stated that existence of khap panchayats is one of the great mysteries in world's largest democracy. According to them, members of khap panchayat are caste leaders. Authors finds that divergence evolution, strong bonding in upper caste against lower caste, high tolerance among villagers, weak Panchayati raj system, high degree of politicisation are the few factors which continuously provide strength to khap panchayats. Khap panchayat follows the rule of endogamy and works as custodian of honour. In recent years khap has emerged as brutal machinery to perpetrate injustice at the name of shariyat and gotra depriving the individuals especially women from their life and personal liberty. Quoting the various definitions of honour killing and honour crimes authors express that honour-based violence are the result of clash between tradition and modernity. According to them, women empowerment, high degree of independence and liberty in thinking are the main reasons for increasing honour-based crimes in society. Besides killing for the sake of honour, chapping the nose, compelling to hold red hot iron rod in hands, huge financial penalties, excommunication from village, humiliating the family members publicly, outstripping are the few other inhuman punishments imposed by khap panchayat on the people.

In the seventeenth chapter of the book titled **'Role of Khap Panchayat in Promoting Honour Killing'** author ***Ruchi Dhyani*** details about the organisation of khap panchayat and how it is different from village panchayat elected under Panchayati raj system. She has also differentiated between honour killing and domestic violence. She has compared the khap panchayat with the Talibani raj where nobody has any individual right. Author has mentioned the report of National Commission of Women, according to which about 700 females are brutally killed in different parts of the world for the sake of restoring honour of family, clan, village community and religion. According to author, khap panchayat makes their way of punishing more and more brutal as to set an example so that the one who violates the rules of khap has to face the consequences today or tomorrow in the same way. She has mentioned a number of couples those were killed in the name of honour. She finds that in recent years police and criminal courts have played a positive role in reducing the cases of honour killing after the apex court of India has issued certain guidelines against khaps.

Dr Deepa Awasthi in her chapter titled **Media Standing Tall Against Feudal Khap Panchayats** mentions that media has always provided best possible solution to various socio-political and socio-economic problems, the mankind has ever come across. She stated that in last century media has gained unlimited strength and emerged as most powerful tool to regulate the society. Just like all other issues media has always helped the society to continue its war against feudal khap panchayats and its century's old stagnant ideologies. Through various ways media has challenged the khaps and created an unfavourable environment against the existence of khaps not only in region but all over the country and abroad too. According to author whether it may be formal media like Newspaper, Magazines, Radio, Electronic news channels or informal media like Cinema, Internet and Social media e.g. Twitter, Whats app, Facebook etc. have always provided courage to women and youth of country, who are worst affected by the inhuman dictates of the khaps. She finds that although media has made tremendous efforts to minimise the impact of khap panchayats and such type of other institutions active in the country but something more was expected from media. War against khaps will never come to an end until media plays its decisive role of educating and awaring the common man especially people living in rural areas. She further suggests the media to take extra precaution while handling the news related to khaps, they must evaluate the impact of airing or publishing news on society.

Manvi Manisha Tigga in her chapter titled **'Khap Panchayat as Parallel Judicial System'** has explained the existence of khap panchayat as caste panchayat which used to act as parallel judiciary system at village level before introduction of Panchayati raj system in India. According to her, in some parts of North India these khap panchayat co-exist along with formal panchayat system. These khap panchayat use to indulge in solving small disputes at village level or regulating the behaviours of individual or group, which have wider social impact. She has mentioned that black face of khap panchayat was exposed before the world when came forward with news of some of their decisions which clearly violate the human rights and law of land. The power of these khap panchayat comes from herd mentality – a tendency among mob to follow the other without using their discretionary thinking. She further finds that people have no other option than to go to khap panchayats as they cannot bear the high expenses of formal judicial system of the country. She further suggests that khap panchayats will automatically lose their relevance when a better option for resolving disputes will be available in rural areas.

Twentieth and the last chapter of the book titled **'Khap Panchayat, Inter-Caste and Inter-Religious Love Marriages'** author ***Preeti*** mentions that functioning of khap panchayat is based on principle of 'bhaichara' and 'Hukka - pani.' In her review based study she finds that khap panchayats are strictly patriarchal in nature and undemocratic as well because hardly one can find any women administering any khap panchayat. Khap emerged as social organisations for administering justice to its people by taking undisputed and impartial decisions on multiple issues like transaggressions, marriage offences, and disputes related to inheritance and sharing of properties but with passage of time illegal decisions taken by khap leaders raised the question mark on the existence of khap like institutions in civil society. Apart from that, these khaps are unacceptable to society especially among young generation, even Supreme Court of India has declared them as 'kangaroo courts' yet the terror of these illegal khaps continues in the minds of people living in the areas where they are dominant. Author has quoted the study of National Commission for Women, according to which about 600 peoples have been affected by the crime of 'honour killing' between year 2005 to 2010. She further finds that strong deep- rooted caste and religion system, conservative mindset of people, lack of governance, traditional value system, community feeling, *bhaichara* factor and indirect political support are the few prime reasons for khap's influence on marriages.

Section–A

Understanding the Khap Panchayats

Chapter – 1

Past and Present of Khap Panchayats: Social and Cultural Perspective

—*Vidya Vati*

Abstract

Khap panchayats have hogged media limelight because of ruthless murder of young couples at their order. Khap panchayats are gotra-based social organisation among jats which are undemocratic in structure and functioning. These organisations are against same gotra marriages and inter-caste marriages. They claim to have long history but historical evidences do not support their claims. These panchayats are very powerful and have become pressure group to make political power yield to their demands fair or unfair. The author has tried to analyse socio-cultural factors lying behind their strength and dominance.

***Key Words**: Khap panchayat, Gotra, Marriage, Village, Society.*

What is Khap Panchayat?

Khap panchayats are gotra-based social organisations of jats in northern belt of India which support caste endogamy and gotra exogamy. It means jats will marry within their caste only but will avoid marrying in same gotra.

The gotra system have genesis in Rig Veda and are named after Rishis and Mahrishis among Brahmins. The Rishis kept cows and literally gotra means cowshed. Over time gotra has been used to identify lineage from rishis. The boys and girls of same gotra are treated like brothers and sisters. Hence, sagotra marriages are not allowed. Clannish life of jats seems to have prompted them to develop their own gotras on the line of Brahmins.

There is confusion in minds of people over khaps. Generally, khap panchayats are taken as caste panchayats, but khaps have different entity. Since khaps are creation of jats, they are active in states like Haryana, Western Uttar Pradesh, Punjab and Rajasthan where jats are dominant. Caste panchayats may be social organisation of any caste. As we find Vaishya Samaj, Balmiki Samaj, Brahmin Sabha or panchayats of Rajputs and Gujjars. These panchayats are not based on gotras of their caste. Khaps are gotra centric organisation of jats. Different gotras have their own khaps. Several khaps of a province constitute Sarv Khap. Satrol Khap is largest khap in Haryana.

Origin of Khaps

Historians diverge on the origin of khap panchayats. Vidhatha was the earliest folk-assembly of the Indo-Aryans attended by both men and women, performing all kinds of functions, military, religious and social. This earliest folk-assembly was followed by Sabha and Samiti which mean gathering and assembly (R. S. Sharma). We find reference of 16 Janpadas/republics in the texts of Panini and late Buddhist text but there is no proof that khaps have any relation with them. Some scholars find janpads to be khap like entity but some claim that khap panchayats are offshoot of sabha and samiti. These are far-fetched ideas propagated to justify the antiquity of khaps. In reality the origin of khaps is shrouded in mystery (D. R. Chaudhary).

Apparently, khaps origin is related to Jat community. No written record of jats is found in ancient history. Many theories prevail. Some modern scholars claim that jats are descendents of Yaudheyas, a tribe mentioned in Mahabharata. Historians like Sir Alexander Cunnigham and Vincent Smith say that jats are Indo-Scythian hordes that invaded India from 200 B.C. to 600 A.D. The word Jat is derived from Jatta, a generic term for cattle grazers and camel breeders moving into a group (jatha). They seem to have first of all entered the Indus Valley as far down as Sindh. Gradually they occupied the entire fertile doab area of Haryana, Western Uttar Pardesh and Rajasthan. By the time of

Delhi Sultanat this pastoral community had settled in agriculture sector. 'Many of jat gotras were formed on the criteria of jat localities and profession not ancestors. Identity of jats strengthened only after 10th century'. (S. B. Bhardwaj)

At early stage socio-economic insecurity may have prompted them to develop khaps on clan basis. Today, more than 500 gotras are found among jats. According to Bhim Singh Dahiya the word khap is perhaps derived from the saka word 'khatrap' and it means an area inhabited by a particular clan. The political unit of khap is defined as a group of 84 villages. This unit of measure is found as far as the saka invasions on Indian sub-continent around 200 B.C.

There is no data available about the khaps. A meeting organised by king Harshvardhan at Kanauj in seventh century is being taken as sarv khap panchayat. The king had advised the people to sort out small matters in village panchayats headed by responsible people. If the matter was not sorted out at village level, they could call a conclave of the same gotra villages. No historical evidence supports this claim.

Sarv khap's information about their history is based on the unpublished handwritten pothi of Pandit Kanha Ram, resident of village Shauram in the district of Muzzafarnagar in Western Uttar Pardesh. The pothis consist of 16 handwritten pages describing the dates and locations of khap panchayats' meetings. These pothis are in now possession of Chaudhary Qabul Singh of Shauram village. According to these pothis, first meeting of khaps was held twelth century in a forest between villages of Bhaju and Bhanera. It is also claimed that khaps had army in medieval period in order to defend against foreign invaders. This seems to be fictitious as there is no corroborating evidence to support this claim. Another meeting (1398 A.D.) is said to be held in the forest of Chaugama the district of Muzzafarnagar to resist the attack of Tamur Lane. But the autobiography of Tamur does not mention any opposition from jats. Chaugama khap claims that it helped Rana Sanga in fight against Babur. One meeting (1661 A.D.) is claimed to be held in Chaprauli near Meerut to oppose jazia imposed by Mughal Emperor Aurangzeb. The date does not tally with the date of jazia. Aurangzeb imposed jazia in 1679 A.D. The revolts were against burden of land revenue. There was fierce battle between Mughal army and jats under the leadership of Gokul near Mathura. Emperor Aurangzeb publicly beheaded Gokul and ruthlessly suppressed jats. Mughals had strong local system of governance with officials like Chaudhary, Quanungo, Amin, Amil, and Faujdar. Had there been khap's meetings, these would have attracted the attention of administration (Suraj Bhan Bhardwaj). The authenticity of Pothis needs to be examined on the basis of linguistic character. These claims have no historical evidence. These writings are likely to be an attempt to dominate other castes. Both Suraj Bhan Bhardwaj and Prem Chaudhary suggest that khap panchayats often make claims to historical lineage to gain contemporary legitimacy.

The dominant section of Jat peasants became part of revenue collection mechanism in the posts of chaudhary, numbardar and muqaddams in parganas. They helped officials in collecting revenue and with passage of time became owners of large land holdings. Later on they were incorporated in the system by the British rulers with different designation. The post of chaudhary was replaced by Ziledar. It is this section which seems to have played role in khaps. The jats helped the British in crushing the rebellion led by Banda Bahadur who raised the slogan of land redistribution. (Singh, 2006) This powerful section deprived dalits and other castes of ownership of land.

Khaps in Modern Age

The word 'khap' was used first time in the Census Report of the year 1890-91 in Jodhpur which was based on religion and caste (S. B. Bhardwaj) but khaps came into limelight recently after a spate of murder of young couples at their behest. The earliest sarv khap panchayat of jats is said to be held at Barona on March 7, 1911. It is said this conclave passed 28 resolutions related to social issues. Some resolutions were anti-women and some were against lower castes. To commemorate the century old sarv khap panchayat held at Barona in 1911, a similar gathering took place on March 7, 2011, which also passed 28 resolutions in order to bring about social reform. But there is no evidence of khap panchayat taking any action against anyone. These panchayats have become notorious for meddling into marital affairs only. (D. R. Chaudhary, Khap Panchayat and Modern Age, pp. 25-26)

Functioning of Khaps

Khaps are controlled by a group of 10-20 people from similar gotra of Jat community. They have autocratic approach and are generally rich and powerful. They have neither formal structure nor any formal membership unlike village panchayat, the oldest democratic administrative structure in India. Every male member of the village has right to attend, and to express views.

Contrarily khap panchayats are undemocratic in approach. Panchayat is called to decide some issues. Brotherhood is the basis of khap panchayats (Jat bhai approach). The heads of khaps are hereditary or some respectable elder is declared as head for a particular sitting of panchayat. Khap panchayats are patriarchal in nature. There is no female participation. To face of attack by women organisations and media sarv khap decided to constitute a women wing on April 13, 2010 at Kurukshetra. These bodies are against same gotra marriage and same village marriage which are called incestuous relationship. Marriage is taboo in 'gawand' (neighbourhood) also.

Khap Panchayat is the union of a few villages in North India, though councils in similar forms exist in other parts of the country also. We find gotra based councils among Munda and Gond tribes of central and Eastern India. These kinship groups determine social norms and customs by holding assembly. In Munda tribes of Jharkhand all gotras have their headman. We have village councils of different tribal communities in Andhra Pradesh which manage village affairs. The councils adjudicate the disputes and often distribute the village resources on the basis of customary laws and methods. Most of the tribes in North East states of India have a judicial machinery to deal with disputes and resolving social offences at the village level. Sexual offences are dealt with their clan elders. (Evolution of Panchayat Raj in India with Special Reference to Andhra Pradesh by Gandhi Siga) Katta Panchayats in Tamil Nadu are also customary village councils. But they are not as strong as khaps.

Lately, 'they have emerged as quasi- judicial bodies that pronounce harsh punishments based on age old customs and traditions often bordering on regressive measures to modern problems.'(India TV-

11.10.2012) They enforces summons through social prohibition and sanctions, imposes heavy fines, get couples killed if they are found to violate so called norms/flouting their rules or force them commit suicide.

Cases of Honour Killing

Some cases of honour killings are being given the writer could lay hands on.

The Manoj- Babli Case

Manoj-Babli case found greatest space in media regarding honour killings in Haryana. It is the case of same gotra marriage. They both belonged to village Kirora in Kaithal district. Manoj and Babli eloped on April 6, 2007 and married at Durga temple. They boarded a bus to reach Kaithal. On the way the couple was dragged forcibly and pushed into waiting Scorpio car. They were killed the same day and their bodies were thrown into the canal. The decomposed bodies were recovered after nine days. The case was heard in the court at Karnal. The court pronounced the historic judgment awarding life sentence to the culprits. The village panchayat of Kirora declared social boycott of Manoj's family.

The Satish- Kavita Case

Satish who was Berwal by gotra of village Kheri Meham in Rohtak district had married Kavita Beniwal of village Bhagi-Behror in Bhiwani district. They had different gotras and different village. After two Beniwal panchayats of Kheri Meham declare the marriage void and declared the couple as siblings. When Kavita refused to accept the verdict, was expelled from village permanently. (The Times of India, Chandigarh, February 1, 2010)

The Vedpal – Sonia Case

Vedpal Maun belonging to village Mataur in Kaithal district and Sonia Bhanwala got married. Vedpal had apprehension that Bhanwalas of Singhwal would not accept this marriage, for it was neighbouring village of Mataur. He shifted to Punjab. Bhanwala khap panchayat declare the marriage void and pronounced the death for couple. Sonia was brought back and put under house arrest. When Vedpal went there to take his wife back, he was lynched to death.

The courts of the country clamped down heavily on khap panchayats and passed rigorous punishment to the culprits. 'This is wholly illegal and has to be ruthlessly stamped out. There is nothing honourable in honour killing and other atrocities and, in fact, it is nothing but barbaric and shameful murder. Attempt of interference in personal lives of people by brutal, feudal minded persons deserves harsh punishment. Only this can we stamp out such acts of barbarism and feudal mentality. Moreover these acts take the law into their own hands and amount to kangaroo courts which are wholly illegal,' said the Bench of Justices Markanday Katju and Gyan Sudha Mishra.

Reasons behind the Strength of Khap Panchayats

Khaps have huge support. Now moot question is why they are so powerful? India is a vast country with huge population. Clashes and disputes are natural in a society. Khaps seem to hold their sway in areas where elected panchayats are either weak or non-existent. Khaps have filled the void. State cannot reach society in every matter. Many people even among jats may dislike dominance of khaps but they remain mute spectators. Here the issue needs to be analysed from other perspective to understand this phenomena.

Human beings live in society because necessity compels him to do so. The need of self preservation makes an individual to accept social norms. It liberates and limits our personalities as individuals, moulds our attitudes and our beliefs. There are conscious or unconscious means of control. Generally people are heard to say that they are not afraid of 'samaj' but the reality is they are. We have in mind 'log kya kahenge' i.e. 'what people will say'. These three words have always been more powerful than law in Indian society and have controlled the behaviour of people in positive or negative way. Sometimes fear of social structures lead one to make great sacrifices. In villages people have fixed habitations unlike in urban areas and interdependent lifestyle. None wants to become the target of ridicule. Everyone wants praise, appreciation, honour and recognition by society. Khap panchayats fully exploit this psychology of members of society.

The other reason of khap panchayats regaining position in society is lacuna in our judicial system. The sheer volume of disputes in courts is whopping. According to data revealed by NDTV, more than three crore cases are pending in courts across the country. In Supreme Court alone the number of pending cases is 46919 as on December 1, 2014. Our judicial system is sluggish and laws are ambiguous. The entire process of seeking justice ultimately is harassing, as is the perception of common man. People support these khaps because of expedite dispense of cases. These panchayats deliver the verdict in a single sitting as against court cases which linger on for years.

Socio-economic factors also lead people to support and respect these panchayats. Though these organisations are highly patriarchal and in a way anti-women. They have put ban on wearing jeans and using mobile phones by girls/women. They have taken some positive steps also. There is no check on dowry and liquor sale in villages and these have been ruining families. Fathers have been selling land to get daughters married. These panchayats have put ban on giving expensive gifts like tractor or motorcycle as dowry and not having DJ music in marriage ceremony. Khap panchayats have muscle power. The way they get couples eliminated is reflection of this. Leaders of factions and relations rule these bodies. They mobilise and polarise other caste groups in the village in favour of their own caste. People give importance to power and dominance. That is why they play decisive role in settlement of caste conflicts.

Another strong factor in revival of khaps is likely to be political. In 1960s, jats began to regroup to find space in politics of the country under the leadership of Chaudhary Charan Singh. Powerful landlords etched fertile ground to gain political power through khaps. Earlier the khaps seem to exist but were not in limelight. Their meetings used to low key affair. When Chaudhary Charan Singh was Prime Minister, Khaps became powerful tool in rallying round the jat community for political interests. The jats even began to bully and deride the people of other castes who supported Congress.

Through khaps they arouse 'herd- instincts' to build pressure group being fully aware that their tactics would work in vote-bank politics. So jats remain in forefront in staging dharna and organising blockade on road or railway track. It is clear on the issue of reservation in government jobs or compensation in lieu of land acquisition. Jats have become aggressive in the face of challenges posed by other backward caste groups like Sainis and Yadavs and other weaker sections of society.

Modernisation and Khap Panchayats

Haryana is in the vicinity of capital city Delhi and has greatly been benefitted by education, urbanisation and modernisation. With the onset of economic liberalisation Gurgaon and other adjoining towns of Haryana has become hub of economic activities. Changes in life style of people have set in. Youth are throwing the baggage of norms and traditions so called upheld by jats as community. Assertion of khaps is an attempt to hold the power structure both at clan level and family level and to stem the wave of modernisation which has its own positive and negative aspects. On flip side corporate life is promoting free sex, love, marketability of females, trend of live-in-relationship, gay marriage etc. which are against the core of Indian society on which it has been existing for centuries. These factors also are driving them to preserve clannish culture.

Reflections on Some Issues

If position of women is reflection of health of society, then Haryana may be called deplorably sick even in condition of richness. In male-dominated Haryana there is devaluation of women's life. Female child is considered as a curse. Female foeticide especially among rich strata is rampant here. One wonders where the norms go when a life is killed for no fault. Today skewed sex ratio (1000:832) is posing grave threat to social balance and harmony. Sale and purchase of girls has become flourishing market. According to data with NGO Shakti Vahini and the UN about 10000 girls are sold who are brought from Jharkhand, Chhatisgarh, Nepal every year. Under the pressure of women organisations and to improve image sarv khap in Bibipur village in Jind district of Haryana passed resolution to work in the direction of Anti Female Foeticide Campaign.

Now khap panchayats are raising demand to bring about amendment in Hindu Marriage Act and want ban on sagotra marriage and same village marriage. These are not new concepts in Indian society. Other castes also avoid sagotra marriage but they do not announce 'fatwa' to kill couples if they deviate from this norm. They have become flexible in view of present socio-economic conditions. Sometimes middle path is etched. For instance, the Bhardwaj gotra of Brahmans have three branches 'shashans'. Marriage is solemnised if the boy and the girl belong to different shashans even when they have same gotra.

Same village marriage is avoided in our society for ages. This practice has social implications in village life which is interdependent and close-knit. A girl is respected as 'beti' (daughter) of entire village. This practice goes in favour of females. The girls are generally more immune from sexual harassment in villages, as it controls the basic instincts of both boys and girls and helps in keeping the atmosphere of village healthy and harmonious. Some issues are never resolved at the level of Law or State. It is only society that can settle the matter peacefully. Perhaps it is these characteristics of village life which inspired Sir Charles Metcalf (1832) to comment:

> The village communities are little republics having nearly everything they want within themselves, and almost independent of any foreign relations. They seem to last where nothing else lasts. Dynasty after dynasty tumbles down, revolution succeeds revolution, but the village community remains the same. This union of village communities, each one forming a separate little state in itself, has, I conceive, contributed more than any other cause to the preservation of the people of India, through all the revolutions and changes which they have suffered, and is in a high degree conducive to their happiness, and to the enjoyment of a great portion of freedom and independence.

Conclusion

Khap panchayats have glorious history is a myth woven deliberately to gain legitimacy for them in modern age. In reality it is caste panchayats or village panchayats which have been pillars of Indian society. These social organisations may have been weakened in particular age but no ruler could ignore them altogether. Khaps have been created in modern age to solidify brotherhood (*bhai - chara*) among jats. Now they have become powerful lobby for taking larger share in economic and political life. They are raising other issues only as face saver.

References

- Charles Metcalf, Indian Society and Social Institutions by Sachdeva and Gupta, K.S. Singh, Ajanta Prakashan.
- Chaudhary, D. R., Khap Panchayat and Modern Age, National Book Trust, India.
- Gandhi Siga, Evolution of Panchayat Raj in India with Special Reference to Andhra Pradesh.
- R. S. Sharma, Aspects of Political Ideas and Institutions in Ancient India, by D.R. Chaudhary.
- Suraj Bhan Bhardwaj, Myths and Reality of the Khap Panchayat: A Historical Analysis of the Panchayats and Khap Panchayats, www.sih.sage.pub.com
- Singh, (2006). Khap Panchayat A Socio Historical... www.academia.edu
- http:/www.khappanchayat.com/history.htm/

Chapter – 2

Socio-political Role of Khap Panchayat in India

—*Dr Mehnaz Najmi*

Abstract

The word 'khap' in northern part of India is used to denote the feeling of community and affiliation. Khap panchayat is the union of a few villages, mainly in north India though it exists in similar forms in the rest of the country...Khap panchayat governs the khap formed by same gotra *(clan) families from several neighbouring villages. Khap panchayats are prevalent in Haryana, western Uttar Pradesh and parts of Rajasthan...They are known to order sexually violent punishments against women. In 2011, in the case of Arumugam Servai versus State of Tamil Nadu, the Supreme Court of India described these panchayats as 'Kangaroo Courts' and said their decrees are illegal...Many young couples have been killed in the past for defying khap rules. Khap panchayat imposes its writ through social boycotts and fines and in most cases end up either killing or forcing the victims to commit suicide..." The problem arises when the dispute resolution is done through cohesion...when the law of land is broken or when killings and murders are defended in the name of some adjectives like honour killing, etc...Supreme Court went on the extent of calling khap panchayat as "kangaroo courts." It further stressed that they are unconstitutional and illegal...The sheer indifference of politicians and vote-bank politics allow the khap panchayat's writ to run amok...The khap panchayats end up usurping the judicial powers of the courts of the land even though they have absolutely no status under the Constitution of India...Irrational opinions and extreme measures... Threat to law and order...Conclusion.*

Keywords: *Khap, KhapPanchayat, Kangaroo Courts, Violence, Women, Cohesion, Supreme Court.*

The word 'khap' in northern part of India is used to denote the feeling of community and affiliation. It is a strong thread that binds the communities in such a way that they look intertwined. Khap panchayat is the union of a few villages, mainly in north India though it exists in similar forms in the rest of the country. Lately, they have emerged as quasi-judicial bodies that pronounce harsh punishments based on age-old customs and traditions, often bordering on regressive measures to modern problems.

The notion of 'belonging' lies at the heart of all communities, real or imagined — whether on the basis of birth, blood, proximity, or of choice. Everyone 'belongs', and a sense of belonging is often crucial to a person's well-being. At the same time, we dispute belonging, vociferously. Such disputes can be competitive, in the sense of 'my community is better than yours', or they can occur when different ideas of belonging intersect and overlap, with different ideas of belonging competing for primacy. Wars, riots, sports rivalries, some forms of electoral politics, and certainly many family disputes, are ultimately about competing visions of belonging. Given its overwhelming centrality to human life, it is somewhat surprising how little attention is paid to unpacking this idea. We use the word often enough, but, do we really know what it is to belong?

In the English language, the word "belonging" has two meanings: one, to indicate an affective sense of identification with a place or people, and the other, to suggest possession. In one sense a person belongs to, as in has a great deal of affection for and identity with, a place or people (or an institution). In the other sense, a person who "belongs" is deemed to be the possession of a place, people, or institutions. This is not simply an idiosyncrasy of the English language. In Hindi/Urdu too (the only other languages with which I am familiar), the words *apna/hamara* or *apnapan* function in very similar ways.

Khap is a cluster of villages united by caste and geography. It is as old as fourteenth century started by upper caste Jats to consolidate their power and position. The main rule is that all boys and girls within a khap are considered siblings. Khap panchayat governs the khap formed by same *gotra* (clan) families from several neighbouring villages. Khap panchayats are prevalent in Haryana, western Uttar Pradesh and parts of Rajasthan. The 10-15 men of dominant caste constitute a khap to settle disputes and control the lives of young people. They prescribe rules for social behaviour and interaction in villages. They are known to order sexually violent punishments against women. In 2011, in the case of Arumugam Servai versus State of Tamil Nadu, the Supreme Court of India described these panchayats as 'Kangaroo Courts' and said their decrees are illegal. Many rural people defend these caste panchayats as they deliver verdict in one sitting whereas court cases drag for years. According to them, in many cases innocent people get harassed in the court and by police. Here as everyone is known so they cross check everything to ensure neutrality.

Love marriages are considered taboo in areas governed by khap panchayats. Those living in the khap-dominated areas are not allowed to marry in the same *gotra* or even in any *gotra* from the same village. Many young couples have been killed in the past for defying khap rules. Khap panchayat imposes its writ through social boycotts and fines and in most cases end up either killing or forcing the victims to commit suicide. All this is done in the name of brotherhood and honour. It is due to the inherent weakness of democratically elected panchayati raj institutions, khap panchayats have become so powerful. Even the government does not have any control on them.

In some villages of Haryana, the young girls are threatened, abused and killed on routine basis, all under khap verdicts. It is acceptable for the families to feed pesticide pills to the teenage girls and then dispose off their bodies by burning them without any police records. The entire onus of siblinghood rests on the girl. She is the keeper of village honour. Sometimes rules are relaxed for the boys but a girl is never allowed to pass the rules. If a couple runs away then the families risk the boycott and hefty fines in lakhs of rupees. Even the other women of the house can also suffer abuse.

In keeping with the khap rules, older villagers try to keep the young people apart. Some schools are also forced to have separate timings for the boys and girls. Fearing their daughters would go astray, many parents marry them off at an early age. People have unquestionable faith in the justice of khap. The question of rights for women does not exist anywhere in the territories ruled by khap panchayats.

There was a news that, "A khap panchayat near Narwana in Haryana's Jind district issued a diktat declaring a married couple siblings, five months after they had an arranged marriage. The kangaroo court issued a diktat 'annulling', Praven Kumar a 25 year old male and 30-year-old Poonam's marriage, saying their gotra fall under 'bhaichara' category and as so they should be treated as brother and sister."

A khap panchayat in Barmer issued a diktat, that girls of the village will not use mobile phones and social media and has also warned girls not to wear jeans and bridegrooms to wear 'Dhoti' when getting married. This diktat comes as the entire world has moved on and has been witnessing technological revolution for decades now. This development almost coincides with Prime Minister Narendra Modi launching his flagship Digital India project through which the entire country would get high speed internet. Beyond the reach of social media, the old conservative mindset remains strong.

The Aam Aadmi Party (AAP) also defended the existence of the khap panchayats, but said that it opposes any kind of decision given by them that violates the law of the land. Yogendra Yadav the erstwhile former AAP member had said, "All castes tend to have their social organisations, for internal dispute resolution. (February 1, 2014, Indian Express) *"We certainly acknowledge the right of all such organisations to exist. They have a right to exist and perform a legitimate role because we do not want every social dispute to go to the court of law,"* he said. Mr Yadav, who played a major role in formulating party's policy on crucial issues, said that the problem arose when the khap panchayats violates the law with their decisions.

The problem arises when the dispute resolution is done through cohesion, when the law of land is broken or when killings and murders are defended in the name of honour. Mr Yadav further stated that, "We are absolutely unopposed to compromising any cohesion, violation of law or any killing." Slamming other political parties for succumbing to the khap panchayats, he said that the AAP will not fall before the feet of these community organisations for the sake of votes. "Other parties go and ask for vote, fall before their feet. They say if there is a murder due to the order issued by the khap panchayat, we will not keep quiet. AAP has not done this before or do not intend to do this in future," he said.

On one hand he is rejecting the cohesion and diktats of khap but at the same time he is supporting the idea of the khap. This kind of ambiguous stand by the politicians is making khaps more powerful and unlawful authority. The other idea about khap panchayats is that it is a form of direct democracy that has been around in western India for centuries now. The problem is that it hasn't really evolved with the times and people who are in charge of these khaps do not have an open mindset.

Now coming to the judgments and controversial decisions made by these khaps, we need to remember that they have absolutely no legal standing. So if they make a decision that infringes any rights provided by the constitution one can approach the court. The problem is that most of the people of that particular region suffer because of the judgments of khaps, but when they approach police, they generally take sides with the khap panchayat. Also, people who stand up against them, they are socially ostracized, which they cannot afford to face. People who are on the receiving end of these controversial decisions are mostly from the weaker sections of society so migrating away from village is not a solution for them either.

Next question arises why does the government do not ban them outright? After all, these khaps are parallel governments that make decisions that are completely unconstitutional. The politicians in our country don't have the will to make such big decisions. Making khaps illegal will invite so much wrath that their party will suffer in the elections. So the only way khaps can be ended is by intervention of courts. Unfortunately that has not happened yet in appropriate way.

The khap panchayats are all male unelected village councils and while there have been one or two instances of khap leaders doing constructive work. (e.g. the sarpanch of Bibipur village, Haryana running an Anti Foeticide Campaign) These institutions have mostly been orthodox, anarchic, irrational, and dangerous.

Supreme Court went on the extent of calling khap panchayat as "kangaroo courts." It further stressed that they are unconstitutional and illegal. Some of the reasons in support of this analysis are –

Unelected and Undemocratic in Nature and Functioning

The khaps are neither directly elected by the people nor do they have any legal sanctity. Khaps are unelected bodies simply composed of the village elders mostly on the basis of caste prejudices or money. They do not represent the population residing in the village and modern outlook as a whole in the majority of cases. For them modernity is deviation from purity to impurity, which needs to be checked and in extreme cases crushed mercilessly. They are quite distinct from the gram panchayats that hold elections and function (or attempt to function) as institutions of democracy at the grassroot level. Thus, calling them panchayats and people accepting them as some kind of governing authority in it poses dangerous equations, threats and questions in front of us. The khaps have no developmental role to play in the modern era. Their appointment is based on traditional power structures in the village. They are helping in prolonging and increasing traditional forms of exploitation by issuing diktats. The question then arises is from where have they got the status and sanctity to give such draconian judgments? Is society equally responsible? The kind of power they enjoy and the way their orders are followed by the society are evidence enough of their unholy nexus.

Politicians represent the collective will of society. They cannot defy the unwritten rules and prejudices prevalent in the system. Like for example in Uttar Pradesh, khap panchayats have ruled against women carrying or using mobile phones or wearing jeans or other western attire. To pacify their traditional vote banks, politicians too become supportive of this structure. Most often than not, it is seen that votes are garnered and demanded on the issues of protecting the existence of khap panchayats. Elected representatives support such issues to maintain their vote banks. Delhi Chief Minister

Arvind Kejriwal, in a recent interview, had said he does not see the need for banning khap panchayats or unelected all male village councils that often endorse harsh treatment of women because they serve a 'cultural purpose.' Dangerous connivance between the elite, sub-elite and the people of village is visible as far as khaps are concerned. The sheer indifference of politicians and vote bank politics allow the khap panchayat's writ to run amok.

Usurping Judicial Powers

The khap panchayats end up usurping the judicial powers of the courts of the land even though they have absolutely no status under the Constitution of India. Supreme Court of India has declared khaps as unconstitutional and illegal in very strong words. It has no legal powers to take decisions that could affect the lives of innocents.

This defect becomes even more glaring as none of the members have any legal training or qualifications. Further, there is no appeals procedure or prescribed method to integrate these institutions into the country's established judicial structure. There isn't even an obligation on them to give a legal rationale for their judgments. All these things make them a threat to civilisation and society. Their diktats are to be followed by all. There is no concept of appeal or re-hearing of the case. They can declare any married couple as brother and sister for the reason of belonging from the same village. They can go to the extent of murdering either girl or boy or both for bringing dishonour to the clan. Whenever such crimes are committed not even single eye witness comes forward to report. When someone or the affected family tries to file a report they are stopped by the care takers of law itself, and if complaint is registered by putting huge efforts the whole khap and its followers turn the lives of complainants into hell. They are treated in the worst possible manners. They are ex-communicated from the society where all the ties with other members of society are broken with them. Even their own blood relatives and extended family members discriminate against them. They are blamed for bringing dishonour to the family. Keeping relationship intact with them might deteriorate the thinking of their children. They might get deviated from the path they are supposed to follow - the path of prejudice and irrationality!

Irrational Opinions and Extreme Measures

Recent statements by members of these 'panchayats' such as eating noodles leads to rape, lowering the marriage age will lead to a fall in sexual offences etc. is evidence of the unjustifiable and irrational opinions. They also end up taking extreme measures to discipline their members such as excommunication and in some cases authorising death punishments or sexually violent punishments. There was a case in Baghpat, Uttar Pradesh, where Minakshi Kumari and her 15 year old sister fled the village with their family, fearing violence after their brother eloped with a Jat (dominant class) married woman. After five days their house was ransacked and members of village khap panchayat - an unelected all male village council- ordered that Minakshi Kumari and her sister be raped and paraded naked with their faces blackened, as punishment of the actions of their brother. The woman who eloped with the brother of these girls has also received the threat of killing along with her new born.

In another case a couple dared to appear in a television programme called 'Satyamev Jayate' where they stated their sufferings at the hands of khap panchayats. Their identities were revealed on Television and within a month the man was murdered. The woman was then forced to go back to her parents in the same village.

If we examine the measures used by khaps to check the young generation we find that it is always the women of the family who are at the receiving end. These people live in conservative and prejudiced societies, where intermingling of sex is not allowed. Men and women are from two different sections of society in which one is in dominant position and other in submissive one. As a result, men of dominant caste behave in any perverted manner they want. It is more of a crime committed against women where a group of people enjoy such sexual crimes which involve women. All sexual frustrations are vent out on the women of society.

Threat to Law and Order

Recent controversies over the status of khap panchayats have shown that if their authority is questioned or challenged even by lawful government authorities the reaction is violent and a threat to public order rather than submission to the constitutionally recognised authorities. Thus, khaps can often act as obstacles in the path of modernity. Notorious for pronouncing bizarre verdicts on social issues, Haryana's community councils, the khaps, asked the 'Arya Samaj' not to solemnize weddings at its temples between couples from the same gotra (lineage) and village. The khaps have objected to such marriages being solemnised, saying that these violated the century old custom. The khaps have also warned Arya Samaj, a reform movement that has its own temples that they would not hesitate to launch a state wide stir against them if they did not stop formalising weddings within the same *gotra* and village. The decision to caution Arya Samaj was taken at a meeting of sarva jatiya khap held at Chhotu Ram Dharamshala in Haryana's Jhajjar town, about 70 km. away Delhi. The meeting presided over by Jai Singh Ahlawat, chief of Ahlawat khap, was attended by various khaps of Yadav, Balmiki, Dhanak, Prajapati and Saini communities, except Jats. Om Prakash Dhankhar, chief of Dhankhar khap, said, "The Arya Samaj temples are turning out to be safe haven for those youth who wish to get married within the same *gotra* and village by ignoring custom." He said that youths getting married this way were using the Arya Samaj to complete legal formalities of their marriage even if these were against social norms. They wanted the priests to call the Sarpanch (village headman) or any other functionary of the village of the man and woman before formalising the wedding so as to ensure that the marriage was being solemnised as per custom. Media saw it as a peaceful threat to Arya Samaj temples. It is evident that they follow no rules when it comes to protecting their existence. They are prone to take law and order in their hands as and when required.

Arise in Political Vacuum to Foster Communitarian Politics

Khaps exercise relatively more authority in regions where the political representatives do not have a substantial popular political hold. In cases where the regional political elites do not hold a large majority they arrive at informal power sharing arrangements that are based on pledging support of caste groups represented by the khaps. On the one hand it leads to greater internal cohesiveness in the caste thus prolonging the life of khaps, and on the other hand it leads to divisiveness between these caste groups. This is another counterproductive effect of the persisting power of khaps.

Considering the ill effects of khap panchayats to personal liberty, modernity and social unity and progress they must be replaced by recognised democratic institutions. But, this does mean that the political and administrative authorities will have to adopt a stricter stance against the khaps.

Conclusion

Khaps are governed by medieval age people, who treated women as commodity. It is still prevalent in various parts of the country, especially among Jats, Muslims and tribal. Most of the uneducated or economically dependent women are living in sub-human conditions where violence against women is common. Khaps are encouraging such violence and honour killing.

Such evils of our culture and traditions must be ended. Killing people for marrying their choice of partners is not the way to deliver any sort of justice. It's totally an inhuman practice which tends to take away the fundamental rights of a human. We comprise a "Young Nation" and if still those old and obsolete norms rule our lives, then what is the majority, i.e. the YOUTH of the nation doing to bring the change? There is a need for progressive and healthy norms that can come to power only through some new social reforms.

The Judiciary undoubtedly can play an important role for the banishment of such practices but to certain extent, even the judiciary has its own limitations. Justice K.S. Ahluwalia of the Haryana and Punjab High Court, on June 23, 2008; on hearing simultaneous cases relating to the marriage of young couples, remarked, "The High Court is flooded with petitions where…judges of this Court have to answer for the right of life and liberty to married couples. The State is a mute spectator. When shall the State awake from its slumber and for how long can Courts provide solace and balm by disposing of such cases?"

The legislature can only be made more effective with the will of the political parties, the leadership of social activists, the working of democratic forces, consolidation of organisations like AIDWA, but most importantly, the pressure of the masses to take action against the wrong. If there has to be a change, then the young generation needs to come forward and struggle for a reformation in an otherwise feudal society.

It is imperative to highlight the fact throughout the country that no one stands a chance to be above the Constitution and thus cannot defeat the purpose of the laws of land. The khap panchayats are actually a curse on the nation and with the way they are functioning, these are dividing the nation at a time when we need to be united to stand ahead in the world race.

Extreme neo-liberalism cannot provide a solution for it. As Indians we cannot completely ignore our culture heritage which forms the customs and traditions, which have their roots back in the times of our great grandfathers. But considering the other argument as well, we have to get rid of those flawed policies formulated by our ancestors. So the answer comes with balancing the human values of liberty and equity without the uncivilised moral degradation of the public based on neo-liberalism.

References

- www.thehindu.com
- www.en.wikipedia.org
- www.indianexpress.com
- www.firstpost.com
- www.azadindia.org

Chapter – 3

Barbaric Acts of Khap Panchayats – Who is Responsible?

—Dr Deepa Awasthi

Abstract

In recent few years khaps have been exposed by media for imposing illegal barbaric acts on the people living in khap ruled areas. It is ironical that every responsible agency in the country is known to fact that they are illegal social organisation based on anarchy, continuously violating the fundamental rights of common man yet they are functional. News of killing the couples, excommunicating the family members of victim, raping the female member of victim's family or naked parade of women against the incidents of love marriages are shocking in twenty first century in civilised society. This chapter discusses that inspite of continuous perusal from media, judiciary and civil society, the inability and inefficiency of government, police, administration, political leaders these khaps and such type of institutions are flourishing in the country. For checking the barbarism of khap panchayat collective efforts are the need of the hour. Chapter also explores that low sex ratio of the region is the prime reason for khaps getting too sensitive and strict on marriage related issues.

Key Words: *Illegal, Barbaric, Fundamental rights, Inability, Collective efforts.*

Introduction

In last few years khap panchayats have emerged as threat to modern ideas which are gaining more and more popularity in society especially among young generation due to exposure to rest of the world.

Young generation of the country do not want to remain stick to old illogical ideas while khaps are known to exist for guarding the ideology based on tradition and culture. Khap functions on the basis of gotra, caste and religion while youth of country opposes the division of society on the name of caste, community and religion, they consider the whole world as a global village. Even the boundaries of countries are meaningless for them. Popularity of these modern ideas has compelled the young generation to stand in contradiction with number of old traditions and customs guarded by khap and such type of old orthodox institutions.

Choosing a life partner as per their choice is one of the most prominent issues which makes the youth against the khap panchayats. As per tradition prevailing in country usually marriages are decided and arranged by the parents and the family members of bride and bridegroom matching the socio-economic status of families but the young generation is not ready to accept such type of arrange marriages any more as according to them it is a restriction on their liberty and right to choose their life partner. Usually young boys and girls fall in love affair at very young age, even before adulthood and few of them who are more committed with firm will power, decide to become life partners for rest of their life. The concept of love marriages is not new to Indian society. A number of ancient literature mentions that it was popular in India; its some forms were acceptable while others were considered as socially unacceptable.

Twenty or thirty years before love marriages were considered taboo in society, usually family members of boy and girl who opt for love marriage, boycott them and end all the relations with them but with passage of time and observing that youths are not ready to take back foot, families are gradually accepting these love marriages. Love marriages in which boys and girls belong to same caste, sub-caste and religion get the early acceptance while inter-caste or inter religious love marriages are still hardly accepted in conservative Indian society. Caste and religion is still playing a vital role in fixing the marriages. Apart from caste and religion issue, marriages within same Gotra or within same native village are the other issues which make the khap panchayats to pass an order or dictates against the couples who violates the rules of khap.

Involvement of Khap Panchayats in Marriage Related Issues

Many people in society have myth that khap interferes in marriage issues only but that is not true. Khap interferes in almost all the social, economic and political issues in which they find that somebody is bringing dishonour to khap, caste, community or religion by violating the old traditions and customs. For them marriage issues are more important than any other issue because they believe that marriage is the only instrument which ensures the purity in caste, community and religion. Sometimes during implementation of rules regarding marriages they violate the law of land through their inhuman barbaric acts against the couples and their family members. Here are the rules of marriages which are protected by khaps at any cost –

- Bride and bridegroom must belong to same caste, community and religion.
- Marriages between boys and girls belonging to similar gotra (clan) are fully banned whether love marriages or arranged, because they are considered as siblings.
- Marriages must not be settled between the boys and girls residing in same village, as they believe in concept of 'bhaichara' (brotherhood).

According to khap panchayat all the people who reside in khap governed areas must follow the rules strictly belonging to any caste, community or religion. As per the views of khap supporters, it is necessary for maintaining diminishing moral values in society especially among young boys and girls. With the passage of time a number of khap panchayats has allowed the love marriages but the love marriages which violate the above rules are still against the social norms.

Khap's supporters know it very well that these abnormal rules can only be implemented when they will be able to create fear of ill consequences in the minds of common man. For creating the fear they present themselves more inhuman and barbaric. As soon as khap members find that any couple or their family member has violated the rules regarding marriages then they call a public meeting, most of the time only male members of society residing in that khap area sit together to discuss the issue and punish the culprits. In the cases where issue is of much serious nature or concerned to large area then sarva khap panchayat is called in which representatives of number of khap participate to pass the resolutions which have even more powerful impact.

Usually these panchayats functions on the ideology of 'dishonour for dishonour.' As they believe that over passing the prevailing customary rules brings dishonour to caste and community so the person responsible for this has no right to have honour. At an instance khap panchayat issued a verdict of raping the female members of family of an individual accused of raping the girl of same village. Sometimes female family members of accused whether girl or boy are paraded naked with face painted black. Apart from this compelling the individual or their family members to drink urine of own or others, touching the feet of every person present in panchayat are another example of humiliating the individual who is held responsible for bringing dishonour to community or caste. Beating by public, compelling the individual or their family member to leave the village, relatives, friends for the sake of safety, fear of getting murdered for the sake of honour are the issues which require the attention of authorities.

Reason for Involvement of Khap in Marriage Related Issues

It is well known that khap interfere in all the issues whether social, political or economic but they seem very strict on the issues related to marriages. Question arises why they strictly ban inter-caste and inter-religious marriages and in case of violation do not hesitate in killing the girl or couple. The reason behind their too much involvement in marriage related issue is the low sex ratio of khap governed areas. In khap governed areas Haryana, Western UP, Rajasthan, Delhi the sex ratio has fallen alarmingly, even much lower to average sex ratio in country. On every 1000 males more than 125 females are short in Haryana. In such a situation it is hard for the male youth to find life partner belonging to appropriate age group. Even stories of bring brides in exchange of money from other states and remote areas of country like Bihar, Odisha, Assam are also common in the region. Estimating the situation khap leaders think that situation can even worse when girls of jat community will chose their life partner from other caste. Due to this they strictly abandon inter-caste and inter-religious marriages.

News of allowing inter-caste marriage is completely misguiding, they have relaxed the norms for getting the males married. They only allow when girl of any other caste is married to Jat Boy but as soon as the issue of a girl marrying the boy of different caste arises, they again become strict.

Evaluation of Role of Government and Non-government Agencies Responsible for Nourishing Khaps

Everybody in country knows that the khap and such type of other institutions are illegal yet they are active all over the country in one or the other form. Obviously, question arises from where they are gaining the strength, who is responsible for their nourishment?

- **Government:** It is the responsibility of government both State or Central to protect the rights of individual provided to them as per law of land. Bill drafted by Women Commission to prevent the honour crimes is still lying on table. None of the government whether UPA or NDA, seems to be in hurry on the issues related to women. Ministers, Member of Parliaments everybody remain silent, even sometimes makes fun of such incidences. Neither the state government nor the central government has ever tried to put ban on khap and khap panchayats while they are continuously acting like parallel government.
- **Political Parties and Political Leaders:** Politicisation of issues related to women is another reason why the activities of khap panchayats are still unchecked. None of the political party or their leaders have ever openly criticised the barbaric acts of khap panchayats. From time to time political leaders belonging to various political parties, stand in favour of these khap like institutions or prefer to remain silent. Understanding the influence of khaps in regions they start behaving as true spokesperson of khaps, in return the khap arranges vote bank for them. Political leader how strong he may be knows it

very well that few words against khap can terminate their political carrier. How ironical it is that when media questions the need of khap panchayat, the chief minister of Haryana comes forward in favour of khaps advertising their positive aspects neglecting their unlawful acts.

- **Police:** Police is another major stakeholder who is not performing their duty honestly. Hardly police has courage to stand against khap panchayats and the officers who want to take action against khap leaders have to withdraw their hands due to political interference. It is hard to believe that police remain unaware to such type of illegal gathering where these khap leaders are going to deliver their verdict as judge. If police really want, they can easily stop such type of gathering in advance for maintaining law and order in area, as these meetings are called with the intention of violating the laws and freedom guaranteed to every individual under Constitution. Cases where victims approached to police, the reaction has always been negative. Most of the time due to lack of timely police protection the couples and their family members have to face the humiliating acts of mob governed by khap.
- **Judiciary:** Judiciary has been the last hope for the victims of khap panchayats. Various courts have really shown their concern by taking positive action against khap leaders but unfortunately Indian judicial system is based on witness and trials. Most of the time no eyewitness come forward against mighty khaps. How ironical is that the family members of the victims also remain silent due to fear of khap. Courts have taken suo moto actions and punished the responsible persons. Even Supreme Court of India has declared them as 'kangaroo courts' and illegal.
- **Media:** Media has also played a positive role in war against the social evil knownas khap. Media has created an environment where people can at least raise their voice against illegal acts of khap panchayats. It is due to media that even common man have the courage to criticise the harmful acts and verdicts of khap panchayats.

Suggestions

Here are few useful suggestions to control the barbaric acts of khap panchayat –

- Bills drafted by Law Commission with the intention to curb the menance of khaps must be enacted immediately. These Bills have no relevance until they become law.
- Police should not wait for incident to happen they must react immediately to take all necessary preventive steps to stop the gathering intended to humiliate aman, woman, couple or family.
- It must be ensured that as soon as any individual or couples approaches to police, they must be given police protection and necessary action should be taken with immediate effects.
- In the cases related to crime committed under the umbrella of khap panchayat the woman police officer must be appointed for investigation on priority basis. Such type of steps will make the victim confident and believe in system.
- A toll free number can be issued for the victims of khap panchayat. Anybody can dial the number for informing/ complaining about the illegal activities of khap panchayat.
- All the Police officers must be ordered to deal the issues related to khap sensibly with open mindset.
- Police must take extra precaution and remain on high alert in khap governed areas; they cannot be excused for lack of pre-information about the khap meeting called by khap leaders when everybody in area knows about the panchayat except police. How ironical it is that police can identify a individual for not wearing helmet or not using seat belt among the mob of thousand but fails to identify the individual committing a serious crime by violating the human rights.
- An awareness campaign is needed in districts where khap and such type of institutions are over active. Every father and brother must be realised to understand that his family members are most important for them above caste, clan,

community or religion. It is their responsibility to take all possible care on priority basis rather slaughtering them on the name of honour.

- Every brother should be always ready to give equal share to his sister in ancestral property, why a sister falls in the situation where she has to indulge in the court case with the brother who promised her every year on occasion of *Rakshabandhan* to lay down his life for saving her life, honour and respect but fails to share the ancestral property.

Conclusion

Khap panchayats in India and abroad commonly known for killing the girls and couples on the issues of sagotra, inter-caste and inter-religious marriages. They are against the modern way of living giving priority to personal liberty and choice. They do not want the young girls to mix up or communicate with boys. Khap are strict on marriage issue due to low sex ratio in region. Although media, judiciary, civil society members are continuously putting the pressure to ban such type of organisations but lack of will power and intention of government, political leaders and police such institutions are surviving and imposing their illegal dictates on common man by creating fear in their mind. A collective effort is badly needed to have control on khap panchayats, ultimately none of the such institution can be allowed to encroach in personal space and life of individuals. Apart from this awaring the people against khaps can also play a decisive role because without public support khap will lose their relevance.

References

- Abdulla, Essay on Honour Killing in India. www.civilserviceindia.com
- After Rohtak Killing, Khap start spying on College goers, tell girls above 10 years to wear Salwar Kameez. (2013). www.intoday.in
- Bhardwaj, S. B.(2012), Myths and Realities of Khap Panchayat: A Historical Analysis of Khap Panchayat, *Studies in History*, Feb 2012, Vol. 28, No. 1, pp. 43- 67, www.sih.sagepub.com
- Bhardwaj, A. (2014), Are Khap Panchayat as Vile as Media Portrays Them? www.dna.com
- Burdak, L., Khap. www.jatland.com

- Dwedi, A., What is Khap Panchayat, What are its Function, Why it is criticised, Should Khap panchayat be banned in India? www.quora.com
- Girls not to use Mobile Phones: Barmer Khap (2015). www.thetimesofindia.indiatimes.com
- Jagmati Sangwan (2011). Khap Panchayat: Signs of Desperation, www.thehindu.com
- Khap Dictates: Rajasthan Women Claiming Property Share to be Outlawed for 10 Years, (2015). www.timesofindia.indiatimes.com
- Malik, S., Should Khap Panchayat be Banned in India. www.quora.com
- Raina, P. (2012). Does India Still Needs Khap Panchayat, www.mytimes.com
- Sakshi Abrol, The Hegemony of Khap Panchayat – A Case of Culture and Tradition at Extreme. www.youthkiawaaj.com
- Sehgal, M. (2013), No Jeans, Mobile Phones, Porn…or Same Gotra Marriages: Khap unveil banned list, They say will Stop Rape and Honour Killing, www.dailymail.co.uk

Chapter – 4

Affirmative Aspects of Khap Panchayat

—*Goldy Gupta*

Abstract

The khap has been prevalent Indian system of social administration in India. In ancient time, Indian society was organised in various forms, such as tribal, village, republican etc. With the passage of time, society organised around the villages. Khap generally means a group of villages made for set rules, giving decisions. Each khap has its own dispute redressal body known as a khap Panchayat, usually comprised of elderly men from khap. Like in family, disputes are resolved with the help of elders, and if it involves more than one family of a clan then the khap panchayat steps in. Inspite of being unsanctioned body by law, it still persists in India. Judicial delay, distrust on normal judiciary system by common people and weak panchayati raj institutions are the major reasons of its dominance. Media creates negative image of khap panchayat but there is some positivity lies in it. Banning of loud DJ music in wedding, stopping lavish show off in marriages, banning expensive items in dowry are far important and worth of respect. It works to protect our society from cultural invasion. It opposes marriage in same gotra. Even, scientifically it is proven that same gotra marriages are not good for the progeny. A khap Maha panchayat, attended by leaders of over 300 khaps took a stern stand against female foeticide. Several daughter empowerment campaigns were launched. Khap panchayat is an advisory body; it only guides what is right. Whatever honour killing instances have taken place, always the family members who have taken this step. In sharp contrast to the hardened stance taken by the khap panchayats, we have the examples of flexibility too in the context of customs and traditions related to marriage. We need to learn from them rather castigate them.

Key Words: *Gotra, Marriage, Daughter campaign, Honour killing.*

Introduction

Khap panchayat is the union of few villages, mainly in north India, though it exists in similar forms in the rest of the country. Lately, they have emerged as quasi-judicial bodies that pronounce harsh punishment based on age old customs and traditions, often bordering on regressive measures to modern problems (India Today Onlinc, 2012).

The khap has been prevalent system of social administration in India. In ancient time, Indian society was organised in various forms, such as tribe, village, republic etc. With the passage of time, Indian civilisation has been shifted to settled agricultural practices from nomadic culture. Then, society too organised around the village. At that time period, the mode of government was a council of five people, called a 'panchayat'. The republican government existed from that period and continued to exist. One of the terms used to denote the republic was 'khap'.

Khap is the term denotes socio-political grouping in a geographical sense. Originally, a khap consists of unit of 84 villages. A unit of seven villages was termed as 'Thamba' and 12 Thambas would form the unit of 84 villages, though khaps of 12 and 24 villages also existed. Their elected leaders would determine which units would be represented at the khap level. These khaps are found to be spread all the way from Northwest India down to Madhya Pradesh, Malwa, Rajasthan, Sindh, Multan, Punjab, Haryana and Uttar Pradesh (Wikipedia, 2015).

The Sarv khap is a political organisation, consists of all the clans, communities and caste of the region. The individual khaps send their delegates to represent their khaps at the Sarv khap or 'all khap'. Since it is a socio-political organisation, it comprises of the clans, castes and communities at the regional level.

The exact origin of it is lost in the mists of time but popular belief dates this social structure back to 600 A.D. These are social institutions that have no sanction under the law, having no legal status (Hindustan Times, 2010) still exists in Western U.P., Eastern Rajasthan but are most powerful in few districts like Rohtak, Bhiwani, Jhajjar, Sonepat, Jind, Kaithal, Karnal and Hissar districts of Haryana. It consolidates its position and power covering area comprising a cluster of villages and set rules. Each khap has its own dispute redressal body known as a khap panchayat. Like in any family, disputes are resolved with the help of elders, and if it involves more than one family of a clan then the khap panchayat steps in. Khap panchayat is an ancient, democratic and socially sanctioned institution. (Singh and Singh, 2013) The historic past indicates that it has been playing a vital role and indulged in such things which may threat to its social values.

Reasons of Dominance of Khap Panchayat

Khap panchayat is a popular system of resolving the disputes since ancient time. Even today, when India is heading toward modernisation, people living in rural areas still follow it. They consider it as a guiding body on social issues. Members of khap panchayats are hereditary. There exists many customs and rules set by these guiding bodies, beneficial for society in positive way. Following are the some other reasons of its dominance:

- **Judicial Delay and Distrust of the System**

It is due to delay in justice by normal courts, the villagers trust in system of khap panchayats. They deliver the verdict in single sitting, whereas courts drag case for years. Many innocent people face harassment by the police when they go to police for protection or to complain. The 'panchs' leaders of panchayats, are all well known to every one of them, so the villagers trust them and are confident that the panchayat will cross check everything to ensure neutrality to administer justice.

Weak Panchayati Raj Institutions

India is a democratic country. The members of Panchayati raj Institutions are elected democratically. Even there is provision to insure participation of women in good number via 33 per cent reservation for them. In reality these elected female members function as rubber stamp only. The failure of Panchayati raj system to deliver what was expected from it is one of the reasons for emergence of khaps as strong socio-political units.

Consideration of Socio-economic Issues

Khap panchayats oppose the lavish show off on the name of ceremony. They also decide not to give expensive gifts in the name of dowry. All the villagers have to follow code of conduct honestly and equally. These are the some examples for the popularity of khap panchayats among the rural people. A young girl told that because of the khap diktat her father would not be able to gamble and drink alcohol and also due to the steps taken by the Khap Panchayat the incidents of sexual harassment is also expected to decrease. (Jamia Millia Islamia University Report, p. 25)

Merits of Khap Panchayat

The main motive of khap panchayat is to maintain peace and harmony by settling social disputes or passing the resolutions for social welfare. Its functioning affects the society in a great way. Their effectiveness depends on the type of issue, number of persons involved, the nature of decision etc. The strong points of any khap panchayat are co-operation, objectivity and mainly *bhaichara* (brotherhood). In our society, the portrayal of khap panchayat in media creates negative image about its functioning. But, in true sense, there is some positivity lies in it. The following are the points which support the positive role of khap panchayat:

- **Acts as Social Reformer**

Khap panchayats have taken up the issues like banning of loud D. J. music in wedding, stopping lavish show off in marriages, banning gifts of expensive items like tractors or motorcycles as dowry. These are far important and worthy of respect (Jamia Millia Islamia Report). There was a gathering in the sixties of the twentieth century in village Sisana regarding the excess expenditures in marriages, size of *baraat* and number of days spent on celebrations of marriages (Dahiya, 2010). There are now instances of the bride being brought to her in-laws house immediately after '*Chunni Udhaai*', thereby foregoing the traditional custom of taking seven rounds of the holy fire.

- **Jury of Common Men**

Every khap panchayat has a jury for common men. The decision at which level, the panchayat should gather depends on the gravity and magnitude of the problem. The larger the area or the intensive the problem, the higher is the level of panchayat gathering for the concerned issue. They provide the equal right to attend the meetings and express their views. The elected leaders at panchayats maintain records of the decisions taken in the proceedings (Law Teacher). Many of the disputes are solved through *bhaichara* (brotherhood) while our Indian judicial system seeks solid proofs and interpretation of laws through lawyer and judge. The consequences of that verdict affect him in no way.

- **Preservation of Ancient Culture**

In this age of westernisation, khap panchayat acts as a strong preservative of our culture and traditions. It protects our society from cultural invasion. Customs and traditions have to be maintained to sustain our society. The design may be changed but the fabric sustains. Society reshapes and reinvigorates itself with the passage of time. Customs and traditions are not to be treated as being a given, ever - constant category that brook no change. Khap panchayat does not stick to custom without any reason. It is flexible in nature. In todays life, we hardly see any example of "*Latta Udhaana*" (Forcible marriage of widow to her husband's brother), child marriage etc. (Dahiya, 2010). The '*Ghoonghat*' or the full veil is obsolete in urban area and ready to disappear in rural area (Bhardwaj, 2014). We should not forget that society is a living organism, and also has the capacity to find a new and healthy balance.

- **Opposition to Same Gotra Marriage**

Khap panchayat governs the rule that all boys and girls within a khap are considered siblings and hence cannot marry. It opposes marriage in same gotra, which is our culture. Marriage, within the same gotra, may lead to the problems related to health issues on account of genetics (Dahiya, R. S., 2010). Even scientifically it is proven that same gotra marriages are not good for the progeny. To understand it, firstly we have to understand the term gotra. The gotra is a system which associates a person with his most ancient or root ancestor in an unbroken male lineage. So, gotra refers to the root person in a person's male lineage. The word gotra is formed from the two Sanskrit words 'gau' and 'trahi'. Gau means cow and trahi means shed. So, gotra is like the cow shed, protecting a particular male lineage. A girl and a boy belonging to the same gotra are considered to be siblings and hence it is prohibited for them to marry even if they belong to distant families and the reason given was since they belonged to the same ancestor. So, it would like a brother marring to his sister and it may cause genetic disorders in their offspring. Manusmriti also discourages same gotra marriage. It is the important and earliest work of the textual tradition of Hinduism. Burdak, Laxman (2012) stated that in Manusmriti, Chapter-3, Verse-5 mentioned that the girl who is not from mother's clan of six generations and who is not of father's gotra is suitable for marriage amongst dwijatiya people - Brahmana, Kshatriya and Vaishya.

- **Promotion of Education**

Khap panchayat promotes the education through many institutions. Jat communities are known for social reforms. Jat community has opened many educational institutions specifically in north India, without any government aid with their own charity. These institutions are democratic in nature and there are no boundations of caste and religion among the teachers and students (Sunita and Yudhvir, 2013). In 1911, in Barona villasge of district Rohtak, Haryana, there was a panchayat on the issue of education – an effort that led to the establishment of the Jat educational institutions over a period of time in Rohtak. (Dahiya, 2010)

Positive Steps Taken by Khap Panchayats

Khap panchayat has constantly been in the headlines for the wrong reasons, be it honour killing or barbaric murder of innocent lovers for falling in love with someone outside from community or of same gotra, banning the use of mobile phones by young girls, restrictions on wearing western outfit or not giving freedom to female. It is quite alarming that, India being a great democratic country, there still exists a pseudo judicial institution like khap panchayat. Recently their role has been constantly under the scanner not only because of the controversial diktats but also for regressive comments made by them. To overcome from the negative image of Khap Panchayat, a conscious effort is also made to refurnish the make up of the dented image by doing something for social welfare. Some of them are -

- **First Women Driven Khap Panchayat**

Due to the intense public uproar and awareness, the Bibipur village of Haryana, decided to bring a positive change in their panchayat system by hosting the first women driven khap panchayat and the issues like female foeticide and sex determination tests were discussed (Mukut, 2012). This Khap Maha Panchayat was attended by leaders of more than 300 khaps from Haryana, Rajasthan and Uttar Pradesh, took a stern stand against female foeticide and demanded that murder charges be slapped against those who indulge into the heinous act (Press Trust of India, 2012). For the first time a large number of women participated in Khap Maha Panchayat. It was seen that the population of girls has decreased; female foeticide may be responsible for it. The meeting signified its role as Haryana has very poor sex ratio. Ex Chief Minister of Haryana, Mr Bhupinder Singh Hudda also encouraged this effort. This type of meetings at large scale create mass awareness about social evils.

Fig. 4.1: Photograph of Maha panchayat on female foeticide in Bibipur Village

Picture courtesy: www.vegmomos.com

- **Allowed Inter-Caste Marriages**

The largest khap in Haryana the 'Satrol khap' allowed inter-caste marriages. In a departure from the norm, more was an agent to a big change in this neck of the woods. In a landmark event, presided over a Maha khap in April, 2014 decided to allow inter-caste marriages, putting an end to a six-century old ban on matrimonial alliances among people living in the 42 villages under this khap. Elders of the villages said that the skewed sex ratio and a rise in bachelors were the driving force to allow inter-caste marriages with the exception of marital ties in the same gotra.

- **Daughter Empowerment Campaigns**

A Sarpanch in Haryana's'Bibipur village, Sunil Jaglan, had come up with idea of saving girl child. He started the 'Selfie with Daughter' initiative. All fathers must click selfie with their daughters and post it on social media. The 'Beti Bachao, Selfie Banao' campaign, now christened 'Selfie with Daughter', is Jaglan's campaign. He launched more than 100 programmes on women empowerment. In 2012, he held the first women's khap panchayat, on female foeticide. Khap claimed that female infanticide is a matter of the past. Today everyone sees a girl as an asset. Still if a person is not capable of looking after a girl child, he will ask the family to take care of her for one year after which, as the panchayat head, I will arrange for the adoption of the girl to a new, better family. This new programme will be christened as 'Beti Pao, Dharm Kamao' (Katiyar, 2015).

Conclusion

For a society to move ahead, it is necessary to have certain degree of elasticity. In sharp contrast to the hardened stance taken by the khap panchayats within Haryana among the Jat community we have the examples of flexibility too in the context of customs and traditions related to marriage. We need to learn from them rather castigate them (Dahiya, 2010). Khap panchayat is an advisory body; it only guides what is right. Coming to honour killing or more clearly to say 'dishonour killing' instances have taken place and always the family members who have taken this step. It is a misleading representation by media.

Such type of killings has also been reported in Tamil Nadu and Punjab states that don't have khap panchayats adjudicating matters of marriage. Families oppose couples, who choose themselves often violently (Bhardwaj, 2014). Who can forget famous Aarushi - Hemraj Murder case? It can also be named as Honour killing. Murder committed by parents for the sake of honour. There was no role of khap panchayat. It is not the appropriate time of blaming. Khaps never rule to kill anyone.

India is not the Taliban ruled Afghanistan. Opportunities for educating females are available. Haryana has always been in limelight due to khap diktats but it is also true that girls are not prevented here from studying, working or even taking up sports as their career. They are in fact encouraged by these khap panchayats. Wrestling Champions Babita, Geeta Phogat, Mountaineer Santosh Yadav, Golden girl Mamta Kharab and many others winning medals for the country are also from khap-dominated rural area of Haryana. None of them would have been possible if the Khaps would have the kind of influence suggested by media. Mukesh Lohan, President of the Youth Wing of Satrol khap, presents another reality of khap. The kind of work that khaps have done can't be compared with politics or politicians. If khap comes to an end, *bhaichara* will also come to an end. In our land, people don't fear the administration as much as they dread social boycott. A court takes 10 to 20 years for delivering a verdict, but khaps give a verdict in 20 minutes. (The Economic Times, 2015).

Khap panchayat should break silence over common issues like domestic violence against women, family planning, dowry menace, drinking liquor and drug addiction, agriculture crisis, forced occupation of common lands, farmers suicide etc. Khap panchayat should take such stands that have social positive impact and benefit for the entire society. All the decisions should be in favour of common man. Some reforms are required, to make the khap panchayats as problem solver rather than problem creator. There should be periodic elections for selecting head of khap, so that a right person with good leadership can be elected to provide constructive guidelines. Youth should also be involved in khap panchayat so that generation gap would not create problems. This old age institution must continue with some modifications according to changing scenario.

References

- Bhardwaj, A. (2014). Are khap panchayats as vile as the media portrays them? www.dnaindia.com (Retrieved on Sep. 02, 2015)
- Burdak, L. (2012). Jat Marriages. www.jatland.com (Retrieved on Sep. 06, 2015)
- Dahiya, R. S. (2010). Khap Panchayats: Need to review their role in society. *Mainstream Weekly*, 48(30). www.mainstreamweekly.net
- HitXP-A Blogzine (n.d.). Science of Genetics behind the Hindu Gotra system-The Y chromosome and the Male lineage. www.hitxp.com (Retrieved on Sep 04, 2015)
- Initiatives against Female Foeticide, (Image) The Tribune, Chandigarh (Published on July 13, 2013) www.tribuneindia.com
- Jamia Millia Islamia University Report. Descriminative and derogatory practices against women by Khap Panchayats, Shalishi Adalats and Kangaroo Courts in India: An empirical study in the states of Haryana, Uttar Pradesh (West),West Bengal and Rajasthan. www.ncw.nic.in (Retrieved on Sep. 02, 2015)
- Katiyar, Prerna (2015). Beti Bachao, Beti Padhao: why it will take a lot more to change mindsets in India's hotbeds of misogynism. The Economic Times, www.m.economictimes.com (Retrieved on Sep. 08, 2015)
- Khap History, Wikipedia, The Free Encyclopedia www.en.m.wikipedia.org (Retrieved on Sep. 02, 2015)
- Law Teacher (n.d.). Khap Panchayat. from www.lawteacher.net (Retrieved on Sep. 03, 2015)
- Mukut (2012). Khap Panchayat: A medieval India under the shining cover. Mukut's Journal. www.worldpulse.com (Retrieved on Sep. 04, 2015)
- Polson, Isha (Image), www.vegmomos.com (Retrieved on Sep. 19, 2015)
- Press Trust of India (2012). Slap murder charge for female foeticide, says Khap Maha panchayat. www.indianexpress.com (Retrieved on Sep. 05, 2015)
- Singh, S. and Singh, D. (2013). Identifying the centripetal and centrifugal forces through Khap Panchayats in Haryana-An analysis. IOSR Journal of Humanities and Social Sciences, 4,109-116. www.Iosrjournals.org
- Sunita and Yudhvir (2013). Khap Panchayats: Changing perspectives. Asian Journal of Multidimensional Research, 2 (7), 14-20. www.tarj.in
- What is khap panchayat (2012). India Today Online, Published on Oct. 11, 2012, New Delhi. www.m.indiatoday.in (Retrieved on Sep. 05, 2015)

Chapter – 5

Threatening Khap Panchayats

—*Palwinder Kaur*

Abstract

Khap is a cluster of villages united by caste and geography. It is as old as fourteenth century started by upper caste Jats to consolidate their power and position. The main rule is that all boys and girls within a khap are considered siblings. Khap panchayat governs the khap formed by same gotra (clan) families from several neighbouring villages. Khaps mainly belong to states of Haryana, Rajasthan and Uttar Pradesh, are originated from the ancient system of 'Panchayats' as a social administration and organisation. Love marriages are considered taboo in areas governed by khap panchayats. Those living in a khap are not allowed to marry in the same gotra or even in different gotra from the same village. Many young couples have been killed in the past defying khap rules. Actually, the word 'khap' itself denotes a regional area or 'Janpad', now equivalent to a 'tehsil'. Khap actually wield much more power than the statutory panchayats in these states. Survival of the institution of khap during such a long passage of time demonstrates not only its resilience but also its suitability for the people inhabiting the long tract extending from Madhya Pradesh and Malwa to Sindh, Punjab and Multan. Besides fathers and brothers of the girls, there is direct involvement of their mothers, paternal or maternal uncles, family friends and even contract killers into the murders. It has been observed that the centuries old conformist mind set prevailing in the patriarchal society does not accept the girls to establish pre-marital relations or to find males of their own choices to marry with.

Keywords: *Khap Panchayats, Women, Honour Killings, Caste, Injustice.*

Introduction

During the last few years extensive reports have appeared in newspapers and television channels all over the country about the brutal killing of young boys and girls in the name of honour killings. Khap panchayats performed positive role during the ancient and medieval periods such as promotion of education, settling the community disputes, donation of lands for the opening of schools, curbing lavish display of wealth during marriages. At the same time, these khaps over the centuries have not approved inter-caste or class marriages. These marriages were and are considered immoral, deserving rigorous reprimand, and developed a culture of intolerance. The socio-economic dominant castes are usually accountable for these unlawful, callous acts against inter-caste relationships. "In the name of preserving 'social order' and saving the 'honour' of the community, caste or family, all kinds of justifications are pressed into service." Khap panchayats have recently been in news for either their diktat judgments or because of their justifying crimes in the name of saving the 'honour' of the families and community at large. These socio-cultural norms are especially imposed on youths, especially on young women, mostly in Haryana or some parts of Western Uttar Pradesh. Despite the growing global attention on 'honour crimes', the issue remains an uncomfortable one as some delegations are concerned that a focus on crimes against women committed on the name of honour is selective, rather than comprehensive in its treatment of violence against women.

Khap and Sarv khap was a system of social administration and organisation in the republics of north-western states like Haryana, Rajasthan and Uttar Pradesh in India since ancient times. People living in its village units since the days of Rig Veda, are called as khaps. Their social, administrative and organisation structure comprised of a republican society headed by the council of five. It is also popularly called as panchayat, earlier 'Sabha' or 'Samiti' lead by an elected 'Sabhapati'. Thus, khaps are a social - political grouping of a particular geographical tract, now extending from Madhya Pradesh and Malwa to Sindh, Punjab and Multan. The word khap is probably derived from Latin word 'corpus' which means an organisation of individuals. Other parallel terms are Pal, Ganas, Janpada or republic. For some reasons the political unit of khap was defined as a group of 84 villages. This unit of measure is found as far back as the Saka migrations/invasions in 500 BC into the Indian subcontinent.

Moving from various forms of governance, tribal to village to monarchical and then modern republican mode, khaps have demonstrated their social resilience and political suitability of their organisation for the masses governed. In Indian subcontinent a unique and crucial basis of stratification is caste system which can be seen as an elaborated hierarchy of birth-based groups. If we look back in history, these status groups were closely linked to the control over resources and thus broadly congruent with class. The extra-constitutional bodies of Khaps are not only creating moral pressures by limiting the choice of youth in getting married to the person of their choice but also creating fear in them and their families. Not surprisingly, even police protection fails to help the poor victims as policemen and politicians fully subscribe to and openly endorse the values underlying opposition to such marriages. They, therefore, allow revenge and condone punishment of the so-called transgressors. Khaps are found not only in one particular region, religion or community. It is found in almost all the regions or communities in Haryana and Uttar Pradesh with different times.

For instance Ahlawat Khap, Rathi Khap, Balyan Khap, Gurjar Khap, Bhadana Khap, Kalsiyan Chauhan Rana Khap, Kasana Khap, Khatana Khap, Bainsla Khap, Bhati Khap, Karhana Khap, Panwar Khap, Batar Khap, Chhokar Khap, Rawal Khap, Nagar Khap, Dedha Khap, Tomar Khap and Chouhan Gurjar Khaap are the main khaps exists in region. It is to be noted that love marriages are considered taboo in areas governed by khap panchayats. If a married couple's gotra is same or if they have married in the same or neighbouring village, they are told to cease being husband and wife and live as brother and sister. To the khap panchayats, it does not matter that their parents may have arranged the marriage, a child may already have been born out of the marriage and that in the eyes of the law they have done no wrong. Yet, the same law is unable to protect them and it bows to what are claimed to be sacrosanct social norms. Parents, brothers and cousins who avenge such "wrong" marriages instead find legitimacy and support from local law enforcement authorities.

What is the Khap System?

The Khap panchayats are village councils usually comprising of 10-15 elderly men from the Jat community that set the rules in an area comprising of one or more villages inhabited by the members of a single clan (caste). A number of khaps form a 'Sarva khap' embracing a full province or state. Their elected leaders would decide which units would be represented at the khap level. A khap originally consisted of 84 villages. A unit of seven villages was called a Thamba and 12 Thambas would form the unit of 84 villages, a khap, together. However, there are also khaps of 12 and 24 villages.

Their elected leaders would determine which units would be represented at the khap level. These khaps are found in North Western India, primarily in Haryana, Eastern Rajasthan and Western Uttar Pradesh. The khap panchayats have unwritten laws, and their decisions are clearly illegal and extra constitutional. The khap panchayat is a creation of the Jats. Each caste has a separate caste council and a leader for every gotra or lineage. Khap panchayats are one of the most mediaeval groups of elders in rural areas which have got handed down from pre-independence times. It then suited the (British) colonizers that the villages handle their own matters rather than clog the courts. But times have changed. The educated civil society in India is finding them repelling.

But one must not forget these khap panchayat murders are also a loss of control over its shrinking pool of women, with sons being preferred. It's impossible for them to digest that women could decide for themselves. Khap is the informal institution of each gotra in the Jat community of North India which determines the customs and practices as well as religious norms for its specific gotra. The members of each gotra elect their headman. This headman convenes the panchayat of his village. It is obligatory for all members to comply with the decisions taken in the panchayat. There is a supreme organisation of the entire Jat community which is called the Sarv khap, it includes all gotra khap. This gotra-based institution is not peculiar to this region. Such types of institutions existed in Munda and Gond tribes of central and eastern India. Gotra-based institutions are product of that tribal age when human society was in its primitive stage. The society was divided into Kul (clan or gotra) based groups at that time. These kinship-groups independently determined their social norms and customs. Rig Veda refers to many clans (Kul). The society of that period was primarily based on pastoralism, though some amount of agriculture was also carried out. However, the concentration of power was checked by various assemblies of the clansmen, in particular, the vidatha, sabha and samiti. As long as the gana-sangha system of polity existed; these clan-based institutions were responsible for regulating the society. The assembly of the clan-chiefs used to wield the power of governance. Their society was organised on the basis of clans, of which the larger unit was the tribe. This form of organisation distinguished them from the peasants and the caste-based society.

Functions

The functions of various units of khap and the Sarv khap panchayat fall into three categories, namely, adjudicative, legislative, and executive. The khap council are various political units now, mostly they do not have legislative functions because they have no legal sanction or authority as they enjoyed earlier, under their legal charter, then the khap panchayat could frame rules and regulations to be obeyed not only by the Jats but also other castes and communities of the khap area, and their infringement was punished by the khap panchayat which was supreme in internal matters. Several instances from the historical records of the khap panchayat of Baliyan and from the minutes of the panchayat meetings can be cited where certain rules of conduct for inter-personal, inter-group, and inter-caste relations, rules guiding land revenue collection, and general policies of social welfare for the people, were framed and executed by the khap panchayat. However, the khap panchayat and its units now function only as adjudicative bodies and executive bodies in so far as the implementation of their decisions is concerned, by virtue of what may be called the traditional charter.

The Sarv khap panchayat still functions as a legislative body when it meets for its formal session every five years since its revival in 1950. An informal meeting of the Sarv khap panchayat of neighbouring khaps may also function as adjudicative and executive bodies when they judge cases of infringement of resolutions adopted in the formal meetings of the sarv-khap panchayat or decide to implement these resolutions in the various khaps of the area or when they decide cases and disputes between persons, groups or castes, and implement their decision on the parties concerned, Executive power, particularly in implementing the sanctions passed by a panchayat, is generally used in extreme cases of default or flouting the social norms by a person or a group, and its success depends upon a strong public opinion behind the decisions of the Panchayat.

A council of higher political units may be summoned if a smaller unit is not successful in settling an issue. Among the territory-based councils, a khap, an inter-khap, or a Sarv khap panchayat, is considered more effective than lineage, patti, village, ganwand, and thamba panchayats. To make a council effective and successful important persons like the headmen, of maximal lineages and the leaders of villages, ganwands, thambas, khap leaders, and sometimes also of the neighbouring khaps, are invited to attend the meeting and to act as judges or mediators. With their judgement and experience and also because of their prestige and political influence, they are considered in a better position to put forward such proposals as may lead to the settlement of a dispute or to implement the decisions of a Panchayat.

Advantages

In our society there is a huge discussion about khap panchayats but only in a negative sense. Some positive aspects are also there -

1. They are having a jury for common man and from common man which has thorough knowledge of issue, both parties and implication of the crime and its verdict. Our Judicial system is only seeing the instance with the help of written and solid proofs and that also is the interpretation of advocates and judges. He bears no implication of crime and verdict he would pass.
2. It's good that they have taken up issues like dowry harassment and oppose lavish show of money in marriage functions.
3. Khap panchayat is based on social respect and responsible for protecting our society from cultural invasion by alien societies.

4. Khap panchayat helps in preservation of culture and traditions from one generation to the next.
5. They played vital role in social activities like widow marriage, poor girls marriage, provide help to poor families by giving them land for agriculture, solving disputes among the families, etc.
6. Khap panchayat promotes the education through many institutions like Jat Institutions. Jat communities are known for social reforms; they have opened Gurukuls, throughout India (North India in specific) and that too without any government aid with their own charity. These institutions are democratic in nature and there are no restrictions of caste and religion among the teachers and students.

Disadvantages

1. Violation of the gotra rule usually invites death for the offending couple, while family members are ostracized. It has served as a motive to terminate many young lives, either through murder or forced suicide. The Maha panchayat recently justified their actions by sending a message to the government and courts saying that the khap panchayats are independent of the laws of the land. As a result, these medieval village level panchayats function as parallel courts. They govern social norms and pronounce verdicts, which are in contravention of the modern, equitable laws that post-independence India adopted as a democracy. The khap panchayats take over the authority to act as prosecutors and judges without having the legal authority to do so.
2. The political and judicial power that the khaps have affects the life of many to a great extent. In order to act according to the rules elder villagers try to keep the young people apart. Some schools are also forced to have separate timings for the boys and girls; or girls are not allowed to go to school at all. Fearing their daughters would go astray, many parents marry them off at an early age. People have unquestionable faith in the justice of khap. The question of rights for women does

not exist anywhere in the territories ruled by khap panchayats. That girls are seldom sent to schools is especially harmful because education can empower various sections of society, and women in particular, more than anything else. In some Haryana villages, the young girls are routinely threatened, abused and killed all under khap verdicts. It is acceptable for the families to feed pesticide pills to the teenage girls and then dispose of their bodies by burning them without any police records. The entire onus of siblinghood rests on the girl. She is the keeper of village honour. Sometimes rules are bending for the boys but a girl is never allowed to bend the rules. If a couple runs away then the families risk a boycott and hefty fines in lakhs of rupees. Even the other women of the house can suffer abuse. In general, women are not well off under the rule of khap panchayats. In some other parts of India where there are khap panchayats, women are considered by them as a commodity. The reproductive roles of women are highlighted under this fold. They are not given any rights and expected to obey their fathers before they are married and fulfil their duties as a wife and as a homemaker after they get married. Women are not even allowed to enter, for participation in these khap meetings. Complete exclusion of female counterparts reflects that it is a highly male-dominated sphere where women are considered mere objects.

3. As a result of the power of the khap panchayat, Haryana remains completely feudal and patriarchal in terms of attitudes to labour, marriage, inheritance, and caste and gender relations. The predominant Jats, as a wealthy farming community, zealously guard their land, females and customs. Exercising control is the key to their social formulations, and khap panchayats serve as instruments towards this end. They are also found in other States, harbouring Jats. For this reason, labourers who do not belong to the Jats do not get a chance to develop in economic respect. The influential khap panchayats also affect the local economy in another way. To a great extent they exert control over the labour market: indirectly they have a say in who gets what kinds of jobs.

How Khaps can Play a Vital Role in Standardisation and Reformation of Society?

1. In earlier times, all these khap panchayats have played a leading role. As they are not elected bodies, their decisions are not supported by law but their terror continues unless they are banned. There is nothing honourable in the killings or inflicting violence on the innocent people. It is very important to punish the people responsible and involved in such kind of exercise in order to prevent cultural and religious practices that are offensive in nature and abuse human rights and dignity. Therefore, the government and social organisations would have to assume the changing mindset of people.
2. TV is not only the source of entertainment; they also provide knowledge to children. So khap panchayats can unite on this platform, there is no better medium other than TV to make the children of modern age aware about our custom and traditions too. This is not only the way of emphasising khap panchayats role and goodwill to society but many more too like in schools through moral classes, in families through grand-parents, in villages through respective and honourable elders. All these have to come ahead and take their responsibility for the society and then see there would not be any crime in future neither from the side of young generation nor from the khap panchayats. There is a need to establish the village-wise committees in every khap to awaken the society against the prevailing social evils. These committees would have equal number of men and women representation.

Conclusion

In the present scenario of globalisation, youth always believe in the change or modification of the tradition with respect to the advancement of technology, urbanisation, education and nuclear families. There is also need for some modification in the thousand years old traditions and should amend the certain rules by inducing some flexibilities according to the norms of present society to make them more significant and more acceptable to the mass. It is about eliminating the constant fear of being killed at any moment by such kangaroo courts even when we are living in a democracy with a fully functional judiciary. In last, the central government has to step in and ensure that the powerful and the retrogressive khap panchayats are dealt with firmly. Both the state and central governments need to strengthen the observance of reformed marriage and inheritance laws and stem the exercise of archaic customary law. Doing so will address the twin horrors of female foeticide and honour killings. Equal inheritance will lead to equal value of sons and daughters and help in balancing the sex ratio.

References

- Agarwal, Partap C. (1971). Caste, Religion and Power: An Indian Caste Study. New Delhi: Shri Ram Centre for Industrial Relations.
- Kaur, Ravinder, (2010). "Khap Panchayat, Sex Ratio and Female Agency", Economic and Political Weekly, Vol. XLV, No. 23, June 5, 2010.
- Malaviya, H. D. (1956). Village Panchayat in India. New Delhi: Economic and Political Research Department, All India Congress Committee.
- Pradhan, M. C. (1966). The Political System of Jats of Northern India, Delhi: Oxford University Press.
- The Tribune, Chandigarh, 9 July, 2013, p. 3.

Section–B

Khap Panchayats and Discrimination Against Women

Chapter – 6

Khap Panchayats and their Discriminative Practices against Women

—*Dr Rashmi Singh*

Abstract

The term honour has a gendered meaning in patriarchal society like India. It is the women who bring honour to her family by adhering to the socially sanctioned behaviour. The concept of honour, especially with respect to women is a deeply entrenched belief amongst all sections of Indian society. In India, centuries old traditions of caste and tribe remain little diluted till date, hence women have to face a number of social diktats issued by organisations like khap with a strong patriarchal mind set. Khap is a centuries old socio-political organisation in states like Haryana, Western UP and Rajasthan. Now-a-days these khap panchayats have received all the negative media coverage for issuing their illogical and barbaric social diktats against women. Honour killing is one of them. There is nothing honourable in honour killings; in fact, they are nothing but the shameful acts of murder committed by brutal, feudal minded persons who deserve harsh punishment. It is the phenomenon of the structured thoughts planted in the traditions of the society. Hence gradual change in the mindset of people is the only cure. This can be done by mass education campaign on gender issue and gender sensitisation which can eradicate the evils of gender discrimination. This has eventually turned Khap panchayats into institutions which can work for empowerment of women rather than making them victims of rotten age old traditions.

Key words: *Honour, Khap Panchayat, Gender Sensitisation, Gender Discrimination, Women Empowerment.*

Introduction

On one hand we are talking about the Vision of India 2020 while on the other hand we are still adhered to the old, outdated and illogical traditions, which are of no use in the twenty first century. Women comprise almost half of the Indian population. How can we think of our nation as advanced, developed and progressive unless and until its women are deprived of the basic human rights, such as live with dignity and freedom. Indian society is embedded in the core of patriarchy. Gender discrimination lies in its soul. Khap panchayats are the typical example of patriarchal mindset. They have issued various social diktats for women from time to time, to restrict their movement, the right to choose their life partner and keep them away from their right in ancestral property.

Historical Background of Khap Panchayats

Khap is an ancient concept which has written references found back from the Rig-Vedic times. The origin of the word 'Khap' is derived from the word 'fank' meaning an offshoot or fraction. Ancient society had arranged itself into clan or under panchayat system. Basically a clan was based on one large gotra or a number of closely related gotras. 'Gotra' is a lineage that is associated to an individual at his/her birth. The father's gotra is carried forward by the child following the norms of a patriarchal society. A number of villages grouped themselves into a Guhaand. A number of guhaands forms a khap (covering an area equal to form a Tehsil to a District) and a number of khaps formed a 'Sarva khap' embracing a full province or State. For example, there was a Sarva khap each for Haryana and Malwa.

It is commonly believed that khaps came into existence sometimes around 600 AD. These are basically socio-political groups, which usually comprise the upper caste and elderly men who are united by geography and caste. Hence, khap is a term for socio-political grouping and used in geographical sense. Khap panchayats have had a long innings in the Jat-dominated areas of North Western India. It is believed to have been started by the upper caste Jats to consolidate their power and position in the community.

Khap is a cluster of villages united by caste and geography. Each village is governed by the panchayat, which is an elected council and the elected members of all the villages in the cluster would then choose a khap leader, who would then convene the meeting of khap panchayats. The main feature of a khap is that all boys and girls within a khap are considered as siblings. Love marriages are considered taboo in areas governed by khap panchayats. Those living in a khap are not allowed to marry in the same gotra or even in any gotra from the same village. Same gotra marriage is a sensitive issue and has helped the khaps to gather massive public support. Khap have become more powerful than elected Gram Panchayats as one unit of khap takes care of the social affairs of almost 84 villages from the same caste. Khap Panchayats are collective patriarchal bodies which function as extrajudicial bodies and hold political influence in the area. The people affected by khaps i.e. Haryana and Western U.P. defend khap as being a part of their tradition and age old culture. Khap is a way of honouring their culture and the values their ancestors taught. Khap panchayat imposes its writ through social boycots and fines and in most cases end up either killing or forcing the victims to commit suicide. This is done in the name of brotherhood and honour. Honour is generally seen as residing in the bodies of women. Frameworks of 'honour' and its corollary 'shame', operate to control, direct and regulate women's sexuality and freedom of movement by male members of the family. It is the woman, who is the subject of honour and not her male partner.

Reasons of their Dominance in Mass

These khap panchayats have a long history and they have attained full support in their villages in spite of their issuance of various social diktats. Such as to ostracize families, declare marriages as void, declare husband and wife as brothers and sisters and give different other discriminative and derogatory orders, and worst of them is honour killing. In spite of all these practices, khap panchayats enjoy a more dominant position over the panchayati raj institutions in the local area. There are various reasons behind their dominance which are listed here one by one:

- **Weakness of the Elected Institutions**

Weakness of the existing government bodies -the panchayati raj institutions boasts of having 33 per cent reservation for women. But such a reservation seems to be a joke on our system as the elected women candidates are mere proxies of their male counterparts. In addition to this the deep-rooted patriarchal system has denial of any system which is governed by females. Because of this till date these institutions have not garnered much public support. Localities turn towards Khap panchayats for the resolution of their disputes.

- **Politicisation of Khaps**

Although Supreme Court of India has issued certain guidelines to not to interpret constitutional laws by their own, khap-related blatant disregard of basic human rights are increasing day by day. The most striking fact is that no political party or leader is in position to oppose brutal acts of khap. The reason behind this is the vote bank of Jats in Haryana. Every leader knows in advance if he/she goes against the khap ideology then his/her political career come to an end. Hence they keep a silence over this matter. This tendency also strengthens the position of khaps.

- **Delayed Judgment by Courts**

Indian judicial system is based on evidence. It provides total opportunity to the victim for clarification of his stand. It will take time in providing justice. Sometimes even innocent people are harassed by judiciary and police. This also produces distrust for the government system.

- **Socio-economic Factors**

Leaders of the khap panchayats are the influential and elite people. Hence the local poor people have no option but to accept their orders. Not only this, women are subordinated to that much extent in our society by hundreds of years that their conscience is lost. They happily bear to live with all the discrimination for them, accepting that it is their naseeb (faith) to born as a girl and to face all the silly things in their life.

Discriminative Practices of Khaps

People have unquestionable faith in the justice of khap. The issues of rights for women, gender equality, gender sensitivity does not exist anywhere in the territories ruled out by khap panchayats. The common discriminative practices of khap panchayats against women are:

- **Female Foeticide**

According to census data, the child sex ratio (0-6 year age group) in India was 927 girls per 1000 boys in 2001, which dropped drastically to 918 girls for every 1000 boys in 2011. Haryana has the distinction of having the worst male female ratio among all states. According to Census-2011, the number of females per 1000 males in Haryana stands at 879. This indicates a general trend of sex selective abortion in India and specifically in Haryana. In Haryana, the patriarchal mentality is deeply penetrated in the hearts of people, hence they don't want to even give birth to the girl child. It is just because of the fact that a girl may become responsible for bringing dishonour or shame to the family by her acts.

Moving in this light the present Prime Minister, Mr Modi launched the "Beti Bachao Beti Padhao" programme on 22nd January, 2015 from Panipat, Haryana for eradication of female foeticide and safety of women in all over India.

- **Honour Killings**

The right to marry or form matrimonial alliances is a fundamental right flowing from the right to life which every individual is entitled to enjoy. In 1994, the historic convention on the elimination of all forms of discrimination against women (CEDAW) in general recommendation no. 21 protects the women's right to enter into a marriage and her right to choose her partner. Culture and tradition cannot be used as a tool to defeat the right to life or choice of marriage partner in accordance with law. Inter caste marriages have been validated in India as early as in 1949 by the Hindu Marriages Validity Act, 1949. The Special Marriage Act, 1872 and 1954 legalise marriage between members of different castes and religions. The Hindu Marriage Act, 1955 against the marriage rules in India, offers more freedom in marriage and permits both sa-gotra and inter-caste marriages. Preventing a woman from marrying a person of her choice is an emotional abuse under the protection of women from the Domestic Violence Act, 2005.

But the ground reality is far from different. Marriage in our society is seen as an institution to be controlled as a means of controlling the sexuality of women and as a means of closing ranks over caste or class. The essential and innate nature of women is identified with her sexuality represented as sinful, thereby requiring male control for protecting and preserving the patrilineal succession of property, patriarchal caste hierarchy and caste culture. Due to these religious texts and their misinterpretation create an impression in the society that woman has to be subordinate to man. For better understanding of the concept of marriage in Indian perspective, we have to go through the concept of honour which is purely gendered in nature.

This means that honour has different meaning for different gender. Gender is the social connotation of the biological sexes, i.e. male and female. Both male and female embody notions of honour in totally different ways. Male honour is quint essentially deemed to be dependent upon female honour. Female honour is passive in nature, completely centering around the expected behaviour of sub-ordinance, modesty and endurance, whereas male honour is by nature, dynamic, centering around qualities of self assertion, dominance and heightened propensity towards flaunting social status. A man's honour lies in his ability to impose control on his women, be it his daughter, wife or mother. Honour is generally seen as residing in the bodies of women. All decisions regarding the body of a woman are made by the male members of her family and caste. The whole clan, caste and community are the co-shares of this honour as blood ties of the family extend to them (Chowdhary, 2007, pp.16-17). Emphasis on family honour is basic to the Indian social framework, in other words it can be said that notions of honour serve as barometers of familial worth.

Shame, as a corollary of honour, operates to control and regulates women's sexuality and freedom of movement by the male members of the family. It is the male member who by the policing of younger woman decides which act is honourable and which brings dishonour to the family. Those women, who dare to fall in love and further choose their life partner, seek to move out of an unhappy marriage, engage in extramarital affairs and last but not the least enter into sa-gotra and inter-caste marriages are seem to transgressed the boundaries of appropriate i.e., socially sanctioned behaviour and bring inexcusable shame to their family. Issue of sagotra marriage is very sensitive and helps to khap in attracting massive support. Man has an inherent power to punish woman for the same. This may result in coercion or violence perpetrated by the woman's biological family, ranging from bullying and beating even to their ruthless killings. These killings in the name of supposed honour is termed as honour killings. Thus, honour killings are murder committed by family members who believe that the acts of the victim have brought extreme dishonour on the family name. These killings are given shape by the ruthless rules of khap system which takes away their lives with barbaric ferocity.

- **Compromised Marriages**

Article 16 of the Universal Declaration of Human Rights (UDHR), guarantees the consent to marriage as a basic human right. But in the areas governed by khaps, the rights of women and girls, to control over their own life, right to liberty and freedom of expression, association, movement and body integrity, their consent to marriage means very little or we can say it means nothing. Marriage is a private domain here concerning the family and the community only, irrespective of what Indian laws direct. Leaders of khap panchayat easily issues diktats for forced marriages where a girl has to compromise with elderly, widower or even the person who has raped her or humiliated her. This is only to govern the sexuality of girl and the so called maintenance of patriarchal caste domain. There is no point of denial by the girl as it resulted in the social boycott of family or even harder outcomes.

- **Child Marriages**

Legally prescribed age of marriage for girls in India is 18 years and for boys it is 21 years. But in Haryana and western U.P. child marriages are still in practice. As children are unable to give their consent, these marriages are the example of consensual marriage and seem to be making joke of Indian judiciary. Khaps governed societies are cling to the notion of honour and see no mistake in engaging children as couples. This discriminative and derogatory practice against girl is leaving no scope of dishonour by rejecting a match chosen for them by her family. According to khap, this can ensure and regulate the sexuality of girl and maintain their patriarchal ideology.

- **Restricted Mobility of Girls**

Khap panchayats have issued various social diktats for women at regular intervals. Such as the women who are below 40 years of age should make minimal use of mobile phones, always go out with male escort, banned love marriages. Not only this recently several khap panchayats have declared that girls have not to wear jeans. These types of dictum create suspicion in our mind whether we are really living in twenty first century. It is distressing to note that in times when people are using 4G technology, some sections in our country has still regressed to the dark ages.

- **Denial to Property Rights**

Besides approving so many social dictums against the woman, khap panchayats have also mounted a campaign against the Hindu Succession (Amendment) Act 2005 that gives equal inheritance rights to women. Activists in Haryana have claimed for a long time that the opposition to same gotra or inter-castes marriages or other prohibitions on girls is actually aimed at preventing the economic empowerment of girls. They want to suppress even the thinking of girls to such an extent that they never dare to raise their voice against any injustice imposed over them. It is assumed that if girls have the right to choose their own marriage partner, they are more likely to go on and demand their share of ancestral land which is equivalent to gold in present time. In Haryana, all woman are expected to leave their property share, if anyone dares to ask for, blood relations ceases to exist. To avoid any conflict after a girl's marriage, the recent tradition in the Haryana is to transfer her property share in the name of male members of the family. Which type of silly tradition is this? The poor girls happily transferred their property to maintain the inner peace of their home to their brother or someone else and these so called protectors of girl's honour brutally kill the innocent girl in the name of honour.

Rationale Behind these Practices

The rationale behind all the discrimination against woman lies in the deep-rooted patriarchal ideology of Indian society. Patriarchy (derived from patriarch in Greek) is a term for societies in which men hold power, dominion, privilege, moral authority and control of property. That position is reinforced by societal, cultural norms and religious teachings. In the domain of family, fathers or father figure hold authority over women and children. Being the repository of the family and caste honour, a woman is rendered an object of protection and violence at the same time. The fear of losing this honour makes the men rationalise and justify masculine aggression and violence against her in the name of restoring his family honour. Violence against woman within the four walls of the house in the capacity of a daughter, sister, wife and even mother is widely accepted and legitimized under the patriarchal order and ultimately transcends caste division.

Any move of woman which is out of the socially sanctioned norms, mainly mixed marriages such as sa-gotra marriages or inter-caste marriages are treated as an attack upon family honour. This has eventually led to confrontations, violence and honour crimes. This point has another angle too. The concept of caste honour is usually appropriated by the upper castes in India, who do not recognise any honour being possessed by the lower caste group (Chowdhary, 2007, p. 19).

Since inter-caste marriages tend to weaken the differences existing among the different caste groups and disturb the caste hierarchies. So the leaders of high caste group perceive it as dangerous for sustaining their power and hegemony. The result is that the mixed marriages and love affairs between a high caste girl and a low caste boy is always contested and criminalised. This type of social thinking leads to either killing the woman or forcing her to commit suicide by the family members under the impression of khap panchayats. These panchayats have forced the family to sacrifice their daughters in the collective interests of the caste. This has been done for re-establishing the family honour and set an example for others. Usually it is difficult for a victim girl to getting back into the *biradari*, her physical elimination seems to be a better honourable option to her family. It has been easily understood that localities have how much unquestionable faith over these panchayats. It has created such strong commitments amongst people, where killing of their own child has no emotional barring to protect the tradition.

By creating the false impression that all marriages of choice between young couples are incestuous, what khaps are actually opposing is the right to choose marriage partner. As couples are selectively targeted, it is clear that the real motive is to control women's sexuality to ensure that property remains within the patriarchal caste domain. Thus, property appears is the root cause for discrimination faced by women. The men in the family feel that if the women are given their due share they will become a threat to their power.

Suggestions

However, sheer negative dialogues and thoughts for khaps are not enough. The main problem is of gender discrimination, which is the outcome of patriarchal ideology. More important is to explore a way out to reconstruct the concepts to reach a solution. Only law could not make any change because khap is not about one person, it is the tradition which is thousands of years back deeply embedded in the core of Indian society. Concentrated efforts by polity, civil society, academicians and media are required to put in order the anachronistic institutions of khap. Only then a social revolution can occur and gender discrimination in any form can be removed from our society. Suggestions for each stake holders have been discussed separately for better understanding.

Suggestions for Law Makers

- There should be uniform definition of honour killing, so that there is no chance of ambiguity in accepting it as a crime.
- There should be amendment in the Evidence Act in order to punish every culprit involved in honour killings behind the prison.

- Strict and deterrent law must be enacted to deal with honour killings.
- Each woman of the country has to protect from each type of discrimination under the Act CEDAW (22) by the Government of India.
- Nobody is above our legislature hence khap panchayats have to follow our constitution and there is proper monitoring over their dictums by law and order. The powers of the caste panchayats need to be curtailed by appropriate legislation.
- There should be joint responsibility i.e. the khap panchayat ordering killings and the person who carries out the killing would be jointly liable for punishment.

Suggestions for Policy Makers

- First of all provide education to all. Education is the most potent tool for socio-economic mobility and a key instrument for building an equitable and just society and is only means of bridging the gap of gender inequality.
- Mandatory education on gender issue, gender sensitisation through mass education campaign by the state is required to combat the evils of gender discrimination.
- The general public ought to be enlightened about the importance of the female population, the value of life and the horrors of honour crimes through massive and large scale campaigns, public debates and discussion, media coverage etc.
- Education is also the cure for declining sex ratio. If girls are educated, self-sufficient and productive members of the society then there will be no difference between a boy and a girl. Eventually evils like female foeticide will gradually disappear.

Conclusion

Now it is the time to liberate and emancipate women from the shackles of age old, outdated laws, traditions and customs which are of no use in present globalised and technology-based society. Women not only have to aware of their rights but have to live with their rights on the lines of equality, dignity and non-exploitation of any form. Events like honour killings bring only dishonour to our democracy and have to eradicate totally at any cost. It should be the joint effort of each section of society to make Indian society a gender just society so that women can also live with freedom to excel in accordance with their inherent talent.

References

- Gupta, Juhi (2014). Caste, Culture and Khap: No honour, only killings. *International Journal of Research in Humanities, Arts and Literature.* 2 (7), pp. 39-48.
- Report by Jamia Millia Islamia dated Jan 18.2013. Discriminative and Derogatory Practices against Women by Khap Panchayats, Shalishi Adalats and Kangaroo Courts in India: An Empirical Study in the States of Haryana, West Uttar Pradesh, West Bengal and Rajasthan.
- Report by Indira Jaising. May 2013. Freedom to Marry: The Constitutional Choice and Khaap Panchayats.
- Vishwanath, Jyothi and Palakonda Srinivas, C., (2014). Patriarchal Ideology of Honour and Honour Crimes in India. *International Journal of Criminal Justice Sciences.* 6 (1&2). 386-395.
- http://www.legalservicescindia.com/article/article/khap-panchayat-adjudicating dishonour
- http://en.wikipedia.org

Chapter - 7

Equally Unequal: Gender Discrimination by Khap Panchayats

—*Dr Meenakshi Dwivedi*

Abstract

Khap panchayats is a form of direct democracy that has been around in North-Western India for centuries now. They are quite distinct from the gram panchayats that hold elections and function as institutions of democracy at the grass root level. These khaps have no developmental role to play in the modern era. Appointment of their office bearers is based on traditional power structures in the village they might end up prolonging traditional forms of exploitation. The problem is that it hasn't really evolved with the times and people who are in charge of these khaps do not have an open mindset especially towards women. This chapter discusses about the judgements and controversial decisions made by these khap panchyats and how they are anti-women.

Key Words: *Democracy, Exploitation, Mindset, Decision.*

Introduction

Gender discrimination is the unfair treatment of an individual because of gender. Gender discrimination affects both men and women. It is apparent in work situations where one gender is given preferential treatment or one gender receives less pay or job responsibilities because of gender bias and unfair stereotypes. Gender discrimination also exists in sports, educational institutions and political organisations.

Genders also experience sex discrimination when applying for housing or applying for credit.

In today's society gender discrimination is commonly meant only for women, because females are the only victims of gender discrimination. Gender discrimination is not biologically determined but it is determined socially and thc discriminatory situation can be changed by the proper and perpetuate efforts. Denial of equality, rights and opportunity and suppression in any form on the basis of gender is gender discrimination. Half of the world's population is constituted by females. They are doing two-third of work of the total work in the world but received only one-tenth of the world's total income. Nearly two-third of the women are illiterate and they posses only one per cent of the total world's assets. In the world only one-fourth of the families are headed by female.

India is a male dominant society where gender discrimination is customised habitually. The long history of inequality among the genders in the India is the basis for gender discrimination. Historically, women were underrepresented in every field of life. The residual effects of favourism towards men and unfair treatment of women is the primary cause of gender discrimination.

In Indian literature women are considered pure, divine and worshipped but on the other hand, she is discriminated and victimised by the norms created by male-dominant society. It is believed that in past (Vedic period) women had enjoyed equal status as men. The Upanishads and the Vedas have cited women sages and seers. But the practices like sati, jauhar, devdasis and purdah were also prevalent. This proves that gender discrimination existed in India since Vedic period and is still prevailing directly or indirectly.

Girls in India are discriminated in several ways – fewer months of breastfeeding, less nurturing and play, less care or medical treatment if they fall ill, less special food, less parental attention. As a result, girls are far more susceptible than boys to disease and infections, leading to poor health and a shorter life span. It is this life long discrimination in nurturing and care that is the real killer of girls – less visible and dramatic, but as unequivocally lethal as female foeticide and infanticide.

Causes of Gender Discrimination

If we think of causes of gender discrimination then we can come up with number of responsible factors. The first and foremost cause is society itself which made male as male and female as female. The most important causes of gender disparity such as poverty, illiteracy, unemployment, social customs, belief and anti-female attitude are discussed here.

Poverty

In India out of the total 30 per cent people who are below poverty line, 70 per cent are women. Women's poverty in India is directly related to the absence of economic opportunities and autonomy, lack of access to economic resources including credit, land ownership and inheritance, lack of access to education and support services and their minimal participation in the decision-making process. The situation of women on economic front is no better and men still enjoy a larger share of the cake. Thus, poverty stands at the root of gender discrimination in our patriarchal society and this economic dependence on the male counterpart is itself a cause of gender disparity.

Illiteracy

Despite the notable efforts by the countries around the globe that have expanded for the basic education, there are approximately 960 million illiterate adults out of whom two-thirds are women. Educational backwardness of the girls has been the main cause of gender discrimination. The disparities become more visible between male and female literacy rate, during 2011. The progress towards education by girls is very slow and gender disparities persist at primary, upper primary and secondary stage of education. They are not able to realise full identity and power in all spheres of life only due to illiteracy.

Lack of Employment Facilities

Women are not able to resolve the conflict between new economic and old domestic roles. In both rural and urban India, women spend a large proportion of time on unpaid home sustaining work. Women are not able to respond to new opportunities and shift to new occupations because their mobility tends to be low due to intra-house hold allocation of responsibilities.

Lack of Awareness among Women

Most of the women are unaware of their basic rights and capabilities. They even do not have the understanding as to how the socio-economic and political forces affect them. They accept all types of discriminatory practices that persist in our family and society largely due to their ignorance and unawareness. Article 15 of the Indian Constitution states that the state shall not discriminate any citizen on the grounds of only sex, the irony is that there still is widespread discrimination which is a form of injustice to women.

Social Customs, Beliefs and Practices

Women are not free from social customs, beliefs and practices. The traditional patrilineal joint family system confines women's roles mostly to the domestic sphere, allocating them to a subordinate status, authority and power compared to men. Men are perceived as the major providers and protectors of a family while women are perceived as playing only a supportive role, attending to the hearth. Boys and girls are accordingly drained for different adult roles, status and authority.

Social Altitude

Though, many social activists and reformers carried their crusade against all social odds to restore honour and dignity to women yet attitudinal disparities still hunt our rural masses. Despite pronounced social development and technological advancement, women in our society still continue to be victims of exploitation, superstition, illiteracy and social atrocities.

India's population still leads traditional lives in rural areas. Religious laws and traditions still determine the lives of many people, particularly women. Even if women are formerly entitled to own land and resources, social and religious factors make many women refrain from this right in order not to cause distortions within the family. The preference for having sons permeates all social classes in India, which sets the standard for girls throughout their entire lives.

In the traditional caste panchayats, village panchayats and in the British scheme of local governments women remained entirely excluded. Though the 73rd Amendment Act has been hailed as an important landmark in the constitutional development in creating wider base for participatory democracy and more space for political participation of women through Panchayati raj system yet women are being marginalised to the forefront and their involvement in decision-making process. The local bodies like khap panchayat play a superfluous role in regulating the rights of rural women by imposing various futile restrictions on them.

Khap is actually the unification of a few villages on the basis of caste and geography. Initially it was started by the upper caste Jats in the fourteenth century to unite their power. But according to some historians the system was present even in 600 AD. As per the original thoughts all boys and girls within the same khap are siblings and hence marriage among them is not possible. The khap is governed by khap panchayat and prevalent in most of the parts of Haryana, Western Uttar Pradesh and some parts of Rajasthan. These community groups consist of elderly men from Jat community.

Khap panchayat is a form of direct democracy that has been around in Western India for centuries now. The problem is that it hasn't really evolved with the times and people who are in charge of these khaps do not have an open mindset. Prior to proper judicial system in India many issues were resolved through khap panchayat but it is believed that with time khap panchayats have become less transparent. Most of the cases are solved by taking traditional values in account especially related to women.

Khap panchayats give greater importance to males than females, traditionally assign them more positive attributes, such as being stronger or smarter. According to them, when men occupy a superior position, they have the power to determine the amount of access women should have, ranging from education and playing sports, to participating in politics and making autonomous decisions about their personal lives.

The khap panchayats are all male unelected village councils. These institutions have mostly been orthodox, archaic, irrational and dangerous. They have even been termed as "kangaroo courts" which are declared wholly illegal by the Supreme Court of India. These caste councils in the states several times hit out at girls for bringing bad name to the community. Khaps are governed by medieval ages people, who treat women as a commodity. Most of the times uneducated or economically dependent women are made to live in sub-human conditions in the areas where khaps rule is on. Violence against women is also common. Khap at many instances promulgate several unlawful and unnecessary demarcations to women. Few of them are briefly discussed below.

Dress Code for Women

Women who come under khap are not allowed to wear the dresses of their own choice. The khap panchayats states that the clothes that our mothers and sisters used to wear few years back were the part of good society. The jeans that they wear today, is spoiling the society and the environment. These things should not be allowed in India, they are part of western culture.The panchayat also claims that eve teasing incidents had increased due to objectionable clothes worn by girls.

Many khap panchayat stirred a hornet's nest on saying women should not ape men blindly and must not attract unwanted attention through their revealing dresses. Khap acclaims that women should not cause trouble to others wearing dresses like jeans, skirts etc. Dresses like jeans, top are against Indian culture. The dress code for women above 10 years of age in some villages is a salwar-kameez. Even wearing chudidar salwar-kameez is offensive as it outlines the legs of the girls. The khap appointed some male members to check whether the girls are following the dress code or not as few college girls were caught changing over to western dresses after leaving their homes for college in salwar-kameez.

Not allowing women to wear jeans or any western clothes is sign of inequality and bias. If men in India can wear the jeans, then why women are restricted from doing the same. It is the right of an individual what to wear and what not to wear. Selective application of rules is nothing but discrimination and bias. The Supreme Court also said that khap panchayat's diktat on dress code for women is unlawful.

Inter-caste Marriages and Same Gotra Marriages

Inter-caste marriages means the union of a man and woman belonging to two different castes, races or clans. It is existed in India since ancient times. But after so many years of independence even in the twenty first century, it is not very common in India. According to a survey conducted in 2014, only 5 per cent of marriages are inter-caste in India. These marriages are opposed by many orthodox social groups and still considered as taboo. For years khaps had an orthodox mindset on inter-caste marriage. The khaps with their conservative values do not allow young people to get married in another caste. They couldn't imagine marriages beyond the same caste. They had a conception that marriages are only possible in the same community and caste. The bride and the groom surely have to match each other's religions, community, language, culture and region. Without matching each other's religious and financial status, the bride and the groom are strictly not allowed to tie marriage knots with each other under a khap.

There are lots of such incidents where we can find the merciless punishments inflicted by the khaps on inter-caste marriages. Those who dared to go for the inter-caste marriage by violating the social norm had to face the consequence in terms of violence, social boycott, family boycott and some time even death also. The cases were reported where khap panchayat tried to kill the married couple who goes for inter-caste marriage. The khap panchayat decided to eliminate the couple.

Few khaps in Haryana are famous for their diktats on same gotra marriages. They believe that the gotra system does have many flaws. People belonging to the same gotra are part of the same extended family, and a marriage within the same gotra is deemed to be incestuous.

Honour Killings

Honour killing is also called as customary killing is the murder of a member of a family or social group by other members, due to the belief of the perpetrators and potentially the wider community that the victim has brought dishonour upon the family or community. It is very common practice in khap governed areas directed mostly against women and girls. In khaps, the perceived dishonour is normally the result of one of the following behaviours, or the suspicion of such behaviours:

- Dressing in the western manner is unacceptable to the khap.
- Wanting to terminate or prevent an arranged marriage or desiring to marry by own choice.
- Inter-caste marriage or same gotra marriage.
- Engaging in heterosexual acts outside marriage, or even due to extra marital relationship is perceived as inappropriate by khap.
- Engaging in homosexual acts. Women and girls are killed at a much higher rate than men.

The most obvious reason for continuance of khaps, is that the caste system continues to be at its rigid best and also because people from these caste councils refuse to change their attitude towards marriage. Recently, there has been a spate of honour killings in the khaps and this has led the government to decide what laws should be put in place to stop this heinous crime.

Early Marriages of Girls

In India, early marriage below eighteen years is illegal by law, but still it exists rampantly across India in many khaps. The practice of girls marrying at a young age is most common in these social caste groups of various states. Around 40 per cent of the girls in these sections of population are married before they reaches 15 years of age and in some cases marriages earlier than puberty are not unusual. This may be due to the fact that young women who are married late have more chances of choosing inter-caste marriages due to the impact of modernisation and development. They also think that their girls can be protected against rapes and abductions by performing early marriages sometimes with much elderly men. Young girls are forced to marry as the pressure is created by khaps on their parents and if young girls or their parents deny from this practice, the whole family is abandoned from the village. The prominent consequences of this malpractice are early maternal deaths of girls, poor infant health, low fertility control and poor fertility outcome, increase rate of physical and sexual violence etc.

Negative Attitude towards Girls' Education

Negative attitudes of khaps towards educating girls is the another cause of poor female status in khaps. There are some overwhelming cultural and economic reasons why female children are not receiving the same medical, emotional and educational attention as their male counterparts in khaps. Normally it is perceived by khap that education has positive effect on inter-caste marriages. In addition, girls with higher levels of education will likely have higher dowry expenses as they will want a comparatively more educated husband. Khaps also imposes restrictions on the girls in the villages to continue their studies in colleges because of security concerns or lack of institutes in nearby areas.

It is reported that few khaps especially in Haryana are taking initiatives for the mission for girls education which is signaling a change in their approach towards literacy among women as a ray of hope for girls. Khap panchayats have initiated a campaign to persuade them to continue education.

No Use of Mobile for Girls

One side the Prime Minister Mr Narendra Modi is launching the Digital India Project through which the entire country would get high speed internet, on the other side there are villages, where these things of technological advancements hardly matter. When the entire world is witnessing technological revolution, the khap panchyats have passed the diktat banning use of mobile phones by unmarried girls. The old conservative mindset is so strong here that there is no identity of mobile and social media. They believe that mass media exposure negatively affects the traditional Indian values and patronise the social evils like inter-caste marriages, modernisation etc.

Solution for Gender Discrimination Caused by Khap Panchayats

Various movements, programmes are being carried out by the government, voluntary organisations and social activists for women's development and against the gender discrimination. To solve the gender discrimination problem caused by khaps a number of initiatives have been taken by the government.

- **Law Enforcement to Khap Panchayats**

Khap panchayats are not legal councils. In India, courts are over burdened with the thousands and lakhs of cases lies pending, it is not possible for common man to go to courts for small day-to-day issues. Even few people remain unsatisfied with the decision of courts. Such type of situation allows khap panchayat to act as quasi judicial system. There should be some set of laws and administration for khap panchayats under which they can be allowed towork so that they would not try to enforce the diktats which violates the fundamental rights of any person.

- **Education**

Women's education plays the key role in reducing discrimination against girls. As per the intentions of khap the female child are often deprived off her right to education. The number of girls dropping out of school far exceeds the boys because girls are expected to help at home, either with household work like washing and cooking or with taking care of younger siblings. Since girls spend more time performing domestic duties, it perpetuates the myth that education is of no help to the girl and her primary job will be to look after the household work, get married early, have children and then raise them. If this is the job she has to do, then education is of no importance to her and it is not imparted and this increases the gap between female and male inequality. It is through education in the early days of a child that we can bring about behaviour changes for opening the doors of opprtunities that will enhance their confidence, personality, and career. Education develops the skills, imparts knowledge, changes the attitude and improves the self-confidence. It provides employment opportunity and increases income. Hence, educating women is the prime factor to combat gender discrimination and for the upliftment of women. Not only the female, the society must be educated to give equal right for female.

- **Empowerment**

Empowered women with the help of laws, education and employment will make the society to accept the women as an equal gender like male. Female also has all the potential and empowerment women will help to use her full capability and mitigate the economic dependency of women.

- **Self-confidence**

Due to prolong suppression of women by khaps they lack the necessary self-confidence, as a result remains uneducated and unemployed. Women need self-confidence to fight against all the atrocities against her and to live self-esteemed life. Hence, boosting the morale and self-confidence of the women, is the key to eliminate the inferiority complex from her mindset.

- **Decision Making**

Even in the family as well as in the society the decision-making power of women is denied. Mostly males make the important decision in the family and in the caste councils. This makes women as voiceless by destroying her self-confidence and she feels less important in the family as well as in the society. So, to end gender discrimination women must empower with decision-making power.

- **Need for Social Awareness**

There is a need of social awareness among all the people of the society. When two people from different communities show the courage to marry, the young and progressive people in the community should unite to support them. If khap kills a girl in the name of honour, families should not associate with them. When police do not record complaints, there has to be action against the authorities those who failed to do their job. In fact, under existing laws, dereliction of duty is punishable.

- **Economic Independence**

In India, mostly, woman in the young age depend on her father, in the middle age she depends on her husband and in the older age depends on her son. Woman always depends on somebody for her livelihoods hence economic independence is imperative for women's development. Economic independence will free the women from the slavery position and boost the self-confidence. Economic independence of women also helps in the national economic development.

- **Employment**

Employment gives the income and improves the economic position of the women. Employed women are given more importance by the family members. Employment gives the economic independence to the women.

Conclusion

A nation or society, without the participation of women cannot achieve development. If we eliminate gender discrimination, women will deliver all the potentials, skills, knowledge to develop the family, the nation and the whole world. Few khap panchayat has also taken some good decisions like saying no to early girls' marriages, sending all children to school, ban on liquor, which are being praised, but ban on using mobile phones and wearing jeans by girls has became a reason for dispute. Generally it is expected that with more development and education, the force of caste factor becomes weak and thereby increase in flexibility in khap's decision is reflected. It is expected that with modernisation, development, increase in educational level etc., the impact of social forces like caste, religion, various taboos etc. will become weaker. The society is expected to become more broad minded, forward looking and tolerant. India will embark on the path of modernisation, development and westernisation against khap like social evils.

References

- Anna Maria Lind, (2006). Struggle and Development: Approaching gender bias in Practical International Development Work, Orebro, Orebro University.
- Berta Esteve Volast, (2004). Gender discrimination and Growth: Theory and Evidence from India, London, London School of Economics and Political Sciences.

- Desai, Sonalde, (1994). Gender Inequalities and Demographic Behaviours: India, New York, The Population Council, Inc.
- Government of India, 2008. Eleventh Five Year Plan (2007-2012), Vol. II, New Delhi, Planning Commission.
- Julie Mullin, (2008). Gender Discrimination – Why is it still so bad and what can you do about it? (Accessed from on 15.08.2008) www.childernin-need.org
- Kalyani Menon Sen and A. K. Shiva Kumar, (2001). Women in India, How Free? How Equal? New Delhi, UNDAF.
- www.aud.ac.in
- www.en.wikipedia.org
- www.psp.sagepub.com

Chapter – 8

Complete Control over Women: The Illegal Intentions of Khap Panchayats

—*Dr Deepa Awasthi*

Abstract

Khap panchayats are the institutions which were established centuries before to regulate the social and personal life of individual both men as well as women. These institutions having limited administrative and quasi judicial powers, used to work on democratic pattern but with advent of civilisation these tasks were taken up by state. Due to various reasons such types of institutions still exist in our country even in twenty first century. In course of development khap panchayats were completely dominated by men and emerged as tool to control or restrict the liberty of women. Although Supreme Court of India has declared them illegal and unconstitutional but still due to mute silence from political parties they have grown as uncontrolled source of power. Any individual alone can hardly have courage to stand against them and those who dare to stand have faced the ill consequences, most of them are either buried in pages of history or they have to live in isolation after hiding their identity. The dictates of khap panchayat issued from time to time have made the life of females especially young girls miserable in the region in which such type of clan, caste, community or village based institutions are active. This chapter details why these khaps are considered as synonyms for honour killing and how the main priority of khap is to control liberty of women ensuring male dominance in each and every field of life. Promoting honour killings, prohibiting sagotra marriages and inter-caste/inter-religious marriages, restriction on wearing jeans top and using mobile phone are the main tools to establish supremacy over women. Major issues in which khap panchayat have encroached in the personal and social life of individual have also been discussed.

Key Words: Quasi judicial powers, Liberty, Illegal, Unconstitutional.

Introduction

In recent few years khap panchayat are seen closely connected with the number of cases of honour killings in country. Despite of strong criticism from media, civil society and various courts, unfortunately this heinous crime could not checked so far. Many couples and their family members have lost their lives who dare to stand against the illegal dictates of khap panchayat. Before exploring the role of khap panchayat in promoting honour killing and various reasons behind, it is necessary that we should try to understand the concept of khap panchayat and honour killing.

Khap Panchayat

As soon as we hear the word khap panchayat, there comes the image of group of old people sitting under the big tree in middle of village with *Hukkas* and *Lathis* in their hand. They have all the power to throw any individual male or female out of village or ban anyone or kill anyone without any possibility of interference from law of land. They have their own centuries old orthodox administrative and quasi-judicial system, not ready to bring positive reforms among themselves. Usually they become centre of criticism in media and society due to their illogical, illegal, unconstitutional, unjust, foolish decisions and dictates.

Going back to history we find that roots of khap, goes behind to early *Rig Vedic* period. These khap like institutions termed as *Jan, Pal, Sangh, Shreni* were the most ancient system of socio-economic and legal administration based on democratic pattern, not only in India but in world also. The term khap means 'clan' or 'caste' and group of people organised on the basis of clan or caste is known as khap panchayat. Each khap panchayat select and send the members or delegates among themselves on the basis of experience and social prestige to a higher level termed as Sarva khap or All khap panchayat. The term khap can also be considered as socio-political groups used in geographical sense inhibited by particular clan or caste.

According to an estimate there are about 465 khap and such type of other organisations active in India, out of which 70 khaps exist in Haryana, 30 khap in western Uttar Pradesh and remaining in Rajasthan, Delhi and other parts of the country. Mainly Jat, Rajput, Gujjar and Kamboj are the main communities which provide a large canvas for existence of khap panchayats.

Honour Killing

Honour killing is the homicide of a member of family by other member of family due to perpetrator's belief that the victim has brought shame or dishonour to family, community or religion or has violated the established principles of society such as refusing to enter arrange marriage, engaged in inter-caste/inter-religious/sagotra marriage, extra marital affairs, inappropriate dressing, homosexuality or becoming a victim of rape. Out of these reasons homicide due to marriage issues has attracted the attention of whole India. Unfortunately, all the time victims of honour killing are the girls who stand against the orders of khap or boy with whom she marries or want to marry and in some cases both of them.

Region covered under khap Panchayat

Although khap panchayat are limited to very small region in India but unfortunately its ideology based on restricting or limiting the rights

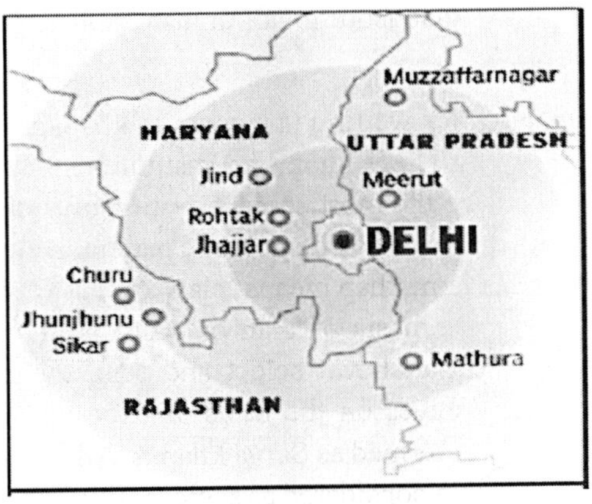

Fig. 8.1: Khap Belt in India

or liberty of women has been extended to all over country especially to state of Haryana, Western Uttar Pradesh, rural belt of Delhi, Rajasthan, Punjab etc. This region of the country is most modernised and developed region of the country. Most ironical thing about this region is that here big shopping malls, multiplex, sky-high luxury housing apartments, world renowned call centres, IT industries, few best hospitals and doctors of country and primitive ideology of khap panchayat establishing male supremacy over women co-exist.

Are these Khap Panchayat Really Democratic?

Khap is a type of autonomous quasi judicial body, although from lower courts to apex court of India everyone has questioned about the existence and working of khap panchayat from time to time but unfortunately the mute silence of government and political parties has given unlimited power to these institutions. These khap panchayats claim that their organisation and working is based on democratic way but in reality they are pure undemocratic. In the views of khap panchayats, women do not have right to take part in democracy that is why they hardly call women in their meetings. Most ironical fact about these khap meetings is that they are usually called to decide matters associated to have check and balance on women and their day-to-day life. Members of khap panchayat have misperception that democracy means dictating the women by the men.

Matters and Issues Dictated by Khaps

Although Supreme Court of India has mentioned in one of its verdict that these khap panchayat have no legal recognition and no right to regulate or administer legal or moral functioning of individual as well as society but unfortunately these khap like institutions interfere with all the issues whether personal, social, political, cultural, religious etc. Some of the main issues in which khap have interfered and dictated are –

- Restricting the unmarried girls from wearing jeans – top.
- Restriction on use of mobile phone by school going girls.
- Prohibiting inter-caste/inter-religious/sagotra marriages.
- Restriction on love marriages.

- Prohibiting extra marital affairs by females.
- Dictates of Excommunication or "*Hukka Pani Band.*"
- Ban on use of DJ in weddings.
- Restricting the consumption of liquor in parties and marriages.
- Implementing dress code for brides and bridegrooms.
- Separate school buses for girls and boys.
- Prohibiting women from claiming rights in parental property.
- Restriction on marrying the boy of same village even if he belongs to different Gotra.
- Restriction on women on maintaining '*rakhi-dora*' relation outside the community.
- Dictates of financial penalty on rapist family.
- Compelling the victim of rape to marry with the accused.

When we go in detail, we find that priority of khap panchayat is to control liberty of women by enforcing various dictates, interfere in the personal and social hemisphere of individual. Usually all the issues dictated by khap panchayat are somehow or other linked with restricting the liberty of women. It is hard to understand that how a girl who has married to boy of other caste/religion or same Gotra with or without consent of family, at that very instance she becomes a subject of pride and prestige not only for family but for community, village and state as well, while the boys or men raping and murdering the innocent young girls never considered to be punished so harsh, they are left free to repeat the crime after paying a mere financial penalty to family members of victim. Here the crime committed by boys are much heinous in nature in the eyes of law of land but khap panchayat consider that engaging in love marriage is crime of much serious nature so that immediate revenge is needed to restore the pride of family and community.

Recently a study commissioned by National Commission for Women, conducted by NGO 'Shakti Vahini' revealed that 72 per cent of 326 cases of honour killings were in fact inter-caste marriages while cases related to sagotra marriages were only three per cent, marriages with in caste were 15 per cent and one per cent were related to inter-religious marriages.

Restriction on marriage issues does not really mean what they say in their dictates, the meaning is much deeper. They want to decide when to marry, where to marry, how to marry, whom to marry and what to wear during marriage etc. They want to decide everything about women limiting their liberty up to minimum so that centuries old male dominance and patriarchal setup of society might not threatened due to growing education level of youth especially girls.

Through organising khap meetings and issuing various dictates with warning of violence to girls are just and instrument to create fear in minds of girls for maintaining control over female members of community. Restriction on wearing Jeans top by girls saying that it provokes the boys is another example of polluted mentality where women itself is held responsible for crime against her.

Although liquor consumption is injurious to health but who are the members of khap to decide who will drink, when to drink? Similarly ban on DJ is symbol of encroachment in the personal life of an individual. How ironic it is when whole India is witnessing technological revolution – Digital India Project (a scheme launched by Prime Minister Shri Narendra Modi) at the same time khap panchayat have restricted the young girls on using mobile phone. According to khap leaders mobile phones especially latest smartphones provides easy access to internet to watch pornography, as a result young girls are losing their moral values even before attaining the age of puberty. To some extent it might be right but it should be enforceable equally on boys not only for girls. They should also know that every girl having smart phone is not watching porn all the time. These phones have emerged as source of immense knowledge in this century.

Sometimes it is seen that families who disobey the khap panchayat face the dictates of excommunication or '*Hukka Pani Band*'. Such type of dictates are most unlawful in twenty first century, who has given them right to interfere in the social hemisphere of an individual. Another major issue is to compel the couple to live as siblings after living a long married life, such type of orders are nothing but the psychology of an insane mind.

Khap wants the women to remain away from property right, they want that women after marriage should not go to court for claiming share in paternal property. Such type of dictates is prima facia against the law of land and not acceptable to more than half population in country. Khap supporters argue that usually after marriage girl shifts to their husband house free from all the liabilities and boys have to take care of old parents so property must be transferred in their favour but this argument is completely baseless, every day in newspaper we come across the news that son and their family members have thrown the old parents out of home and girls came forward to take care of their own parents as well as husband's parents also.

Some of social economist believes that main aim of khap's ideology is to restrict and to establish control over women is for ensuring that property must remain in patriarchal caste domain especially in Jat community. For this reason they want their girls to marry several villages away so that it reduces the chance of establishing claim over parental property. After that a '*fatwa*' restricting the easy mobility of women will further weaken their ability to hold the land, even after that if woman claims her share in parental property, she is forcefully compelled to transfer their share to male member of family, most of the times the male member is her brother.

Khap's verdict to restrict the women from having respectful relation of '*rakhi dora*' from other community members suggest that they want to complete control over women of their community.

Khap panchayat's decision to pay financial penalty by the rapist and their family members to victim of rape is question mark on them being civilised. It is a free passage to criminals with big pockets. Such types of ironical dictate are most favourable for criminal minded males who consider the women as a toy for leisure and pleasure. They are confident that they can save themselves as they have money with them, they can humiliate anybody by raping female members of that family. In some cases khap panchayat have compelled the girl and their family members to marry with the boy who is accused of rape. This decision is to save the accused from legal trials and probable jail because everybody knows that for the sake of marriage relation wife will ultimately withdraw the case.

Challenging the Khap Panchayat

Media has always played a vital role in highlighting the activities of khap panchayat, it may be formal media like Newspaper and Electronic News Channel or informal media like bollywood cinema and small screen television channel but due to negligence from government and lack of political will unlawful activities of khap panchayats could not be checked so far. It is not possible to criticise the decisions of khap on individual level, it might be threat to life of that individual but when media highlighted the issue among public then a number of women and youth organisations initiated to agitate against the dictates of khap panchayat. Not only this court have also taken cognizance of such events and issued the appropriate orders from time to time to protect the society from unlawful interference of khap. Unfortunately mute silence from police, administration and state government has been responsible for the death of several couples. Even khap continued their unlawful acts in presence of police as in Vedpal Moan case. He was beaten by the mob till death when he reached to his in-laws village to receive her wife escorted by police at the order of court. Supreme Court of India has already declared them as 'Kangaroo courts' and 'wholly illegal'.

In most of the cases court always made their best attempt to protect the right of life and liberty of young girls and boys who wanted to marry at their will or already married. Although all the political leaders accept that khap are unlawful institutions and their dictates are completely void but hardly any one of them have courage to accept and challenge them publically. Reason behind such attitude is that no party or candidate can win their election without having financial, work force (volunteers) and vote bank support of these khap panchayat. Usually in Sarv khap meetings they decide collectively, whom to support in election in return they want political security for their members and their ideology.

Although role and prestige of such institutions is shrinking day by day but still they are strong enough to create a fear factor in the mind of youth especially girls. Even young generation of rural areas are getting exposed to modern ideas due to revolution in field of information communication technology, fast pace of urbanisation and positive role played by media.

Conclusion

The controversial decisions made by khap panchayat have a long-term impact on individual as well as society. It is very easy to say that victims of khap can go to the court or police but unfortunately all the victims belong to weaker section of society, they can be females or even male member belonging to lower class in social stratification, they don't have the courage to stand against the mighty khaps. They are left with no option either to accept the unlawful verdicts of khap panchayat or leave their village, community, relatives, property and move to new place. Obviously these khap panchayat are centuries old institution, not going to end in one day, they are weakening day by day and their useless dictates, verdicts, and decisions are losing their value. The word khap is no more acceptable to civilised society. Especially youth of India, male as well as female has to come forward to encounter such type of feudalistic thinking.

References

- Abdulla, Essay on Honour Killing in India. www.civilserviceindia.com
- After Rohtak Killing, Khap start spying on College goers, tell girls above 10 years to wear Salwar Kameez. (2013). www.intoday.in
- Bhardwaj, S. B.(2012), Myths and Realities of Khap Panchayat: A Historical Analysis of Khap Panchayat, *Studies in History*, Feb 2012, Vol. 28, No. 1, pp. 43- 67, www.sih.sagepub.com
- Burdak, L., Khap. www.jatland.com
- Dwedi, A., What is Khap Panchayat, What are its Function, Why it is criticised, Should Khap panchayat be banned in India? www.quora.com
- Girls not to use Mobile Phones: Barmer Khap (2015). www.thetimesofindia.indiatimes.com
- Jagmati Sangwan (2011). Khaap Panchayat: Signs of Desperation, www.thehindu.com
- Khap Dictates: Rajasthan Women Claiming Property Share to be Outlawed for 10 Years, (2015). www.timesofindia.indiatimes.com
- Malik, S. Should Khap Panchayat be Banned in India. www.quora.com
- Raina, P. (2012). Does India Still Needs Khap Panchayat, www.mytimes.com

- Sakshi Abrol. The Hegemony of Khap Panchayat – A Case of Culture and Tradition at Extreme. www.youthkiawaaj.com (Retrieved on Dated 3rd August, 2015)
- Sehgal, M. (2013). No Jeans, Mobile Phones, Porn…or Same Gotra Marriages: Khap unveil banned list, They say will Stop Rape and Honour Killing, www.dailymail.co.uk

Chapter – 9

Co-relating the Existence of Khap with Skewed Sex Ratio in Haryana

—*Dr Deepa Awasthi*

Abstract

Inspite of continuous efforts from government and non-government agencies the sex ratio of the country has not improved to satisfactory level. Unfortunately a number of under developed countries with one tenth of India's economy has much better sex ratio as compared to India. Southern states of country has really worked sincerely in this regard and their report card on sex ratio reflects the same but the sex ratio of Northern and Western states of the country especially Haryana, Punjab, Uttar Pradesh, Rajasthan and Delhi has always been on lower side as compared to average overall sex ratio and average child sex ratio of the country. In this chapter author has tried to correlate the existence of khap panchayat with skewed sex ratio in khap governed areas especially the state of Haryana where khap panchayat are functional in full strength have been discussed in detail.

Key Words: *Skewed Sex Ratio, Child Sex Ratio, Northern States, Developed Countries.*

Introduction

No nation on this earth can claim to be civilised until they ensure end to all type of gender-based discriminatory practices against almost half of the population. Continuous efforts are being made at global level to reduce the gender gap. Gender equality and the empowerment of women were considered as one of the eight Millennium Development Goals by the United Nations. India is one of the countries which have failed to improve its sex ratio. Status of one-sixth population of the world residing in India has a negative impact on global sex ratio. Preference of son over daughters has imbalanced the sex ratio in India. As per census data 2011 India has only 940 females against 1000 males. The situation was even worse in last decade, as per the census data 2001, India has only 933 females as compared to 1000 males. This trend of declining sex ratio is not new in India, sex ratio is continuously showing declining growth even before independence. (Fig. 9.1)

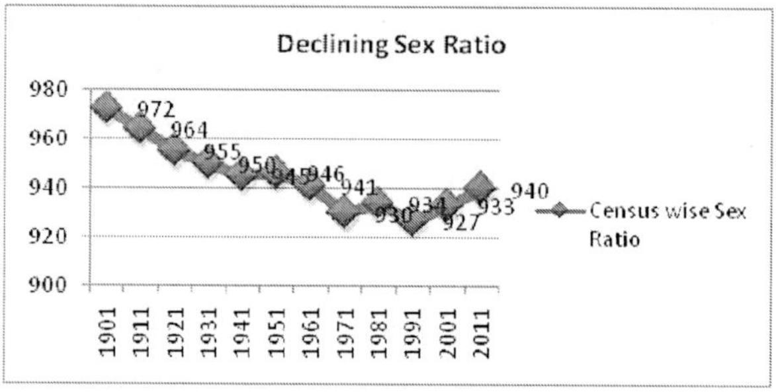

Source: Census of India, 2011.

Fig. 9.1: Continuous Decline in Decade-wise Overall Sex ratio in India.

According to report of UNICEF, China and India only are responsible for almost 80 per cent missing women in the world. If this trend will continue for long time India is expected to have 25 million

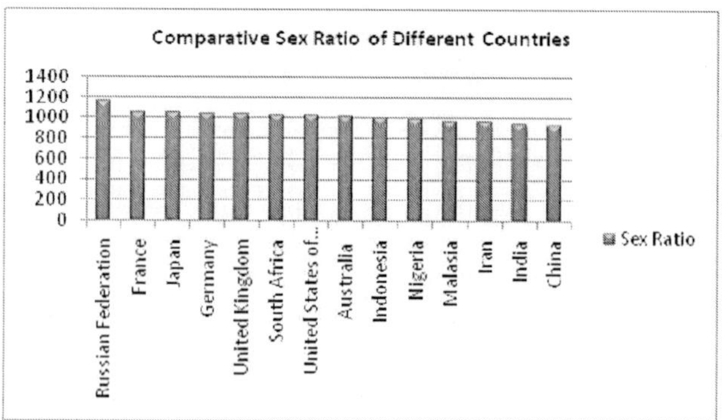

Source: UNICEF Report.

Fig 9.2: Comparative Sex Ratio of Different Countries.

young surplus males till 2020 standing top of the rank of countries having unbalanced gender population. Due to continuous efforts made by government and non-government agencies the overall sex ratio has increased to some extent from 933 to 940, but the situation is shameful when we find that many underdeveloped countries have better sex ratio as compared to India. (Fig. 9.2)

Figure. 9.3 reflects that states situated in northern parts of the country have much lower sex ratio as compared to southern states.

Sex Ratio, 2011 (States/Union Territories)

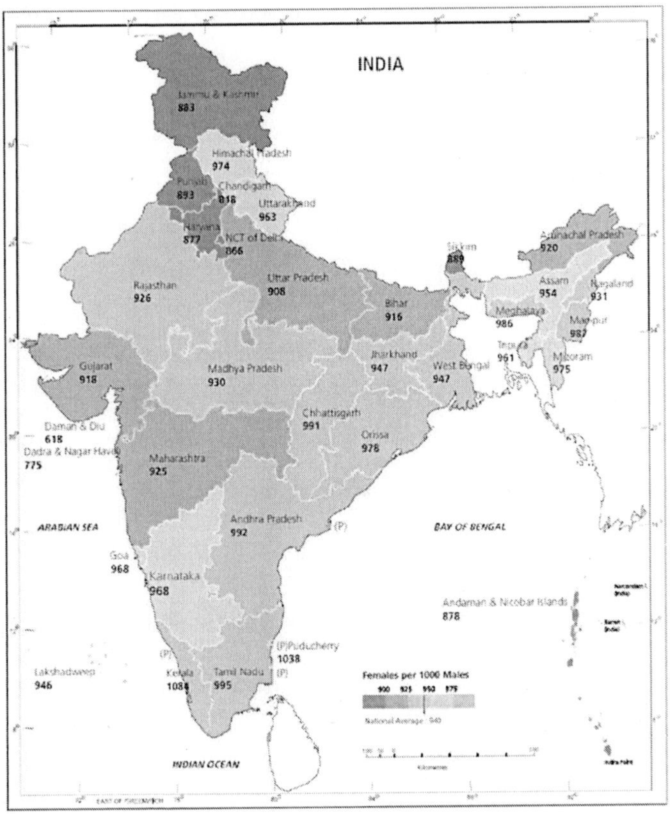

Source: Census of India, 2011.

Fig. 9.3 State-wise Overall sex ratio in India.

Sex ratio of southern states i.e. Kerala, Tamil Nadu, Andhra Pradesh, Karnataka, Goa, Puducherry, Odisha, and Chhattisgarh are better as compared to northern states i.e. Punjab, Haryana, Jammu and Kashmir, Delhi, Uttar Pradesh, Rajasthan and Bihar. Sex ratio of these northern states is even lower than national average sex ratio of 940 female against every 1000 males.

Data of child sex ratio (between age group 0 – 6 years) is even more disturbing, only 914 female child as compared to 1000 male child, almost eight per cent decline. This child sex ratio is all time lowest since independence. It reflects that inspite of huge efforts the sex ratio of country is not going to improve in near future. (Fig. 9.4)

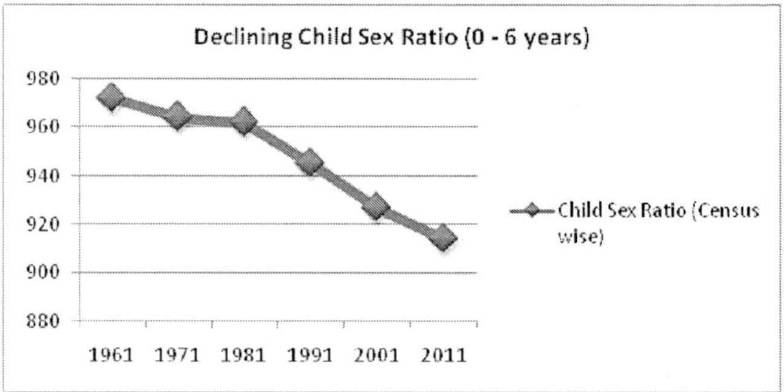

Source: Census of India, 2011.

Fig. 9.4: Continuously Declining Child Sex Ratio (0 to 6 age group).

Although a slight increase is observed in over all sex ratio after 1991 but continuous declining child sex ratio is matter of concern because it puts a question mark on the future of mankind as species. As per the current data released by United Nations Department of Economic and Social Welfare (UN-DESA) for 150 countries, only India and China are the two countries where female infant mortality rate is higher than male infant mortality rate.

The status of child sex ratio is even more alarming in state of Punjab and Haryana. Punjab with 846 female child and Haryana with 830 female child as compared to 1000 male child are situated at the bottom of the table. This lowering of child sex ratio indicates

Haryana is not going to observe any improvement in overall sex ratio of state in forthcoming decades.

When we compare the child sex ratio of various states in India, we find that states affected by khap rulings has lower sex ratio as compare to other non-affected states and average child sex ratio of country. As per census data – 2001 and 2011, the khap governed states, most of them situated in north region of country i.e. Punjab, Haryana,

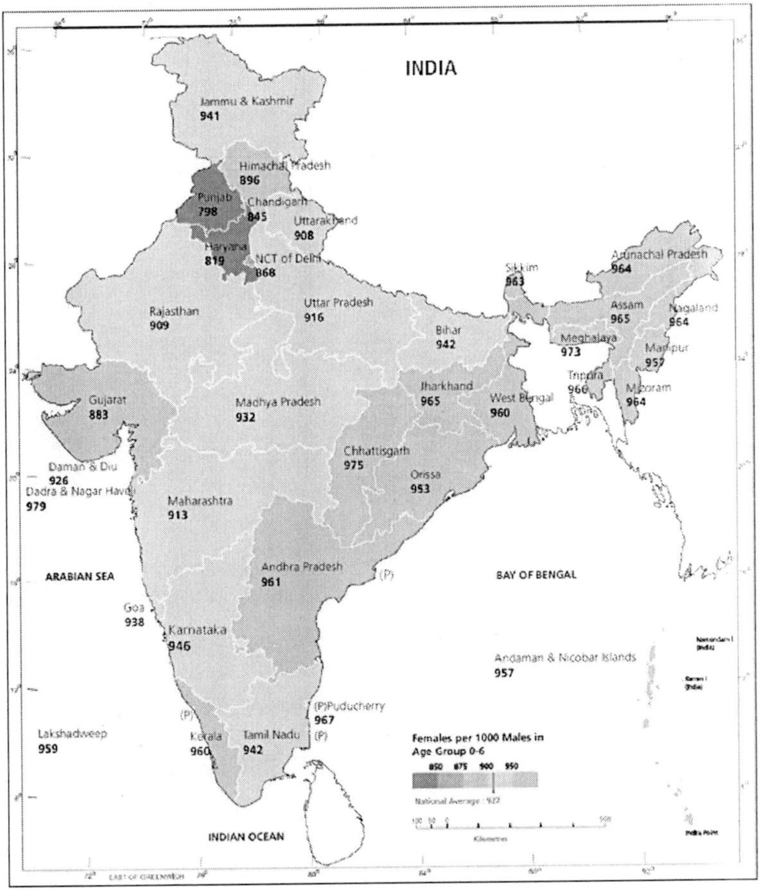

Source: Census of India, 2001.

Fig. 9.5: Child Sex Ratio in India, 2001 (State/Union Territories).

Child Sex Ratio in Age Group 0-6, 2011 (States/Union Territories)

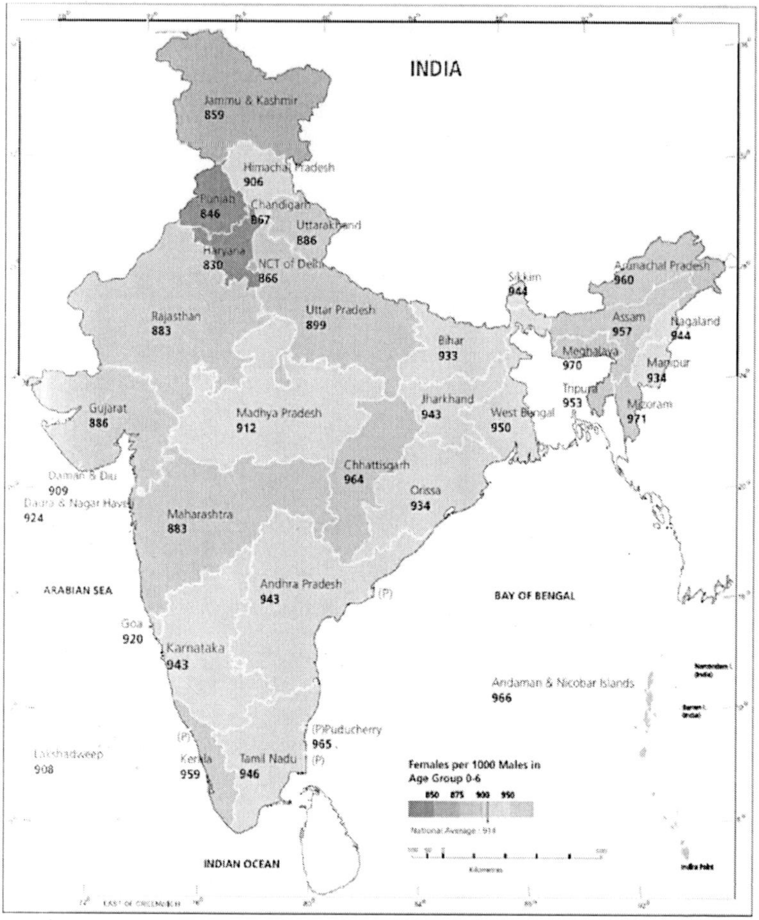

Source: Census of India, 2011.

Fig. 9.6 : Child Sex Ratio in India, 2011 (State/Union Territories).

Uttar Pradesh, Delhi and Rajasthan were the states where child sex ratio (0 to 6 years age group) has always been lower side as compared to prevailing average child sex ratio of country. (Table. 9.1)

Table 9.1: Comparison of Child Sex Ratio of Khap Affected States

States	*Child Sex Ratio/Average Child Sex Ratio (0 to 6 years) As per Census Data - 2001*	*Child Sex Ratio/Average Child Sex Ratio (0 to 6 years) As per Census Data - 2011*
Punjab	798/927	846/914
Haryana	819/927	830/914
Delhi	868/927	866/914
Uttar Pradesh	916/927	899/914
Rajasthan	909/927	883/914

Source: Census of India, 2001 and 2011.

District-wise Analysis of Sex Ratio in Haryana

Almost all north states, where the khaps and such type of other caste-based social institutions exists have low sex ratio as compared to overall average sex ratio of country but situation is alarming in Haryana. fifteen districts identified for having most skewed sex ratio in country, nine of them belongs to Haryana. As per the census data, 2011 the total population of Haryana was 25,351,462, out of which 13,494,734 were the males against 11,856,728 females. It represents that 1,638,006 females were short as compare to male population.

Table 9.2. clearly reflects that none of the Districts of Haryana has overall child sex ratio or child sex ratio equivalent or near to national average.

Table 9.2: District-wise Comparison of Overall Sex Ratio and Child Sex Ratio in Haryana

Districts in Haryana	*Overall Sex Ratio*		*Child Sex Ratio*	
	(2001)	*(2011)*	*(2011)*	*(2011)*
Panchkula	823	870	829	850
Ambala	868	882	782	807
Yamuna Nagar	862	877	806	825
Kurukshetra	866	889	771	817
Kaithal	853	880	791	821
Karnal	865	886	809	820
Panipat	829	861	809	833
Sonipat	839	853	788	790

(*Contd...*)

Jind	852	870	818	853
Fatehabad	884	904	828	845
Sirsa	882	896	817	852
Hisar	851	871	832	849
Bhiwani	879	884	841	831
Rohtak	847	868	799	807
Jhajjhar	847	861	801	774
Mohindergarh	918	894	818	778
Rewari	899	898	811	784
Gurgaon	850	853	807	826
Faridabad	-	871	-	842
Mewat	899	906	893	903
Palwal	862	879	854	862

Source: www.slideshare.net

Unfortunately we are discussing the state which has witnessed highest development in last two decades with comparatively higher per capita income. 65.12 per cent of population of Haryana lives in urban areas as compared to 34.88 per cent people living in rural areas. One can easily expect that with more population living in urban areas with comparatively better education and economic development, the impact of traditional village councils termed as khap will be reduced, but it is a myth. The overall sex ratio and child sex ratio of urban areas of Haryana is lower than the ratio of rural areas. Table. 9.3 reflects that there is no impact of urbanisation on the sex ratio of state.

Table 9.3: Comparison of Overall Sex Ratio and Child Sex Ratio in Urban and Rural areas of Haryana

Indicator	*Urban*	*Rural*
Overall Sex Ratio	873	882
Child Sex Ratio	832	865
Population Ratio	65.12 per cent	34.88 per cent

Source: Census of India, 2011.

Reason behind Skewed Sex Ratio in Haryana

Alarming data of overall sex ratio and child sex ratio in Haryana suggest that all the awareness campaign and crores of rupees spent by government and non-government agencies for improving sex ratio and preventing female foeticide are getting wasted. The main reason behind low sex ratio is ideology based on male dominance where every couple wants to have son rather than giving birth to daughter. Sex selective practices are very common in Haryana. As per official data of Haryana Health Department more than 150 illegal ultra sound machines involved in business of determining and disclosing the pre-natal sex have been seized and sealed, unfortunately there have been only 24 convictions under the Pre Conception and Pre Natal Diagnostic Technique Act. Although shameful but it is fact to be mentioned that Haryana state have the credit of first three cases filed under this Act.

Traditional ideology based on priority to male and male dominance has created a situation where women are considered as second category citizen and deprived of all basic facilities at personal level i.e. better clothing, better food as well as at social level i.e. educational and employment opportunities.

Contribution of Khaps in Lowering the Sex Ratio

Khap is another factor that is responsible for low sex ratio in Haryana. Khap system has always been discriminatory against women, hardly they have any right. They have to follow the verdicts and dictates given by male-dominated khap panchayat. From time to time khap issues their dictums directing the women encroaching in the field of personal life and liberty. They decide that women should not wear jeans and other western tight outfits as they reflect the shape and size of their body. Clarification given by khap leaders is very ironical that such type of clothes provoke the boys and restrictions will help to control the crime against women i.e. rape, eve teasing, abduction, molestation etc. Through such type of '*Fatwas*' the male-dominated khaps wants to control the liberty of women.

They also find that use of mobile phones especially by younger girls leads to moral corruption as they can use it for watching pornography. Even khap challenges the law of land related to marital affairs and inheritance of property. One of the khap leader states that minimum age of marriage should be reduced by government as due to modernisation boys and girls desire to have sex at younger age. Not only this, in Haryana girls don't have the right to chose their life partner, khap strictly bans sagotra, inter-caste, inter-religious marriages and some time even love marriages in khap governed areas. If any girl dares to go against the verdicts of khap for punishing and torturing they humiliate the victim and their family members by parading naked, painting the face black, compelling her to drink urine etc. It is to be mentioned that there is a incident where khap has issued an order to rape the female family members of victim.

Such type of environment makes us think that whether we are living in twenty first century or sixteenth century. What is wrong when couples prefer birth of a son over daughter in Haryana as they already know that if they give birth to daughter then she has to face the ill-impacts of existence of khap and such type of institution? Parents know that today youth require liberty and free space in their personal life they may stand against khap, obviously hardly any person would like to face the humiliation for her daughter or family by khap panchayat.

Being the centre point of khap politics parents especially belonging to jat community wants to marry their daughters out of Haryana where the impact of khaps is less, i.e. jat belt of adjoining states Rajasthan, Delhi, Western UP. Due to this trend the boys who are well employed, even fail to find right life partner for them. Well educated and well employed girls never want to return to Haryana. Due to this vulnerable situation there are number of stories where young males buy the girls from economically poor states like Assam, Bihar, Odisha, Chhattisgarh etc.

Initiatives by Khaps for Improving Sex Ratio

Realising their fault various khaps in Haryana have made their efforts to improve sex ratio. A Maha khap panchayat was held in Bibipur village against the female foeticide. A resolution was passed that female foeticide and infanticide are the issues of olden days, now for every father daughter is an asset. It was also decided that parents who cannot take the responsibility of rearing a girl child may take the help of khaps, khaps will arrange a suitable family for adoption of girl, after passing one year from birth.

This khap panchayat is also remembered for participation of large number of women. These women were sent to Maha khap as representatives of various khaps of Haryana and Western UP. Apart from this another khap has lifted the centuries old ban from sagotra and inter-caste marriages. This has brought some improvement as youth have indirectly given the right to find a life partner of their choice even if it belongs to other caste.

Although such type of positive efforts are appreciable but they will not be effective until women are not given rights equal to men. An attitude of khap panchayats, according to which women are considered as property of male head of family must come to end. If the inhuman incidents against women promoted by khaps will remain continue there is absolutely no possibility of improvements in sex ratio of State of Haryana. Women must be allowed to wear according to their will. They must be allowed to go out for education, employment, entertainment and sports activities.

Conclusion

Due to various reasons India is short of 60 females per 1000 males. Although the overall sex ratio is continuously increasing year by year but the continuous decreasing child sex ratio is great matter of concern. It suggests that heinous crime of female foeticide and infanticide is still prevailing in country. Haryana is the state with lowest sex ratio in the country. Gender-based discriminatory environment created by khaps is the most contributing factor for skewed sex ratio of region affected by khap politics. Various sanctions imposed by khaps on girls from time to time has compelled the parents in Haryana not to give birth to girl child. Realising the problem various khaps in State have changed their ideology and launched a number of awareness campaign. But all these efforts are insufficient until khap panchayats stop targeting the women, stopping all type of discriminatory practices against women especially young girls.

References

- Census of India, 2001 and 2011, www.censusofindia.gov.in
- District-wise Sex Ratio and Child Sex Ratio – 2001 and 2011 in Haryana, www.slideshare.net
- Sharma, N. (2011). Haryana Census Report – Literacy Rate Debunked, www.hindustantimes.com

- Rai, R. K., Singh, P. K. and Parashuraman, S. (2013). Declining Sex Ratio of the Child Population in India: A Decomposition Analysis. www.iussp.org
- Sandhu, K. (2014). Leaders mostly silent on the issue of skewed sex ratio, The Indian Express, Chandigarh (Published on October 10, 2014), www.indianexpress.com
- Sex ratio in Haryana worst among all the states (2013). www.dna.india.com
- Singh, P. (2015). Skewed sex ratio forces Haryana khap to lift 60 year old marriage ban. (Published on February 25, 2015), www.newminutes.com

Chapter – 10

Khap Panchayat and Discrimination Against Women

—*Sharabani Mazumdar*

Abstract

India is identified for its rich culture and tradition across the globe. It is the place where women are worshipped as Durga, Shakti, Saraswati and Lakshmi. At the same time women are considered as means of dishonour culture and tradition. Khap panchayat, the ancient upholders of caste norms have been in the news for all the bad reasons these bodies have been asserting the value of the past, gone by era and stand in the way of the values of Indian Constitution – liberty, equality, fraternity and justice. Most pancha are ignorant peasants, men whose minds are darker than the bottom of the village well and replete with feudal beliefs that haven't been reexamined for centuries. They believe that their honour resides not in their own exemplary conduct but in their wives, daughters and sisters crotch. Now it is the time to realise that our nation can attain greatness by paying proper respect to women. One should never forget that it is the women who bear the child for nine months in her womb and show this beautiful world and give opportunity to live the life in full enjoyment. If khap believes in tradition, culture and shastras, then they should follow the old tradition of giving equal opportunity to women in every walk of life, including the religious and the intellect.

Key Words: *Khap, Tradition, Panchayat, Honour, Women.*

Introduction

In the last few millennia, society in the Indian sub-continent was organised in various forms such as tribe, village, monarchical or

Source: www.kractivist.org

Fig. 10.1: Village Panchayat of Elder People.

republican. As civilisation shifted from nomadic to settled agricultural practices, society organised around the village. The government in the village was a council of five people and was called a panchayat.

The traditional caste panchayats were part of the socio-political life of village communities even in the pre-colonial period. They were essentially informal, decision-making, caste-based bodies of elderly 'wise' men, drawn from their respective castes or from the dominant caste, who commanded universal respect in the community. These members were not elected or self-appointed but were members of consensus and sometimes by heredity. In these panchayat there are two sections of people that are dominant and oppressed. These meetings have always been controlled by the members of the dominant section. The former (due to the integrated nature of the economic system and the virtual monopoly over land) are able to control the later, the lower caste groups and enforced decisions upon them, through threat of economic sanction as well as using or threatening physical violence.

Source: www.hindustantimes.com

Fig. 10.2: Photograph of a Khap Panchayat.

There are twin factors on which lay the strength of traditional caste panchayat are first the numerical strength of a particular caste group and second the landownership it commanded. It means that the landowning class and upper caste population of a village or a religion dominated the traditional panchayats.

The exact origin of khap is unknown. Historically, it has been a decentralised system of social administration in North Western state like Haryana, Uttar Pradesh, Madhya Pradesh and Punjab. It is a tribal, traditional, informal, sociological and political organisation. It regulates not only social customs of the dominant class of the jats but also the members of other class or caste living in its jurisdiction. It is not made of one gotra rather more than three or four gotras assemble together and discuss some issue. Ancient society has organised itself into class or under panchayat system. A class based on one large gotra or a number of closely based gotras. A number of village grouped themselves into a 'Guhaand' and member of guhaands formed a 'Khap' and number of Khaps formed a 'Sarva khap' embarrassing full province or state.

The origin of the word khap is derived from the word 'faank' meaning an offshoot or fraction. It was first used in Rajasthan in the context of Rajput ruler class during the medieval period. In the fourteenth century it was statutory by upper caste jats to consolidate their power and position.

It is an ancient concept which has written references found back from the Rig Vedic times. It is an exclusively male-dominated institution and the women have no share or say on it. The main feature of a khap is that all boys and girls within a khap are considered as siblings. Love marriage is considered taboo in areas governed by khaps panchayats. Punishments imposed by khaps are as follows:

- **Social boycott**- If somebody disobeys the laws or orders of khap then the guilty or their families have to face the social boycott.
- **Fines**- There could be several kinds of fines depending upon the depth of crime.
- **Killing**- Sometimes the khap or even the parents or relatives of the offender, kill them in order to save their honour.
- **Forcing the victims to commit suicide**- In order to save their image and sometimes due to fear they force the victim to commit suicide.
- **Gang rapes**- As a punishment they feel that women deserve rape.
- **Drink urine**-To punish they force the victim to drink urine of their own or someone else's.
- **Naked parade** - For their crime women have to walk naked in front of the khap and villagers through whole village.
- **Beaten up**- The people of khap beat them severely in a barbaric way.
- **Shaving the head.**
- **Dipping the nose in the urine.**
- **Rubbing the nose in the dust.**
- **Touching other's feet.**

Source: www.indiatoday.in

Fig. 10.3: Picture of a khap meeting.

There are different types of khaps and such type of other organisations like 'Kangaroo courts' and 'Shalishi adalat' (West Bengal), 'Tappa panchayat' (Tamil Nadu) as well as 'Sarva khap' who imposes various kinds of restrictions on the people living in that particular area.

Restrictions Imposed by Khaps

- **No love marriages within same gotra [clan]** - As they believe that persons belong to same khap are brothers and sisters.
- **No use of mobile phones by girls** - Khap feels that mobiles are the root cause of misbehaviour with women.
- **Wearing of jeans is banned-** According to their view eve-teasing and rapes are happening because of wearing of wrong dresses in order to provoke the boys.
- **Declare marriages as void** - If they are within khaps even if the family of the girl is ready to accept the marriage.

- **Ostracize families.**
- **Declare husband and wife as brothers and sisters (siblings) after long married life.**

Source: www.thehindu.com

Fig. 10.4: A Cartoon: Representing Implimentation for young Girls.

Reasons for Dominance of Khap Panchayats

There could be number of reasons responsible for dominance of khap panchayats in few particular states of north India, few of them are as follows:

- **Panchayati raj institution is not strong** enough to deliver justice at village level.
- **Vote bank based politics** and **lack of will power.**
- **Judicial delays** and **distrust on system** as court takes very long period to give verdict as a result the innocent people have to wait for the justice, they are harassed by police as well as the court ultimately they go to the panchayat.

People believe that panchayat will cross check each and everything as they know the villagers personally.

- **Socio economic factors** – Women also support khap diktats for various reasons as khap's decisions like not having DJ music in weddings or banning expensive gifts as dowry are far more important because then parents will not have the pressure for daughter's marriage, will stop taking alcohol that will bring harmony in the family and also several harassment will decrease automatically.
- **Female foeticide** – In northern India, still people want male child in their families as they feel that boy will bring goodwill to them and girl child will bestow dishonour to their family.

Discrimination against Women

All the rules of khap are mostly for girls rather than boys. They alone are held responsible for guarding the honour of village. She epitomises 'honours' across societies. It is generally seen as residing in the bodies of women. Women who fall in love, engage in extra marital relationship, seek a divorce, choose their own husbands are seen to transgress the boundaries of appropriate that is socially sanctioned sexual behaviour that may let to horrific violence. The rights of women to control their own lives, liberty and freedom of expression, association, and body integrity mean very little.

The Indian society is highly patriarchal in nature believes in a way of life which is very rigid and based on certain norms including caste system comes with the concepts of gotra. 'Gotra' is a lineage that is associated to an individual at his/her birth. Marriages in same gotra are not considered appropriate because the boy and the girl of same gotra are considered as brothers and sisters which are a sensitive issue that have helped khap to gather public support especially from male members of the society. Notion of honour serves as barometers of familial worth. It is attached to human conditions, just as love, care, affection.

In case of 'honour killing' sometimes formal collective decision made by a council a family member who not only decide whether the girl or women behaviour merits death but also plan how the murder will be done and who will carry out this heinous crime. Honour is frequently if not always gendered. To reserve is to adhere strictly to social norms only by women. They are forced to consider every aspect of their life in the light of 'honour' as a quality which is essential to maintain the reputation of the male members of the family and the entirety of their social worth. Female honour is passive in nature completely centering on the expected behaviour of sub ordinance, modesty and endurance.

A women's role is restricted to be that of dutiful daughter, an obedient wife and self-sacrificing mother. They should work through her life without complaint. They have no desire, wish, dreams, happiness and even sadness. If she tries to move an inch from the so- called customs might result in violence from her parents, ranging from bullying, beating and even murder. However, surprisingly according to the recent study commissioned by Nation commission for women NCW revealed that out of total love marriages there are only three per cent sagotra marriage and 72 per cent are inter-caste marriage. According to the poll conducted by Thomson Reuters in 2011, India is the fourth most dangerous country in the world for women. According to another report, within the span of three generation India has systematically targeted and annihilated nearly fifty million women from its population. The 2011, census found that there are nine hundred forty women for every thousand men and this national figure hides significant national discrepancies.

Punjab and Haryana have the worst sex ratio in the country. They account for 15 districts in the country with most adverse child sex ratio in 2001. According the 2001 census every fifth girl child in Punjab was missing because of gender discrimination.

Outcomes

The actions taken in order to punish women for her deeds are loss of virginity, marriage without consent, premarital pregnancy, and infidelity. Men are less suffered as they have greater bargaining power and may escape death by paying the other family with money or women or might be spared because their tribal or community connections.

Forced marriages are also there where consent of a girl is given less importance as compared to the will of the parents and extended family. It can be also seen that women who are below 40 years of age should must not make use of mobile phones, go out with a male which force us to think do we really living in twenty first century?

Even the khaps are banning women's venturing out for job. When an innocent mother tried to help a couple to move beyond the norms of khaps, she was not only stripped but also beaten up and her face was blackened.

Besides approving honour killings and ban on liberty, khap panchayats have mounted a campaign against the Hindu Succession [Amendment] Act 2005 that gives equal inheritance rights to women. This is done in order to prevent the economic empowerment of girls so that they cannot demand their share of ancestral land. To avoid any conflict after a girl's marriage (arranged or love), the recent tradition in Haryana is to get her property share transferred in the name of the male members. Women have no right to speak for their right, liberty, freedom of thought and equal share in property.

Supreme Court advocate Kriti Singh says that khap panchayat's rulings violated the right to privacy and the family's dignity. Over the years khaps have becomes more and more bold and invasive in their pronouncements about marriage and how women should conduct themselves. The time has come that if not all then at least the women MPs and MLAs must spoke up and stand against the khaps. It is very distressing to note that in times when people chat via 4G technology, Indian society has regressed to the Dark ages.

Ambedkar prophetically said in the year 1948 that currently the state of affairs in India's villages where institution such as khap panchayat not only exist and flourish but also being nurtured by political class of our country.

Discrimination against Women by Khap Panchayats

Khap panchayat in Muzaffarnagar in Uttar Pradesh has banned unmarried girls from wearing jeans and using mobile phones as they believe that it gives rise to crime of eve teasing. Congress spokesperson

Rashid Alvi hit out at the khap saying no one can discriminate against women. He said, "Women are equally free in this country."

The naked brutality of honour crimes against women is in contravention of the spirit of the 'United Nations Convention on the elimination of all forms of discrimination against women [CEDAW]' which has been duly signed and ratified by India. It is difficult to quantify, but India is counted among the countries (Pakistan, Iraq, Turkey, Saudi Arabia, Afghanistan and Iran being others) having very high per capita incidents of 'honour' killings in the world. Recently, 20 years old Santhal tribal woman was raped by 12 men in West Bengal on the orders of a kangaroo court called a Shalishi Sabha. Her crime was to have fallen in love with a man outside her community. The couple were tied up and "tried" and asked to pay Rs 25,000 as payment. The man was able to pay but the woman could not. The headman reportedly declared that she could be "enjoyed" by several men and did the same.

Source: www.timescrest.com

Fig. 10.5: A cartoon reflecting the fear created by khap.

It is said that girl's behaviour and technology are responsible for different types of crime agaist women and it is the women who are responsible to carry the honour of the village and the family. But what about the minor rape cases. In Rajasthan, Kota, a six year old rape victim has been forcefully compelled to get married to the eight year old son of the man accused of the rape.

A step-father in Chandigarh raped his minor daughter (class fifth student) continuously for two days in the absence of her mother.

There are incidents taken place in the areas of Haryana, Western Uttar Pradesh, Rajasthan and the rural belt of Delhi, West Bengal. A Haryana khap leader has come up with his own novel explanation, where he lays the blame squarely on "Chowmin."

A few years back case reported in Baghpat region of Uttar Pradesh, the Asarra khap administrators barred women from using cell phones, going to the market or walking unescorted, boycotting love marriage. Since no constitutional provision restricts anyone from all these. The former Home Minster, P. Chidambaram condemned their decision of imposing unconstitutional burdens in the society.

Similar kind of incident takes place in Sunderbari village panchayat in Kochadham block of Kishanganj district of Bihar where the panchayat restricted women from using mobiles. They also announced if any woman was found using mobile phones, heavy fine as much as Rs 10,000 would be imposed on her. Senior official of the khap believed that "mobile phone is the cause of all evils in our society, including, increasing love affairs and the elopement."

Reacting to the increasing number of rape cases in Haryana, khap panchayat announced ban on TV and in rape case that takes place in Jind district in Hisar, Haryana Khap panchayat has blamed girls for such incidents. They favoured for child marriages and suggested that the marriageable age for girls should be reduced to 16 years.

In another incident, Nawal, a twenty four year old Pakistani women, was accused by her family off behaving dishonourably because people in their village were gossiping about her. Fearing for her safety, she went to police and the police made her brothers sign a pledge not to hurt her. Only three out of four brothers signed the pledge. The fourth killed her by beating repeatedly and then strangling her with a plastic wire around her neck. On June 15, 2012, a girl studying in a Bulandshehar college was allegedly cremated by her family in Bhaipur – Brahampur village.

In Rajasthan, a man named Kaulal Meghwal elopes with the wife of his neighbour, Rajendra. In this case the khap panchayat gave their verdict to Mamta Bai, wife of Kaulal, to stay as spouse of Rajendra or pay him three lakhs as compensation.

Way Forward: The Status of Khap Panchayat

A recent landmark judgment by the Additional Sessions, Court at Karnal in the *Manoj-Babli honour killing case* in which five accused were given the death sentence, as it reminded that khap that they were not above the constitution.

In order to eradicate this social evil it is vital to understand that this archaic set of laws loss together with set of modern and formal institution, like panchayati raj, judiciary, police and the state, should work together. In the light of the above discussion, the following suggestions are submitted:

- Indian Parliament is required to enact a new legislation at the earliest for curbing the malpractices of unconstitutional khap panchayats.
- Various help lines should be introduced in order to help the victims then and there.
- Education – All the people should be given proper education. There must be different form of cell created by the government who will work for the upliftment and protection of women.
- Strict laws – Laws should be as strict as Saudi countries so that before doing any crime offender must think for thousand times.
- Media's involvement- The role of media is very important in this field. It can bring the truth of any event in front of the crowd so that women can fight for justice with the help of media.

- Female literacy- If we want to change the world around us then female should be made literate at any cost.

Conclusion

Generally, the khap leaders are uneducated senior citizens who lack flexibility in their approach. Through education they can be made aware of the existing laws and work in accordance with them. This will help in bridging the gap between the older and younger generation. Participation of women should be encouraged at the core level and everyone should be given a fair chance of defending himself before deciding a matter. Thus, above analysis indicates that the much awaited local institutional justice has dwindled with the passage of time and became an alarming signal to which law as well as society should promptly respond.

References

- Khap panchayat, Sex Ratio and Female Agency, www.aud.ac.in
- Discriminative and Derogatory Practices Against Women. www.ncw.nic.in
- Khap Panchayat: Latest News on Khap Panchayat, www.ibnlive.in.com
- Caste, Culture and Khaap- Journals With Impact Factor, www.impact-journals.us
- Khap Panchayat, www.kractivist.org/tag/khap-panchayat-
- Khap Panchayat: Tradition v. modernity, www.azadindia.org
- Khap- Wikipedia, the free encyclopedia, https://en.wikipedia.org/wiki/khaap
- Khap Panchayat: A Socio- Historical Overview | Economic and.. www.epw.in
- Khap Panchayat- Latest News on Khap Panchayat | Read Breaking...
- Khap Panchayat: The Self- Imposed and (Self) Righteous Judiciary
- www.theviewspaper.net
- zeenews.india.com/tags/Khap-panchayat.html

Section–C

Khap Panchayats, Honour Crimes and Laws

Chapter–11

Nothing Honourable in Honour Killings: A Study of Khap Panchayats, Honour Killings and the Response of Indian Judiciary

—Zainab Farhat and
Dr Nagendra Ambedkar Sole

Abstract

Over a period of time honour killings have attracted the attention of media, policymakers, administrators, academicians and the judiciary. Honour killings have been widely reported in countries like Iran, Turkey, Afghanistan, Iraq, Saudi Arabia, Egypt, Palestine, Jordan, Algeria, Brazil, Ecuador, Morocco, Israel, Ethiopia, Somalia, Uganda, the Balkans, Sweden, Holland, Germany, Italy, Yemen, Pakistan and India. The concept of honour killings is closely associated with the concept of shame. In this chapter an attempt has been made to focus on the important issue of cultural crime, i.e. honour killings. It also looks at the international laws and standards that ensure freedom from discrimination as well as constitutional provisions that allow an individual to exercise their choice independent of caste, religion or gender and protection from honour related crimes. Chapter also presents the landmark judgements of Judiciary in India with regard to honour killings so that legal precedents can be used to put a stop to these honour killings in the country.

Keywords: *Honour killings, International provisions, Law, Judgements, Khap panchayats.*

Introduction

Human beings are associated with society not only socially but psychologically too. The norms of the society are unavoidable moral obligations of the socio-cultural customs, dominantly controlling the psychological behaviour of man. The ideas of honour and dishonour are inbuilt in the way a man thinks by the process of socialisation. For every society, there are certain aspects of social behaviour, formulated according to the status and role of various members of the society.

In the era of globalisation and economic revolution where India is aiming towards development, it is lagging behind in eliminating the deep-rooted social evils. Among them the most horrendous brutal crime committed is honour killing. The people, who think themselves as the so called repositories of the family honour, consider the women as a property, not as a human being, where women are subjected to violence owing to the prevailing cultural norms and socialisation pattern. If a woman or girl is accused or alleged in behaviour that could infect the family status, she has to face brutal retribution. Though such accusations are not based on facts or concrete evidence, any act of dishonour often suffices family members to take matters into their own hands.

The 'honour killings' are an extreme symptom of discrimination against women including other forms of domestic violence – is a plague that affected every country, the United Nations human rights chief says, calling on governments to tackle impunity for this crime on in March, 2010.

The concept of honour that inspires violence and killing has both collective and gender specific aspects, and it is closely associated with the concept of shame. In this context, the concept of honour that inspires violence and raises the expectation of retaliation with violence mainly emanates from the assumption that the honour of the family or group is dependent on the conduct of its members. So, as long as the honour of the group or community is not affected by the shameful and dishonourable conduct the community or group does not necessarily expect retaliation or require killing or violence in return. (Dogan, R. 2011).

The understanding that one's honour and social value are based solely on another person's obedience to cultural expectations creates a strong dependency between those involved. As guardians of female value, men are held responsible for women's conduct because their dignity is closely related to it (Hussain, 2006, 4).

The words 'honour killing' have a strong connotation – whether it is by the media, by NGOs or by governments; an 'honour killing' is something that is understood to be a terrible injustice, a human rights violation and gender subordination, even as users of the term inevitably have different approaches, struggles and agendas. Honour killing is the product of social interactions amongst members of society; and it is qualitatively different from other kinds of murders. It is governed by "the specific logic of an honour culture." (Dogan, R., 2011).

The UN Special Rapporteur on Violence against Women has called honour "a magic word that cloaks the most heinous of crimes." Such murders are not based on religion but on deeply rooted cultural beliefs. (UNAMA, 2010)

According to UNICEF, women who are victims of rape and sexual abuse are also often victims of honour killing because of the perception of dishonour that they bring to their families. The United Nations Population Fund has estimated that as many as 5,000 women and girls are killed by the members of their families or relatives each year for the sake of honour around the world. (UNIFEM, 2007)

The Occurrence of Honour Killings around the World

As honour killing is becoming a global phenomenon, its rising incidence has caught the attention of academicians, civil society, media, and policy-makers and has been widely reported in countries such as Iran, Turkey, Afghanistan, Iraq, Saudi Arabia, Egypt, Palestine, Jordan, Bangladesh, Algeria, Brazil, Ecuador, Morocco, Israel, Ethiopia, Somalia, Uganda, the Balkans, Sweden, Holland, Germany, Italy, Yemen, India and many more countries. (Yazmin, 2008)

None of the world's major religions overlook the honour-related crimes that are increasing at a higher level but the wrongdoers have tried to justify their actions on the grounds of religion where individuals or families involved in committing crimes will at times cite their interpretations of religion so as to reinforce their understandings of honour, regardless of their faith. Religion plays a very septic role as a source of providing meaning in discussions related to honour and violence, though there is no direct link between religion and honour-related violence which is enacted by people of different faiths.

The Middle East and Arabic countries have recorded comparatively high level of honour-based violence and in these regions the formal law codes are most likely to reduce the crime sentence motivated by the feeling of honour. Historically, honour-related violence has been practiced in North Africa, the Middle East, South Asia, Latin America, and Southern Europe, with patterns of violence differing across the regions. The prevalence of honour killing and honour-related violence is very difficult to gauge. (Koteweg, 2014)

In 2009, European Parliamentary Assembly noted the rising incidents of honour crimes with concern. In 2010, Britain saw a 47 per cent rise of honour-related crimes. Data from police agencies in the UK reported 2283 cases in 2010 and most of the attacks were conducted in cities that had high immigrant populations. The national legal Courts in some countries viz., Haiti, Jordon, Syria, Morocco and two Latin American countries do not penalize men killing female relatives found committing adultery or the husbands killing their wives in flagrante delicto. (GOI, 2012)

Honour killing is commonly known as 'karo-kari' in Pakisan. The Human Rights Commission of Pakistan reported 790 cases of honour killing while in the same year about 960 cases were reported by Amnesty international.

In Pakistan and a number of other countries of the Middle East, homicide in the case of adultery is excused because men are gripped by a violent, emotional response beyond their control. The men are considered victims of circumstance and pardoned because the murder is impulsive and passionate. This gendered explanation locates the propensity for violence not in males in general, but in culturally constituted ways of "being a man" which links masculinity with aggression. (Gutman, 1997).

According to local tribal authorities, honour killing is still legal in some conservative Muslim countries such as Iran and Pakistan, although the Central government often condemns such practices. Honour killings are so common and widespread in Turkey that they amount to almost half of all murders in the Eurasian country. These practices are formally prohibited in most of the countries but perpetrators are often treated leniently where honour killings are common, punishable by just two or three years in prison. (Martino, 2010).

The UN Commissioner for Human Rights Navi Pillay observed that "The reality for most victims, including victims of honour killings, is that State institutions fail them and that most perpetrators of domestic violence can rely on a culture of impunity for the acts they commit – acts which would often be considered as crimes, and be punished as such, if they were committed against strangers."

Worldwide, more than half the victims of honour killing are tortured befor killing, they did not die instantly but in agony. In North America over one-third of the victims were tortured; in Europe two-third were tortured; in the Muslim world, half of them were tortured. Torturous deaths include : being raped or gang raped before being killed; being strangled or bludgeoned to death; being stabbed many times; being stoned or burned to death; being beheaded, or having one's throat slashed. (MEQ, 2010).

In some Western cultures, honour killings often arise from women seeking greater independence and choosing their own way of life. In some cultures, honour killings are considered less serious than other murders because they arise from long standing cultural traditions and are thus deemed appropriate or justifiable. An adulterous behaviour of woman or pre-marital relationship or assertion of right to marry according to their choice, are widely known causes for honour killings in most of the countries. (GOI, 2012).

The problem with majority of the countries is that they have confusion of what honour killing actually constitute. According to the international rights and women's group many families report the killings as suicide or reports of missing to escape the punishment under the law. According to UN statistics, the United Kingdom has 12 cases of honour killings every year and the majority of them are from the Asian and West Asian Diaspora.

In the recent times due to the age of migration in the western immigrant receiving countries and also around the world, the cases of honour killing have risen up. For instance, accusation of dishonour may emerge because someone from an older migrant generation remains wholly tied to the culture and codes of their village – and further fails to accept that their children have been brought up in modern British society. Over the past two decades, Western immigrant-receiving countries have been confronted with honour killings and other forms of honour-related violence as the younger generation of immigrants started imitating the western culture and the older generation residing in the US and Europe adhere to their own country's customs, traditions and norms, leading them to react violently.

Honour Based Violence (HBV) is a term described for violence that is committed within the context of the extended family and is motivated by a professed need to maintain standing within the community. Victims of HBV are mostly women or girls and at times men may also be at risk due to their decision of going beyond the ambit of family's honour.

In most of Western and Northern Europe, HBV is almost entirely associated with population of immigrants, where such acts are seen as the survival of tribal and patriarchal values from their countries of origin, although these may be exacerbated by the experiences of translocation and social exclusion.

International Human Rights Foundations

Under the international laws and standards, the State's responsibility is to uphold women's rights and ensure freedom from discrimination which is mentioned in a clear cut manner and includes responsibility to prevent, protect and provide redress – regardless of sex, and the person's status in the family.

- **Article 1** of the **UN Declaration on the Elimination of Violence Against Women** proclaims that "violence against women" means any act of gender-based violence that results in, or is likely to result in, physical, sexual or psychological harm or suffering to women, including threats of such acts, coercion or arbitrary deprivation of liberty, whether occurring in public or in private life.

- **Article 12** of the **International Convention on Economic, Social and Cultural Rights (ICESCR 1976)** ensures that "right of everyone to the enjoyment of the highest attainable standard of physical and mental health." Crimes of honour involving sexual violence, physical or mental torture hamper the rights of women.
- **The Platform for Action on Women's Human Rights from the UN Fourth World Conference on Women** calls upon states for a transformed partnership based on equality between women and men as a condition for people-centred sustainable development and to take urgent action to combat and eliminate violence against women, which is a human rights violation resulting from harmful traditional or customary practices, cultural prejudices and extremism.
- **The Convention on the Elimination of Discrimination of All Forms against Women (CEDAW) 1979** in its preamble explicitly acknowledges that "extensive discrimination against women continues to exist", and emphasises that such discrimination "violates the principles of equality of rights and respect for human dignity." The CEDAW defined discrimination as "any distinction, exclusion or restriction made on the basis of sex in the political, economic, social, cultural, civil or any other field.
- **The International Covenant on Civil and Political Rights (ICCPR)** asserts that the States Parties to the present Covenant undertake to ensure the equal right of men and women to the enjoyment of all civil and political rights set forth in the present Covenant and that "every human being has the inherent right to life" in addition to "the right to liberty and security of person."

Constitutional Provisions

The Constitution of India has many provisions that allow an individual to exercise their choice independent of caste, religion or gender and protection from honour-related crimes including honour killings.

The Protection of Human Rights (Amendment) Act, 2006 made the provision for protection of individual rights, similarly the National Human Rights Commission, State Human Rights Commissions and Human Rights Courts seeks to protect the human rights. Though the Protection of Women from Domestic Violence Act, 2005 provides for an effective protection of the rights of women guaranteed under the Constitution for those who are victims of violence of any kind.

The point to be noticed is that there are no specific laws in India which deals with this horrifying act of honour killings. Honour killing get strong sanction from the society too, as not only the family of the victims but also the community at times support the dreadful act. Honour killings are considered homicide and murder which are taken as serious crimes under the Indian Penal Code, Section 299 of the IPC, deals with culpable homicide while Section 300, deals with culpable homicide amounting to murder.

The honour-based crime violates the Article 14, 15 (1) and (3), 19, 21 and 39 (f) of the Constitution of India. Even today there is no legal definition of honour crime in India. The reason to save honour of the family and giving harsh punishment to the victims so that other's couldn't do such shameful act as considered by them.

The Law Commission of India views that the words 'honour killings' and 'honour crimes' are being used loosely as convenient expressions to describe the incidents of violence and harassment caused to the young couple intending to marry or having married against the wishes of the community or family members. They are used more as catch phrases and not as apt and accurate expressions. (GOI, Prevention of interface with the freedom of matrimonial alliances in the name of honour and traditions, A suggested legal framework, 2012).

The National Commission for Women has drafted a Bill titled "Prevention of Crimes in the name of Honour and Tradition." The Bill is closer in thinking to the law proposed by the Law Commission. It suggests certain prohibitive and penal measures. It provides for recording of declaration of an intended marriage by the couple concerned as a means of seeking protection apart from penalising the acts of harassment etc. caused to the woman or her partner. However, it misses the necessity and desirability of the focus on directly dealing with unlawful assemblies and their vicious influences. Further, the offences under general law are also included in the said Bill. But, certain aspects contained in that Bill have been usefully incorporated in the proposed law. (GOI, Prevention of interface with the freedom of matrimonial alliances in the name of honour and traditions, A suggested legal framework, 2012).

In the light of such shameful incidences the law called The Endangerment of Life and Liberty (Protection, Prosecution and other measures) Act, 2011, proposes to put improved penal sanctions against outraging the modesty of women. It declares public meeting as unlawful assembly if it's done to discuss a marriage matter of a couple who have married by choice. It further removes the requirement of notice under the Special Marriage Act, holding the members of the assembly as liable, where boycott and methods like such are taken up as illegal. This is really a positive step in India to protect the gross Human rights violations in the name of upholding the honour.

India – A Silent Spectator to Honour Killings

The incidence of women exploitation in India is deep-rooted and they continue to become the soft target of it. Women folk have been subjected to such truant practices because of medievalism, male chauvinistic surroundings, influence of religion, social control and fear of being ostracised from the society, rigid caste system, stereotyped mindset, lack of formal governance in the rural areas and the preservation of perceived purity of their lineage. (Kumar, 2012).

Honour killings have become increasingly common in many parts of the country mainly in Haryana, Rajasthan, Western Uttar Pradesh, and even in some parts of Bihar, Delhi and Tamil Nadu.

There are more than 1000 honour killings in India every year says the experts. The NGO 'Shakti Vahini' in its study stated that heart aching incidents of honour killings have been reported from all over the country and in the ninety per cent of the cases known, the perpetrators of crime were belonging to the girl's family.

In Muzaffarnagar district of Western Uttar Pradesh, 13 honour killings cases occurred within nine months in year 2003. In the year 2002, ten such killings were reported, 35 couples when investigated were declared missing.

A study conducted by the National Commission for Women stated that 72 per cent of 326 cases documented over the year 2009-10 involved couples that entered into inter-caste marriages. Among the incidents that have taken place the most barbaric was the brutal killing of a young couple Manoj and Babli in Kaithal district of Haryana in 2007 where they were dragged out of the Haryana roadways bus and were forced to drink poison. Their crime was that they had violated the caste norms of gotra and eloped to get married. The murder was supported by khap panchayats and politicians.

The rising incidence of murders of people marrying outside their caste or religion and other severe offences on caste basis and 'gotra' are matters of grave concern. Those directly involved in the actual commitment of the acts of violence or murder are either people from one's own family or part of the community. The persons who are involved in such incidents and offences are not even taken cognisance by the law and their domineering position and strength suppress the investigating agencies.

The caste or community panchayat's play a constructive role in addressing the common problems related to the society. The famous "Khap panchayats" who see themselves as the custodians of honour, are dominantly active in Haryana, western Uttar Pradesh and parts of Rajasthan where in areas governed by khap, love marriages are considered taboo exceeding their limits, who often impose their decisions in matters relating to matrimony interfering in the rights of youngsters indulging in acts of endangering their freedom of life and liberty.

From time to time voices have been raised against the reign of khap panchayats who are self-elected councils and covertly endorse the killings in the name of saving the honour of the community. The caste system has turned into a social evil. It is just a notion that only women's are the only victims of it, men are also equally treated in the most horrendous ways, once they cross the so called gotra system.

In the case of honour killings by khap panchayats, one can see that if adherence to a particular cultural practice is imposed in the name of 'tradition', the attack is not just on the individuals but on the institution of individual choice based on a conscious agency protected by the tenets of a Rule of Law which is assumed to be based on universal notions of justice and fairness. Thus, it is not just the marriage that is questioned but the exercise of free will in deciding whom to marry. It is obvious that universal notions of justice would deem the denial of such an exercise invalid, and even, horrifying. (Annavarapu, 2010).

Some of the recent and well known inter-caste/community cases of 'honour' killings come from not only rural but also urban regions of India, extending from north to south, cutting across class lines. The media has come a long way from disregarding the news of 'honour' killings and considering it as essentially belonging to the 'Other' India - the rural hinterland - to sensationalise it as belonging to a 'feudal mindset', the media has been forced to accept its existence in educated, modern, urban. (Kumar, P. 2010).

Girija Vyas, then Chairperson of the National Commission for Women, while preparing the draft of 'The Prevention of Crimes in the Name of 'Honour' and Tradition Bill, 2010', had regarded honour killings as violation of certain fundamental rights guaranteed by the Constitution of India, including the right to life, and liberty which, if broadly interpreted, includes the right to bodily integrity, and the right to choose whom to associate with. The actions of the parents of the girls to stop her from exercising her choice also result in curtailment of her freedom to movement and expression. A valid consent to marriage is also an essential requirement under the law.

The role of the transnational media at times of 'honour killings' in a much more sensationalised and simplistic fashion, through the narratives of description of violence, the stories of escape, mode of death, and other are at times poorly researched as the case becomes very convenient once it is highlighted where actually such types of crime don't really need an investigation as to why it was done. The media needs a more focused and long-term attitude in the coverage of socio-economic issues.

Nitish Kataria murder in 2002, Asha, Nirupama, Kuldeep and Monika Murder in 2010, Deepti Chikara Murder in 2012 are some of the murders taken place in the name of honour.

In a recent horrific case of Bhavna Yadav in Nov, 2014 caste and honour again overpowered a women's life where she was allegedly murdered by her parents for marrying her boyfriend. According to the news reports, the victim Bhavna Yadav a resident of Delhi, was beaten up, strangled and her body was dumped.

Indian Judiciary on Honour Killings

Judiciary shows its active role in protecting the individual liberty and also taking strong action against the social evils like honour killing is one of them. It has consistently played proactive role in raising the mantle against honour killings through some landmark judgments. In the words of noted lawyer Prashant Bhushan, "The Supreme Court is the only hope people have and it's the only institution that seems to be doing anything."

Some of the landmark judgements of various courts regarding honour killings are as follows:-

- ***Lata Singh* v *State of Uttar Pradesh and others, AIR (2006) SC 2522***, the Supreme Court has ruled that "*there is nothing honourable in such killings, and in fact they are nothing but barbaric and shameful acts of murder committed by brutal, feudal-minded persons who deserve harsh punishment.*" The Supreme Court has further directed the administration or police authorities throughout the country to see to the fact that if any boy or girl who is a major undergoes inter-caste or inter-religious marriage with a woman or man who is a major, the couple are not harassed by any one nor subjected to threats or acts of violence. Police shall institute criminal proceedings if anyone is found giving such threats or committing acts of violence against such couples. Court also highlighted the expected role of the concerned District Magistrates or Collector and SSPs or SPs by stating that they shall be immediately suspended by the State Government and charge sheet shall be framed against them if they do not prevent the incident having an advanced knowledge of the same or do not properly apprehend the culprits and the others involved.

- In another case of ***Arumugam Servai* vs. *State of Tamil Nadu*, (2011) 6 SSC 405**, the Supreme Court has declared the honour killings based on the perception of the khaps, wholly illegal that must be stamped out. And in the same case classifying honour killings, not as a separate crime, but like any other heinous crime violating a person's constitutional rights as well as in the context of violation of human rights.
- The Supreme Court in ***Bhagwan Dass* v. *State of NCT, Delhi, (2011)* SSC 396**, laid down that honour killings satisfy 'the rarest of the rare' doctrine so as to attract the death penalty for its perpetrators. The bench declared honour killing as nothing but barbaric and brutal murders by bigoted person with feudal minds. In the opinion of the bench, "*if someone is not happy with the behaviour of his daughter or other person who is in his relation or his caste; the maximum he can do is to cut off social relation with him or her.*"
- In the historic ***Manoj-Babli honour killing case of 2007***, the Sessions Court of Haryana had set a new record against the illegal fatwas issued by the khaps and openly sent out the message that nobody is above the Constitution. This case culminated in a landmark judgement delivered by district session judge Vani Gopal Sharma in 2010 and the five accused were given death sentence to life and one of them sentenced to life time imprisonment.
- As a note of caution, former Attorney-General of India, Soli Sorabjee had stated that *"The court is not running the country,*

but it is saying to the executive, 'You should be running the country according to the laws. It's the job of the Supreme Court to see that the executive functions within its power and acts when it has a duty to act – what it is their duty to do is a matter of subjective judgment to some extent."

- Similarly, in ***Trimukh Maroti Kirkan vs. State of Maharashtra, (2006)1 SCC 681***, the Supreme Court observed: honour killings have become commonplace in many parts of the country, particularly in Haryana, western UP, and Rajasthan. Often young couples who fall in love have to seek shelter in the police lines or protection homes, to avoid the wrath of kangaroo courts. We have held in Lata Singh's case (supra) that there is nothing honourable in honour killings, and they are nothing but barbaric and brutal murders by bigoted, persons with feudal minds.
- In the case of ***State of U.P. Vs Krishna Master and others,*** the Supreme Court has awarded life sentence to three persons in an honour killing case, in which six members of a family were gunned down, but said the accused deserved capital punishment. Though judiciary has played its cruicial role but it is surrounded by limitations too.
- In the Noida double murder case where ***Arushi Talwar and Hemraj***, a domestic help being employed by her family in Delhi, where the two were killed in 2008 has also speculations that Arushi was killed in the name of honour where now her parents are behind bar, the case is still a mystery to be solved.
- The recent **murder case of Sheena**, involving ex- star CEO wife Indrani Mukerjee, the case has also been seen as an incidence of honour killing where Sheena was murdered by her mother and her second husband as suspected.
- Justice K. S. Ahluwalia of the Punjab and Haryana High Court on June 23, 2006 made a revealing statement while simultaneously hearing 10 cases pertaining to marriages of young couples that "*The High Court is flooded with petitions where...judges of this Court have to answer for the right to life and liberty to married couples. The State is a mute*

> *spectator. When shall the State awake from its slumber and for how long can Courts provide solace and balm by disposing of such cases?"*

What needs to be done...?

Honour killings for whatever reason, coming within the category of rarest of rare cases deserve death punishment. It is time to stamp out these barbaric, feudal practices which are a slur on the nation. This is essential as a deterrent for such an extreme, uncivilised behaviour. All persons who are planning to perpetrate honour killings should know that the gallows await them.

With society's acceptance to honour killing in life, it would need much more than a tough law to punish the perpetrators. The mindset of the people needs to be changed through Cultural Revolution. An analysis of the honour killings presents it as a gendered notion highlighting inequality and hierarchy where both men and women symbolise notions of honour, but differently. The woman is termed to be the repository and the man is the regulator of this honour.

Violence against women can only be combated if there is a healthy partnership between the women's development groups and the institutions of the state. They have to work effectively on the criminal justice system to further protect the rights of the women victims. Community level programmes should be initiated on the grassroots level to promote gender equality. The section of India which is overpowered by the shackles of honour based killing is outside the ambit of the country's constitutional and judicial values. Social attitudes of the people need to be changed which should reflect more of liberal and human values and equality and protection for all women.

The major problem in finding out the culprits is that the incidences of honour killing are not widely reported by the media since families act in secret. It may be noted that so long as families and communities continue to sustain and maintain a sense of honour with regard to this barbaric act, honour killings will continue.

Though, the civil society and the government have become more vigilant during the course of time due to feminist movements, investigations of the media and the transformation of Indian society from traditional prejudiced to a more legal and rational society, more needs to be done to constitute rigorous laws and rigid punishments to change the mindset of the prejudiced patriarchal society.

It is the responsibility of state and society to protect the human rights of its young citizens, to avoid honour killings, to create new possibilities for the people concerned to find protection, support and aid. Therefore, it is suggested that social evil like honour killing cannot be eliminated through law alone, rather almost every substitution be it social, economic, political and cultural will have to be sensitised against this crime as only law could be one of the important tools to fight this practice.

In the changing discourse the religious leaders should come up to condemn such inhuman acts. First of all the mindset of the people have to be changed. The concepts of empowering the women and their rights should be taken as normal as the empowerment of the males, it shouldn't be treated as something alien or giving some extra freedom to them. The agencies like State Women's Commission, Social Welfare Department with some other NGOs should develop some preventive measures and active policing in such cases.

Apart from legislation to effectively curb honour-related crimes, it is equally important that the steps should be taken to organise counselling programmes for the village communities, for instance to explain to them that sagotra marriages are not opposed to law, religion, sadachar, or medical science. (GOI, 2012).

The Ministries and NGOs who are related to women affair should provide targeted assistance to women to lodge complaints against these traditional practices with the help of police and prosecution. Adequate support by the people should be given to the national and provincial Commissions on Elimination of all types of violence against women so that the matters are investigated well. Nation-wide campaigns need to be organised to raise awareness on the violence against women and women's rights. The rural areas shall be given particular focus and women and girls education shall be an aim in the coming times so that they actually are well educated about their rights.

The khaps cannot be considered beyond the law and it would be really unwise and socially incorrect to leave the life and liberty of the vulnerable people at the mercy of such dominant authorities. Regard and respect for life, liberty and autonomy of persons need to be the focus and the perceived interest of such assemblies. It's time to go beyond the role of just filling the cases and doing investigations; the judiciary should develop proactive mechanisms to protect the rights of these victims.

The Indian judiciary had made it clear time and again through various judgements that there is nothing honourable in honour killings. The time has come that the society should change its attitude towards this problem. For changes to take place from its root, both men and women need to engage in transforming unequal gender relations.

References

- Annavarapu, S. (2010). Human Rights, Honour Killings and The Indian Law scopes 'Right to have Rights'. *EPW.*
- Dogan, R. (2011). Is Honour Killing a Muslim Phenomenon? *Journal of Muslim Minority Affairs.*
- GOI, Prevention of interface with the freedom of matrimonial alliances in the name of honour and traditions, A suggested legal framework, 2012. The Law Commission of India.
- Gutman, M. C. (1997). Trafficking in Men: An Anthropology of Masculanity. *Annual Review of Anthropology.*
- Honour Killing by Region South and Central Asia, www.hbv-awareness.com
- Koteweg, A. (2014). Honour Killing in Immigration Context: Multicultu-ralism and the Racialisation of Violence against Women, Politikon, 2014, 183-208.
- Kumar, A. (2012). Public Policy Imperatives for Curbing Honour Killing in India, *Journal of Politics and Governance.*
- Kumar, P. (2010). Redeeming Honour through Violence: Unrevealing the Concept and its Application.
- Martino, H. (2010). Killed in the Name of Honour. Human Rights International.
- MEQ. (2010). Wordwide Trends in Honour Killing. www.meforum.org
- UNAMA, (2010). Report on Harmful Traditional Practices and Implementation of Law on Elimination of Violence against Women in Afganistan. UNAMA Human Rights.

- UNIFEM. (2007). Facts and Figures on Harmful Traditional Practices. Geneva: Unifem Publications.
- Yazmin, A. (2008). The State and its Implications: An Examination of Honour Killing in Jordan and the Efforts of Local Activist. Alburn University, Thesis, Unpublished.

Chapter – 12

A Critical Jurisprudential Appraisal of Law and Justice in Crime of Honour Killings and Role of Khap Panchayats in India

—Dr Amit Kashyap and
Shashi Bala Kashyap

Abstract

Khap panchayats are the self-proclaimed courts which enjoy full legitimacy and authority among the segments of their caste as the custodian of honour. These panchayats have no constitutional basis and they are not legitimate courts. Under this unconstitutional system, all members crouches around a 'chabutara' in a village in order to take quick, unilateral and incontestable decision on multiple issues like social transgression, marriage offences, property rights or regarding situation threatening tranquility in a village. Today where the society is governed by legal norms and constitutional authorities, the bodies like khap panchayat pose impediment to development and good governance. The dictates of khap panchayat are praised by the people of particular territory or community in which khap exists; this is the most crucial impediment for abolition of khap panchayat. This chapter attempts to find out, why does khaps still exist in India? What is the source of strength of khap? It also presents a detail discussion on the issue of khap panchayat and tries to put forward some possible solution.

Key Words: *Honour Killing, Kangaroo Court, Sagotra Marriages, Unwritten Laws, Dictates, Patriarchal.*

Introduction

Khap panchayat like the caste system is a traditional institution which is basically engaged in a process of dispute resolution in village communities. Traditionally every village has its own panchayat or council. Panchayat literally means assembly of five (panch) prudent and respected elders chosen and accepted by village community. Usually mighty and powerful persons, with the coerced public consensus and without any election, group together declare themselves the "king of the caste", thereby constituting the "caste panchayats." Traditionally these assemblies settle disputes between individuals and villages. However, these bodies lack any constitutional or legal basis. They should not be confused with "Panchayati raj" Institutions. Khap panchayats are undemocratic in origin. They have unwritten laws and their decisions are clearly illegal and unconstitutional. Without application of law and acting on their whims and wishes, they impose self-created norms backed by sanction in the name of preserving morals and values of the society.

It is well said by Indian philosophers that the seeds of divinity grow and blossom in a cultured society where women are given due respect and equal opportunity of rise and dignity. Twenty first century will be known for the society where everyone has their own way of life, whether it is related to the food, dress up, retreating, education, prestige, etc. A well dignified human being puts all his efforts for acquiring the prestige, fame and a position in the society and treat well everyone according to various situations. But when someone made to understand that this prestige, frame, reputation in the society is going to be ruin or finish in a few seconds results i.e. A 29 years old youth dragged his sister out on the street and cut off her head with one stroke of the sword for the protection of the honour.

Khap panchayats, working against the Constitution, are autocratic and less transparent in process. Till the establishment of the judicial system, khaps were socially famous and relevant for harmonious settlements of disputes. With the passage of time they lost their influence but from last few years, the issues like demands of ban on same-gotra marriages strengthened them again. Exact origin of khap panchayat cannot be found out but we may broadly consider the period of its development in 600 A.D. In the ancient times, when the man was living itinerant life, villages were being formed at a rapid rate and the society headed towards civilisation for better standards of living. Khap panchayats are understood to have come into existence as a social system for maintenance mechanism in those agrarian societies. They are the legacies of the tribal councils, formed by various tribes with a purpose of facilitating resolution of intra-tribal disputes and inter-tribal inter-course. Khap panchayats generally consist of powerful elements of the dominant caste. They are generally senior citizens who claim to be considered as upholders of village norms, custodians of rural cultures and guardians of public morality. They have a great hold both at the local as well as provincial level.

Working of Khap Panchayats

Khap panchayats are units of number of villages organised into a political council for the purpose of societal control and decision-making on social issues. The khap area is inhabited by a dominant caste that had a control over most of its agricultural land, and by a single clan or by more than one clan each with a number of villages and being predominant in those villages. When a single clan had only few villages, other clans could also join into a common khap for the purpose of their defense and control over their people. When a khap is dominated by single clan, its headship lay within that clan. When the number of clans exceeds in number, the headship goes to that clan that had more number of villages under that aegis.

Khap panchayat is generally classified on the basis of its territorial jurisdiction. If there is one community and people of that particular community residing in more than one village of patwari level headed by the panchas, it forms 'kheda'. It occupies the lowest position in the hierarchy. The second, level is called 'Patti' where people of a community from villages of revenue inspector level are brought under one head. Patti further has two kinds: 'Chep Patti' and Borah Patti. Simply more the number of villages under the judicature of a khap panchayat, the greater is the strictness observed in imposing its orders, thus higher is the punishment in case of disobedience.

There is also a provision of appeal. In case of appeal, the decision of 'Maha panchayat' is final, unobjectionable and unquestionable. 'Sarv khap panchayat' may also be called for adjudication, if there is conflict between the dictate of two Khaps or dispute in jurisdiction or for any other serious issue. Sarv khap panchayats consist of all khaps prevailing in an area. It is the 'Pradhan' of the khap who calls the meeting of the Sarv khap when an issue between two khaps need to be resolved or when the issue is of the serious nature. The nominated khap pradhan controls the proceeding of the Sarv khap panchayat till a decision is arrived. After this the detailed history of the case is presented, the other khap pradhans are invited to put their views before the meeting. After hearing out all the speakers, a small committee of 10-15 khap pradhans is constituted to reach a consensus. Before a decision is announced, a hand count shows whether the decision of Sarv khap would be acceptable to everyone. If the issue is related to all the khaps, it becomes the duty of each khap to implement the decision in its respective jurisdiction. If the issue is related to a particular khap, then the concerned khap is supposed to abide by the decision of Sarv khap. The main role of Sarv khap is to maintain the peace and harmony between the various khaps by settling disputes between them or by passing resolution related to the social welfare of the people such as education of girls, ban on female foeticide and dowry, limited expenditure of the marriage and so on. If somebody is found violating the decision of the khap, sanction is imposed to maintain the khap's decision. On the basis of constitution of khaps could be classified into following three categories:

(i) Khaps based on single caste and single gotra

A particular geographical area is dominated by a single gotra of a particular caste. The gotra has a sizable number of villages in that area, e.g. Dahiya khap, Hudda khap, Malik khap, Sangwan khap and so on all of which are located in Sonipat, Rohtak, Bhiwani, the districts of Haryana and the Balyan khap in Muzaffarnagar district of Uttar Pradesh. These Khaps include about 40084 villages.

(ii) Khaps based on single caste and multiple gotra

When the entire area is dominated by a single caste, with some of the villages dominated by various gotras, it is considered as single caste and multiple gotra system. Chaubitii organisation of 24 villages of Meham in the Rohtak district of Haryana is an example of such khap.

(iii) Khaps based on multiple castes and multiple gotra

This system is renowned as having villages in particular geographical area of which some villages are dominated by a particular caste and other villages by other castes but different gotras. Bawal khap of Chaurasi in the Riwari district may be considered as this type of Khap.

A single khap panchayat generally consists of 84 villages or 12 thambas. Thus, thamba is considered as a group of seven villages. In its hierarchy Sarv khap (all caste council) is the highest level khap which embraces a full province or a state. Every khap individually elects its leaders who represent the dispute on behalf of that particular village at sarv khap level. It depends upon the magnitude of the problem that at what level a sarv khap would be required to call upon.

Modus Operandi of Khap Panchayat

Khap panchayats forcefully implement their illegal dictates. The following acts are sufficient for compelling us to think that we are still living in barbaric era.

In the boiling oil pot a coin is placed and the accused has to get it out of the pot. If the accused would perform the task he/she will be declared innocent. (Kanuni daanv pencho ke dar se kayam aadivasi adaalaten, 1999, January 15, Dainik Bhaskar, Jodhpur Edition)

Heated hot red iron stick is placed on the palms of the accused. The palms are covered with seven pipal leaves and turmeric. The accused has to walk seven steps with the red hot stick between his/her palms. The accused is considered innocent if the palms are not burnt. This exercise is usually followed if there is any doubt on the character of the accused. (Kalyug me di sita ne agni pariksha, 2002, July 8, Dainik Bhaskar, Jodhpur Edition).

To judge the guilt of a woman she is forced to fry "Puris" with her bare hands in the boiling oil. She will be declared innocent if her hands are not burnt during performing the act. (Ve har saal deti hai agni pariksha, 2002, October 17, Dainik Bhaskar, Jodhpur Edition)

Usually, on the basis of looks of a poor widow, she is declared demon.

Imposing huge fines or penalties, seizure of lands of the accused and forcibly get possession on the same are other verdicts of Self-proclaimed Judges of khap panchayats.

These verdicts include forced divorce and remarriage of the couples against their wishes and sometimes without consent of their family members.

Sometimes the decision of ex-communication of accused personally or with the families results in enormous mental torture and humiliation.

A 50-year-old woman in Rajasamand, Rajasthan was allegedly paraded naked on a donkey on the orders of a self-styled village court that decided that she was guilty of killing her husband's cousin. A tribal girl was allegedly gang raped on the orders of a khap panchayat in Birbhum district of West Bengal. A khap panchayat or caste council in Madhi village in Uttar Pradesh allegedly stripped a woman, blackened her face and beat her for helping young couple to elope. The woman's son who tried to intervene and protect his mother was also beaten up brutally.

Reason for Persistent Survival of Khap

In the British period the nation was divided among many provinces and each province was governed by its own special laws. There was no uniform law for the entire nation. Khap might have been justified relatively at that time but their existence even after independence is questionable because presently we are living in the environment of education, individuals rights and fundamental rights, directive principles of states, Panchayati raj institutions etc. So, it is required to make an analysis of the philosophical foundation of khap panchayat. The concept of khap panchayat is closely associated with the cultural relativism. The thought of societies where khap panchayat exists is that their culture is superior to others. This thought leads them to protect and preserve their culture by their own means and decisions. That is why the societies in which the khap exists follow the decisions of khap without protesting.

Khap system cannot be abolished by statutes or any punitive action because the common conscience of people living in khap governed areas, is with them. If we want to make this dispute resolution system more rational and effective, the members of khap must seek to incorporate some basic moral requirements, in coherence with national laws. The main source of strength of khap panchayat is massive community support of that particular society in which khap exists. There exists huge vote bank in the hand of khaps for politicians therefore lack of political will to abolish this social ill is obvious. For abolishing the khaps, it is needed that people's support to this unconstitutional authority should be dejected by bringing awareness in the khap societies. It is essential to make them start thinking that they are lacking some basic-moral principles and values in their culture.

Contemporary Socio-legal Challenges by Khap Panchayats

- **Honour Killings**

There is no specific definition of honour killing. However, these honour killings are murders committed by family members and the people belonging to concerned caste on the verdict of khap panchayats or family members of such who are believed to have brought shame or dishonour on family name. The apparent shame is caused by a victim refusing to enter into an arranged marriage or for having a relationship that is considered to be inappropriate by the family or community. The perceived dishonour is normally the result of the following behaviours, or the suspicion of such behaviours -

(a) Dress in such a manner which is not acceptable by the community.

(b) Marriage by own choice (against wish of family or community).

(c) Engaging in certain sexual acts, including those with opposite or same sex.

- **Forced Marriages**

In khap regime, sometimes marriages are performed by pressurising one or both the parties and without their free will and consent. The victim of such marriage is forced through coercion, fear, abduction, threat, inducement and deception. A forced marriage can take place, between the people of any group, children, an adult and a child or between adults. The victims of forced marriages experience torture, abduction, threaten, mental and are even forced to commit suicide.

- **Female Foeticide**

Despite of number of articles in newspapers, magazines and efforts made at a large scale by the volunteers, social activists and government and non-government organisations, the female foeticides is growing at an increasing rate in the entire nation, especially in North India. The case of female foeticide is recorded to be the maximum in the North Indian states of Haryana and Punjab.

The sex ratio in the Haryana state is recorded to be a shocking figure of 877 (females)/1000 (males). Boys are considered comparatively superior to girls as per the practices of female foeticides. Giving birth to a girl child is almost a sin in the regions where khap panchayat exists. So, these people resort to kill the female foetus or the moment a mother gives birth to a girl child.

To restrict the killing of female child, the government has passed the Pre Conception and Pre Natal Diagnostic Techniques (Prohibition of Sex Selection) Act, 1994. This provides prevention of the misuse of pre-natal diagnostic techniques for the purpose of pre-natal sex determination leading to female foeticide. To avoid the discriminate abortion of female foetuses, the Medical Termination of Pregnancy Act, 1971 permits abortion only in limited cases. Apart from this Act, the IPC under Sec. 312 to 317 also imposes restriction on termination of pregnancies.

- **Prohibition on Sagotra, Inter-caste and Inter-religious Marriage**

Khap panchayat prohibits sagotra, inter-caste and inter religious marriages. The marriages are governed by khap on three important principles –

(a) Marriages within the same gotras are forbidden since in that case a boy and girl are regarded as brother and sister.

(b) Marriages in the different gotras are forbidden if a boy and girl belong to the same village or physically adjoining villages.

(c) Inter-caste and inter-religious marriages are strictly barred.

Sagotra marriages are not prohibited by law. The Hindu Marriage Disabilities Removal Act, 1946 was enacted with a view to dispel any doubts in this regard. The Act expressly declared that marriage between the Hindus belonging to same gotras or parivara or different sub-division of the same caste is valid. The Hindu Marriage Act, 1955 does not prohibit Sagotra, inter-caste or inter-religious marriage. The views of village elders or family elders or family elders cannot be forced upon the willing couple and none has a right to use force or impose far reaching sanctions in the name of vindicating community honour or the family honour. There are reports that drastic actions including wrongful confinement, persistent harassment, mental torture, infliction of severe bodily harm are resorted to either by the close relations or some third parties against the so called erring couple. Social boycotts and other illegal sanctions affecting the young couple, the families and even a section of local inhabitants are quite often also resorted. In **Arumugam Servai vs. State of Tamil Nadu**, the Supreme Court strongly deprecated the practice of khap panchayats taking law into their own hands and indulging in offensive activities which endangers the personal lives of the persons marrying according to their choice.

Judicial Trends and Recent Developments

The judiciary after the protest of human rights activists, drawn its attention towards the unlawful activities of khap panchayats:

In **Laxmi Kachhwaha vs. State of Rajasthan (1999),** public interest litigation was filed in the Rajasthan High Court to draw the attention of the Court to illegal functioning of caste panchayat on the weaker sections of the concerned communities, especially on women. The Court observed that these panchayats had no jurisdiction whatsoever to pass social boycott order, or to impose fine on anyone and to violate the basic rights of an individual. It ordered the state authorities to take steps for preventing the abuse of social influence by restraining such panchayats from functioning and ensuring arrest and punishment to its members.

In **State of UP vs. Krishna Master & Others (2010)** the Apex Court made an extraordinary move by awarding life sentence to the three accused of honour killing who murdered six persons of a family. The Bench further observed that "wiping out almost the whole family on the flimsy ground of saving the honour of the family would fall within the rarest of rare cases. The Principle evolved in this case was reiterated in **Bhagwan Das vs. State (NCT) of Delhi (2011),** where the Apex Court opined that "there is nothing honourable in honour killings, and they are nothing but barbaric and brutal murders by bigoted, persons with feudal mind. In our opinion honour killings, for whatever reason, come within the category of rarest of rare cases deserving death punishment. It is time to stamp out these barbaric, feudal practices which are a slur on our nation. This is necessary as a deterrent for such outrageous, uncivilised behaviour.

All persons who are planning to perpetrate honour killings should know that the gallows await them. In **Lata Singh vs. State of UP** the Supreme Court opined that the caste system is a curse on the nation and the sooner it is destroyed the better. In fact, it is dividing the nation at a time when we have to be united to face the challenges before the nation. Hence, inter-caste marriages are in fact in the national interest as they will result in destroying the caste system. However, disturbing news is coming from several parts of the country that young men and women, who undergo inter-caste marriage, are threatened with violence, or violence is actually committed on them. In our opinion, such acts of violence or threats or harassment are wholly illegal and those who commit them must be severely punished. This is a free and democratic country, and once a person becomes a major he or she can marry whosoever he/she likes. If the parents of the boy or girl do not approve of such inter-caste or inter-religious marriage the maximum they can do is that they can cut off social relations with the son or the daughter, but they cannot give threats or commit or instigate acts of violence and cannot harass the person who undergoes such inter-caste or inter-religious marriage. We, therefore, direct that the administration/police authorities throughout the country will see to it that if any boy or girl who is a major and undergoes inter-caste or inter-religious marriage with a woman or man who is major, the couple are not harassed by any one nor subjected to threats or acts of violence, and anyone who gives such threats or harasses or commits acts of violence either himself or at his instigation, is taken to task by instituting criminal proceedings by the police against such persons and further stern action is taken against such persons as provided by law.

Similarly, in **Arumugam Servai vs. State of Tamil Nadu (2011),** the Apex Court interpreted law on this matter that in case of age of majority, the young couple has statutory right to marry. What the parents do is that they can cut off their social relations with them, but cannot threat them or kill them.

The Court further observed that "khap panchayats (known as katta panchayat in Tamil Nadu) often decree or encourage honour killings or other atrocities in an institutionalised way on boys and girls of different castes and religion, who wish to get married or have been married. It is wholly illegal and has to be ruthlessly stamped out. .... There is nothing honourable in honour killings or other atrocities and, in fact, it is nothing but barbaric and shameful murder. Other atrocities in respect of personal lives of people committed by brutal, feudal minded persons deserve harsh punishment. Only in this way can we stamp out such acts of barbarism and feudal mentality. Moreover, these acts take the law into their own hands, and amount to kangaroo courts, which are wholly illegal."

Hence, the Court directed the administrative and police officials to take strong measures to prevent such atrocious acts. If any such incidents happen, apart from instituting criminal proceedings against those responsible for such atrocities, the state government has been directed to immediately suspend the District Magistrate/Collector and SSP/SPs of the district as well as other officials concerned and charge sheet them and proceed against them departmentally if they do not:

(1) Prevent the incident if it has not already occurred but they have knowledge of it in advance, or

(2) If it has already occurred, they do not promptly apprehend the culprits and others involved and institute criminal proceedings against them, as in our opinion they will be deemed to be directly or indirectly accountable in this connection.

In **Sujit Kumar vs. State of UP & Others (2002),** Allahabad High Court noted that "In our secular and liberal country, honour killings have been taking place from time to time, and what is deeply disturbing is that police and other authorities do not seem to take necessary steps to check these disgraceful and barbaric acts. In fact, such honour killings far from being honourable are nothing but pre-mediated murder and must be treated accordingly." The court further directs the police in the State to prevent any such honour killings or harassment of people who love each other and want to get married as such practice is a blot on our society. The police must also see that the persons entering into inter-caste or intercommunity marriages are not harassed by their relatives or any others and are free to live at any place and with whomever they like. There is no prohibition of inter-caste or inter-community marriage in the law. If a person who is a major wants to get married to a person of another caste or community, the parents cannot legally stop him/her. That being so, the administration must ensure that nobody harasses or ill treats or kills such people for marrying outside his or her caste, community or class.

Legislative Reforms and Initiatives Against Khaps

Various legislative efforts have been taken by the government to prohibit the unlawful activities of khap panchayat.

- **The Prohibition of Unlawful Assembly (Interference with the Freedom of Matrimonial Alliance) Bill, 2011**

Law Commission has drafted a Bill to prevent interference of any person in the matrimonial alliance in the name of honour and tradition. The Bill also intends to declare such panchayats unlawful. It proposes that "no person or any group of persons shall gather, assemble or congregate at any time with the view or intention to deliberate on, or condemn any marriage, not prohibited by law, on the basis that such marriage has dishonoured the caste or community tradition or brought disrepute to all or any of the persons forming part of the assembly or the family or the people of the locality concerned. Such gathering or assembly or congregation shall be treated as an unlawful assembly and every person convening or organising such assembly and every member thereof participating therein shall be punishable with imprisonment for a term of not less than six months but which may be extended to one year and shall also be liable to fine up to ten thousand rupees." The Bill further says that any member of an unlawful assembly, who alone or in association with other such member counsels, exhorts or brings pressure upon, person or persons so as to prevent, or disapprove of the marriage which is objected to by the said member of the unlawful assembly or creates an environment of hostility toward such couple or either of them or their relatives or supporters, shall be deemed to have acted in endangerment of their liberty.

- **The Endangerment of Life and Liberty (Protection, Prosecution and other measures) Act, 2011**

Shocked by the growing cult of honour killings and swiftly dispersing roots of khap panchayats across the country, the Law Commission of India has also proposed legislation namely The Endangerment of Life and Liberty (Protection, Prosecution and other measures) Act, 2011, to prosecute persons or a group involved in such endangering conduct and activities. Under the proposed law, the act of endangerment of life and liberty shall mean and include any manner of acts of threat, encouragement, commending, exhorting and creating an environment whereby loss of life and liberty is imminent or threatened and shall include:

(a) Enforcement of measures such as social boycott, deprivation of the means of livelihood, denial of facilities and services which are otherwise generally available to the people the locality concerned; and

(b) Directly or indirectly compelling the persons concerned to leave or abandon their homestead in the locality.

Further, it also provides that "it shall be unlawful for any group of persons to gather, assemble or congregate with the intention to deliberate, declare on or condemn any marriage or relationship such as marriage between two person of majority age in the locality concerned on the basis that such conduct or relationship has dishonoured the caste or community or religion of all or some of the persons forming part of the assembly or the family or the people of the locality concerned."

The legislation also speaks that "any person or persons instrumental in gathering of such an assembly or who takes an active part in the execution of the assembly shall also be subjected to civil sanctions." viz, they will not be eligible to contest any election to any local authority and will be treated as a disqualified candidate.

The following legislative steps will contribute to necessary reforms against khap panchayat:

- Fast track courts should be constituted empowering to deal with matters of honour killings and such other malpractices.
- The Special Marriage Act should also be amended in such a way so as to reduce the duration of registration of marriage.
- Apart from that arranging awareness programmes among the people who are follow the verdicts of khap unquestionably.
- Instead of criticising the khap, efforts should be made for lawful functioning of khap. It would also be helpful to minimise the burden of courts.
- The main problem is not the khap rather the problem is towards khap verdicts so, awareness among people is necessary who follow its orders.
- Village Court should be constituted so that khap panchayats will become irrelevant automatically.

Conclusion

It's high time to put a full stop on these prevailing malpractices. The time demands to annihilate harsh and brutal practices of khap and make the people aware about their rights because working of khap in the name of honour and tradition violates the basic human rights of an individual. It is now essential for legislature to legislate on such a burning issue. India being a member of the UDHR, the ICCPR and other international conventions has the responsibility to initiate the mechanism which can curve up this problem. Only stringent legal measures will not be sufficient. This problem is the result of a centuries old society, having the feudal and patriarchal set up, which can do anything for its culture and tradition. Here the need is not only to change the mindset of people but also to step out of the old and outdated traditions so that these unauthorised actions can be prevented.

Due to lack of flexibility in approach of the leaders of khap may be found as uneducated senior persons of the society. Through providing education to them and bringing awareness about present and prevailing laws can make the difference. Women participation is also needed to be encouraged. This can be immensely helpful in bringing social reforms in rural area.

The patriarchal mindset that revels in unnecessary hype of honour residing in woman's bodies can only be changed through the light of education. Education is the most potent tool for socio-economic mobility and a key instrument for building an equitable and just society. It is the only means of bridging the gap between gender inequalities. Since change through mass education programme cannot be brought overnight, we need a law to at least put a leash on the crimes against women in the name of honour. It is being strongly felt that there should be a strict and deterrent law to deal with honour killings/honour crimes. For effective implementation, the law is required to be supplemented by social mobilisation to deal with such crimes.

References

- 2002, 2AWC 1758 www.indiankanoon.org
- 80 year old woman paraded naked on donkey on khaps order, December 7, 2014, www.ndtv.com

- AIR 2010 SC 3071. Criminal Appeal No. 1117 of 2011.
- AIR, 2006 SC 2522.Criminal Appeal No. 958 of 2011.
- Anshul Kumar Pandey, "Kangaroo Courts must go!" www.dnaindia.
- Baij, Nath, Honour Killings; Violation of Human Rights of Women, *Indian Journal of Socio Legal Studies.* 2320–8562. (Special Issue) 2014.
- Bhardwaj, S. B. Myth and Reality of the Khap Panchayats: a Historical Analysis of the Panchayat and Khap Panchayat, www. sih.sagepub.com
- C. J. I. Sathasivam, Special law will deter honour killings, The Hindu, 30th June, 2013.
- Chaitra Arjunpuri, "Honour Killings" Bring Dishonour to India, dated December 27, 2012, www.aljazeera.com
- Chander Suta Dogra, Retrograde avatar of repressive traditions, The Hindu, 11th February, 2014.
- Dhananjay Mahapatra, No Law in Place to rein In Khaps–SC, Times of India, dated July 19, 2012.
- Dishonour killing father burns daughter to death http://zeenews.india.com
- Honour Killing in India, www.academia.edu
- Honour Killing in India, www.civilserviceindia.com
- Honour Killing in Kolkata: Man beheads sister in public view, takes severed head to police station, The Times of India, www.articles.timesofindia.indiatimes.com accessed on 08-09-2015.
- Human Rights Watch, Integration of the Human Rights of Women and the Gender Perspective: Violence against Women and "Honour" Crimes, Intervention Before the 5th Session of the U.N. Commission on Human Rights (Apr. 6, 2001), www.hrw.org
- Jaidip Majumdar, The Injustice of Justice, www.honourcrimes.wordpress.com
- Johanna Bond, Honour as Property, 23 Colum. J. Gender & L. 202 (2012).
- John Alan Cohan, Honour Killings and the Cultural Defense, 40 Cal. W. Int'l L.J. 177 (2010), The Hindu, Aug 6, 2010, p. 11.
- Kachhwaha, Kavita, Khap Adjudication in India: Honouring the Culture with Crimes, *International Journal of Criminal Justice Sciences*, Vol. 6 Issue 1 and 2 January- June / July – December 2011 (Combined Issue), p. 298, p. 301.
- "Khap Panchayats; Taliban? When will barbarism in the name of honour end" www.daily.bhaskar.com
- Law Commission, Unlawful Interference Of Caste Panchayat etc. with marriages in the name of honour, accessed on 25 December, 2012 www.law-commissionofindia.nic.in
- Manusmriti, Ch 3./Verse 56.

- Manveer Saini, "Haryana people prefer khaps over courts", The Times of India, Dec 16, 2012, www.articles.timesofindia.indiatimes.com
- Mazna Hussain, Take My Riches. Give Me Justice: A Contextual Analysis of Pakistan's Honour Crimes Legislation, 29 Harv. J. L. and Gender 227.
- Menace of kangaroo courts or katta panchayats in India. www.jeywin.com
- NCW slams khap Panchayats for imposing customs on young couples, Express News Service: Chandigarh Tuesday, 24th Sept., 2013.
- Sangwan, K. S.,(2012) Khap Panchayat in Haryana, www.Jatland.com
- Singh, Ranbir, The Need to Tame Khap Panchayats, *Economic and Political Weekly* p. 17, Vol. XLV No. 21.
- Srivastava, Sakaar, Honour Killing in India, www.academia.edu
- Stories from the Hindu Methodology, www.hindumytohologyforgenext.blogspot
- Suo Motu Writ Petition (Criminal) No. 24 of 2014, Gang rape on orders of Village Court August 27, 2012 www.ndtv.com
- United Nation Convention on the Elimination of all forms of Discrimination against Women, 1981.
- Woman paraded naked on donkey on orders of kangaroo court in Rajasthan, Nov. 11, 2014, www.ndtv.com
- Women having 3 years-old daughter killed for 'honour' www.articles.timesofindia.indiatimes.com

Chapter – 13

Administrative Crisis in Dealing with the Honour Crimes

—*Sandesh Yadav*

Abstract

Honour crimes especially honour killings are related to inter-caste or self choice love marriages, restricted not only to the States of Punjab and Haryana, Delhi, and Western Uttar Pradesh but also to the other Northern and Western Indian states. Such an orthodox practice of honour crimes especially honour killings are thriving well in Indian society because there are no specific laws related to honour crimes. Though we have several legal provisions viz. Fundamental rights Human rights and sections of Indian Penal Code (IPC), 1860 which deal with violence against women and contain implicit interpretation of honour crimes but our country do not have specific legal provisions related to honour crimes. In absence of specific laws to deal with honour crimes our administrative machinery particularly police personnel become helpless in taking actions against criminals while on the other hand criminals involved in honour crimes remains in advantageous position. To curb the menace of dishonourable crimes in the name of honour, Government of India prepared "The Prevention of Crimes in the Name of Honour & Tradition Bill, 2010" and "The Indian Penal Code and other Laws (Amendment) Bill, 2010." These Bills contain specific provisions, elaborate explanation and comprehensive coverage of minor and major aspects related to honour crimes and if passed successfully, they will be helpful in solving the administrative crisis in dealing with the honour crimes and make police personnel to work more effectively and efficiently. Further, it will protect the fundamental rights and human rights of the Indian citizens especially women.

Keywords: *Honour Crimes, Fundamental Rights, Human Rights, Indian Penal Code 1860, Violence against Women.*

Introduction

Several cases of killings and other forms of crimes in the name of honour have been reported in the past and are continuing to be reported all over India till date. The degree of such honour crimes vary from violent or abusive acts *(Emotional, Physical and the Sexual abuse)* to the murder or killing of victims. The major victims to such honour crimes are girls who wish to do inter-caste or self choice marriages and in the end, killed in the name of honour either by the family alone or in association with some relatives or caste based panchayats. Presently, such honour crimes are acquiring the status of social terrorism and making social environment choky for girls in today's democratic India.

Honour crimes are justified in the name of *custom* and *tradition*. Such honour crimes violates fundamental rights (Article 14, Article 15(1) and Article 21) of the Constitution of India and Human Rights (Article 3, Article 16) and considered offensive under several sections of Indian Penal Code, 1860.

Honour crimes are the means to spread *Social Terrorism* and increasing number of cases of honour crimes are putting question mark on the effective and efficient working of our administrative machinery especially police personnel. Further, there is great deal of demand regarding the enactment of specific laws in order to deal with honour crimes. Though, some offences under the Indian Penal Code, 1860 are invoked to book offenders in these cases but already existing legal provisions do not cover the entire gamut or illegal actions perpetrated in the name of honour.

The Government of India considered honour crimes as the most serious form of crimes against women and drafted the "The Prevention of Crimes in the Name of Honour and Tradition Bill, 2010" and "The Indian Penal Code and Other Laws (Amendment) Bill, 2010." These two bills provides stringent punishment for those indulging in honour killing and making it specific offence under the Indian Penal Code, 1860 and the entire khap panchayats ordering such killings would also be prosecuted for the abetment of the crime and the onus will be on the accused to prove his/her innocence while normally the onus is on the state to prove the guilt of the accused. The proposed laws would not only identify the honour based crime but will be helpful in punishing the offender, whether an individual or group. The proposed laws would define what constitute honour killing and would cover the cases of women being forced to strip in public and people being ostracized from village.

The Prevention of Crimes in the Name of Honour and Tradition Bill, 2010

Section (3). All persons including young persons and women have the right to control their own lives, a right to liberty and freedom of expression, and a right of association, movement and bodily integrity. They have a right to choose their own partners in marriage or otherwise and any action to prevent the exercise of these rights shall amount to an offence under the provisions of this Bill.

Section (4). If any person or persons, whether he or they are members of the victim's family or person or persons acting in concert with, or, at the behest of, a member of the family or a member of a body or group of the caste or clan or community or caste panchayat (by whatever name called), kills or kill, a woman or her partner (or any person/persons associating with her or them) causes grievous hurt or any form of injury or to persecute her or them for exercising the rights stated in Section 1, or participates or incites such an act, shall be guilty of.

Explanation to Section (4) says that for the purpose of this section, all members of the caste or clan or community or caste panchayat, present or participates or incites the commission of an act by which death is caused was ordered, shall be deemed to be guilty of having committed such act.

Section (5). If any person or persons, whether he or they are members of the victims family or person or persons acting in concert with, or, at the behest of, a member of the family or a member of a body or group of the caste or clan or community or caste panchayat (by whatever name called) harasses or harass a woman or her partner (or anyone connected with them) for exercising the rights in Section 1 or attempts/attempt to prevent either one or both of them from exercising these rights they shall be punished with imprisonment for a minimum term of one year and a maximum term of ten years and shall also be liable for punitive fine.

Explanation to Section (5) says that the acts of harassment and prevention in this section shall include both physical and mental acts such as:

- Declaring the couple, as brother and sister, who have got married, inspite of the fact that they are not children from the same natural parent and such marriages are recognised and considered legal by the law or custom for the time being in force,
- Extraditing the couple or their family or relatives from the village or area they live in,
- Asking the couple or anyone associated with them or harboring them to pay a fine,
- Imposing social sanctions or social boycott on the couple or their family or anyone associated with them,
- Imposing economic sanctions or boycott on the couple or their family associated with them,
- Divesting the couple or their family including the family of the male partner of any land or property belonging to them,
- Repeatedly harassing the couple or either of them not to meet or associate with or live with each other, by physically visiting them or through any means of communication,
- Threatening the couple or either of them or their family or anyone associated with them of retributive action of any kind whatsoever,
- Causing harm or injury to the girl or the couple or anyone connected with them,
- Any other act or acts of harassment or intimidation, whether physical or mental or psychological, to stop the couple or either of them from meeting or being in the company of each other.

Section (6). If any person or persons, including a body of persons by whatever name it is called, eulogizes or publicly supports or incites, the harassment or killing or any kind of violence against the couple or either of them or any member of their family, he or they shall be punishable with a term of imprisonment upto two years and with punitive fine.

Section (7). Burden of Proof – Where any person or persons is or are prosecuted for an Offence under Sections 4, 5 or 6, the Burden of proving that he or they have not committed the offence or offences under the said sections shall be on him or them.

Section (8). Power to prohibit certain acts –

Sub-Section (8.1). Where the Collector or the District Magistrate is of the opinion or has received information that any of the offences under Sections (4), (5) or (6) are likely to be committed, he shall by order prohibit/prevent the commission of such offences and further prohibit the meeting of any persons or body of persons likely to discuss the commission of the said offences.

Sub-Section (8.2). Whoever contravenes any order made under Sub-Section (1) shall be punishable with imprisonment for a term which shall not be less than six months but may extend to two years and with fine.

Sub-Section (8.3). When an Executive Magistrate receives information that any person or persons acting in concert with, or, at the behest of, a member of the family or a member of a body or group of the caste or clan or community or caste panchayat (by whatever name called), is likely to commit any wrongful and is of opinion that there is sufficient ground for proceeding, he may in the manner hereinafter provided, require such person or persons acting in concert with, or, at the behest of, a member of the family or a member of a body or group of the caste or clan or community or caste panchayat (by whatever name called), to show cause why he/they should not be ordered to execute a bond with sureties for keeping peace and maintain good conduct for such period, not exceeding one year, as the Magistrate thinks fit. Proceeding under this section may be taken before any Executive Magistrate when either the place where the breach of the peace or disturbance is apprehended is within his local jurisdiction or there is within such jurisdiction a person who is likely to commit a breach of the peace or disturb the public tranquility or to do any wrongful act as aforesaid beyond such jurisdiction.

Sub-Section (8.4). When a Magistrate acting under this provision, deems it necessary to require any person to show cause under such section he shall make an order in writing, setting forth the substance of the information received, the amount of the bond to be executed, the term for which it is to be in force, and the number, character and class of sureties (if any) required.

Section (9). Declaration by the couple about intention to be together. Any two persons desirous of marrying each other, or associating with each other shall be entitled to declare their age and willingness to be together, in oral or in writing, before any government official who shall send the said information to the nearest Police Station and no action shall be taken by the Police and or any other authority or at the instance of third party, against the said couple.

Section (10). Obligation of certain persons to report about commission of the offences under this Bill –

Sub-Section (10.1). All officers of the government are hereby required and empowered to assist the police in the execution of the provisions of this Bill or any rule or order made thereunder.

Sub-Section (10.2). All village officers and such other officers as may be specified by the Collector or the District Magistrate in relation to any area and the inhabitants of such area shall, if they have reason to believe or have the knowledge that any of the offences mentioned under Sections 4, 5 or 6 is are about to be, or have been committed in the area they shall forthwith report such fact to the nearest police station.

Sub-Section (10.3). Whoever contravenes the provisions of sub-section (1) or subsection (2) shall be punishable with imprisonment of either description for a term which may extend to two years and shall also be liable to fine.

Section (11). Bill not in derogation of any other law – The provisions of this Bill shall be in addition to, and not in derogation of the provisions of any other law, for the time being in force.

Section (12). Procedure – Save as otherwise provided in this Act, all proceedings under the Act shall be governed by the provisions of the Code of Criminal Procedure, 1973.

Section (13). Power to make rules –

Sub-Section (13.1). The Central Government may, by notification in the Official Gazette, make rules for carrying out the provisions of this Act.

Sub-Section (13.2). Every rule made under this Act shall be laid, as soon as may be after it is made, before each House of Parliament.

Section (14). Appeal –

Sub-Section (14.1). Not withstanding anything contained in the Code of Criminal Procedure, 1973, or in any other law an appeal shall lie from every judgment or order under this Act to the High Court.

Sub-Section (14.2). Every appeal under this Section shall be preferred within a period of thirty from the date of the judgment or order under this Act.

Sub-Section (14.3). Except as aforesaid, no appeal or revision shall lie to any Court from any judgment, order or decree under this Act.

Sub-Section (14.4). An appeal preferred under sub-section (1) shall be heard by a Bench consisting of two or more judges.

Section (15). Demand amendment in the Section (5) of the Special Marriage Act, 1954. The amendment is related to the omission of the words. The amendment is related to the omission of the words "for a period of not less than thirty days" from the Section 5 of the Special Marriage Act, 1954.

Indian Penal Code and Other Laws (Amendment) Bill, 2010

The Indian Penal Code and Other Laws (Amendment) Bill, 2010 is mainly concerned with the Section 300 of IPC, 1860. The proposed amendments in the Section 300, IPC, 1860 can be summed up as under:

- Section 300 deals with committing an intentional act which causes death.
- To introduce honour killings as the fifth clause.
- Fifth Clause says- if it is done by any person or persons acting in concent with, or at the behest of, a member of the family or a member of a body or group of the caste or clan or community or caste panchayat (by whatever name called) in the belief that the victim has brought dishonour upon the family or caste or clan or community or caste panchayats.
- Explanation- "Dishonour" & "Perceived to have brought dishonour" will include "acts of any person adopting or dress code which is unacceptable to this or her family or caste or clan or community or caste panchayats."
- The murders for choosing to marry within or outside the 'Gotra' (sub-caste) or caste or clan or community against the wishes of one's family or caste or clan or community will also come under the ambit of the honour killings.
- Killing somebody for engaging in sexual relations which are unacceptable to the community or caste panchayats or family will also fall under this category.
- Externment of a person in the belief that he or she has brought dishonour will also be punished with imprisonment of either description for a term which may extend to two years or with fine or with both. On the point that who all come under the ambit of honour killings, the draft suggests that all members of a body or group of caste or clan or community or caste panchayat, ordering or abetting the commission of murder will be deemed guilty of having committed the murder and that would make it liable for the maximum penalty i.e. death sentence.

Further, it also contains certain amendments to Section 354 to include assault or criminal force to women with intent to outrage her modesty.

Indian Evidence Act, 1872

Further, there is proposed amendment in the Section 105 of The Indian Evidence Act, 1872 and they can be summed up as under:

- Burden of proving that the case of accused comes within exceptions.
- Where the onus be on the member of khap panchayats and family member to prove their innocence.

Administrative Crisis

Our Indian administrative machinery, specifically police department, is going through the crisis in dealing with honour crimes. Failing of police department as the main agency to deal with honour crimes held them unanswerable, inefficient and ineffective. The reason behind this ineffective and inefficient performance is the vague definition of honour crimes and the absence of specific legal provisions related to honour crimes.

The major reasons of administrative crisis can be summed up as under:

- The non-specific legal definition of crimes committed in the name of honour.
- Absence of specific legal provisions covering crimes committed in the name of honour.
- Prevailing confusion regarding the legal provisions related to crimes in the name of honour.
- Politicisation of such matters hinders the dealing of such cases by the administrative machinery.

If we go through the legal provisions mentioned in the IPC, 1860 and other related legal documents then we will find that there is no clear cut definition of crimes committed in the name of honour. Sometimes, these are mentioned as crime against women and in severe cases of killings police address such crimes under the Section 302 of IPC, 1860. In other words, such type of definition and description of honour crimes creates difficulty for the police personnel to understand the nature and the degree of crimes related to honour. The absence of crystal clear knowledge of honour crimes results in poor decision-making and consequently resulting in inefficient and ineffective actions by the police personnel.

Till date, the cases of honour crimes are dealt under Section 354 of IPC, 1860 and the cases of honour killings under Section 302 of IPC, 1860 because there are no specific legal provisions to deal with honour crimes in particular. Though the nature and degree of honour crimes varies from minor brutalities to killings but in the absence of specific legal provisions related to honour crimes, police personnel remain in the state of confusion and keeps on searching for the sections of IPC, consequently, improper actions are taken by the police.

Conclusion

These proposed legal Bills will result in defining the crimes related to honour separately and distinctively. Further, specific legal provisions contained in these Bills will help out the administrative personnel particularly police in realising the degree of severity of crimes committed in the name of honour. Police personnel will get acknowledged with the specific legal provisions to deal with different types of crimes committed under the name of honour. It will make the police personnel to deal with the case more seriously than the other cases of murders. Further, the provision will held that onus of proving the guilt of accused will not be duty of the police but it will be the job of culprit to prove his or her innocence. Shifting the burden of onus will make police to register case without any hesitation and without any worry.

Acknowledgement

*I would like to acknowledge, **Prof. Manzoor Ahmad**, Editor-in-Chief, Jan Madhyam, Lucknow, Uttar Pradesh for his guidance and comprehensive understanding related to various aspects of Police Department.*

I would also like to acknowledge, ***Prof. Mohd. Ishtiaque,*** *Honorable Vice-Chancellor, Magadh University, Bodh Gaya, Bihar, for his unending motivation and encouragement during the completion of this research article.*

References

- Baxi, Pratiksha, Rai, Srinivas M. and Ali, Shaneem, Sardar (2006). Legacies of Common Law: Crimes of Honour in India & Pakistan. Taylor and Francis, Ltd. Vol. 27 (7), pp.1239-1253.
- Byreshwar, Pankaja (2014). 'Honour killing' The Menace. *International Journal of Applied Research (IJAR)*, Vol. 4 (1), Jan.2014.
- Deol, Satnam Singh (2014). Honour Killings in Haryana State, India: A Content Analysis. *International Journal Criminal Sciences (IJCJS)*, Vol. 9 (2), pp. 192-208, July-Dec. 2014.
- Indian Penal Code, (1860). Government of India, India.
- Kachhwala, Kavita (2011). Khap Adjudication in India: Honoring the Culture with Crimes. *International Journal of Criminal Justice Sciences (IJCJS)*, Vol. 6 (1&2), pp. 297-308, Jan-Jun/July-Dec. 2011.
- Rana, Pranab Kumar and Mishra, Bhabani Prasad (2013). Honour Killings - A Gross Violation of Human Rights and It's Challenges. *International Journal of Humanities and Social Sciences Invention,* Vol. 2 (6), pp. 24-29, June-2013.
- Sunita and Yudhvir, (2013). Khap Panchayats: Changing Perspectives.*Asian Journal of Multidimensional Research (AJMR),* Vol.2 (7), July. 2013.
- Universal Declaration of Human Rights (1946), United Nations Organisation (UNO).
- Vishwanath, Jyoti and Palakonda, Srinivas, C. (2001). Patriarchal Ideology of Honour and Honour Crimes in India, *International Journal of Criminal Justice Sciences (IJCJS*), Vol. 6 (1&2):386-395, Jan-Dec. 2011.

Chapter – 14

Khap Panchayats: Killing for Honour or for the Ego

—Dr Amit Kashyap, Shashi Bala Kashyap and Dr Amita Raj Gargey

Abstract

In the newly liberalised India still most of the marriages tend to be arranged by families, either through a marriage broker, a newspaper classified advertisement, a web-based marriage portal or the long-established oral tradition: word-of-mouth but when these methods fails then even marriage can be forced to save the honour and women can be murdered for rejecting a forced marriage and marrying a partner of their own choice, usually not acceptable to the family of the girl or boy. Honour killings the illegal decrees by caste/clan/community panchayats to annul or prohibit marriages, social boycotts and even murder of couples have finally drawn the attention of the State, killing in the name of honour amounts to utter rejection of 'egalitarianism'–a corner stone of India's Constitution and testifies how the values of feudalism and patriarchy are rooted in our social systems. Khaps seem to be in no way different from 'Taliban' the feudal lords of Afghanistan who have their own way to deliver justice. The message is flashed all over the world that we still live in dark ages in spite of our super computer knowledge.

Key words: *Challenges, Human Rights, Honour Killings and Khap Panchayats.*

Introduction

On achieving independence, it was believed that India will develop into a modern state where there will be no place for any kind of exploitation and suppression either in the name of caste, religion, sex or language, wherein feudal practices and values of the past will be substituted by values of egalitarianism. The Founding Fathers, thus, gave India a Constitution committed towards values of equality, liberty and fraternity for assuring Human dignity. Everyone has the right to life, liberty and security without any limitation due to race, nationality or religion, have the right to marry or to have a family of their own choice. They are entitled to equal rights as to marriage and its dissolution. Marriage should be enter into only with the free and full consent of the attending spouses. The family is the natural and fundamental group, unit of society and is entitled to be protected by the society as well as state.

However, disturbing news is coming from several parts of the country that young men and women who undergo inter-caste/inter-religious marriage are threatened with violence. If the parents of the boy or girl do not approve such inter-caste or inter-religious marriage the maximum they can do is that they can cut-off social relation with the son or the daughter, but they cannot give threats or instigate acts of violence. Women who marry a man of their choice moreover take recourse to law, placing themselves outside the traditional scheme. It is common myth that through the nature of their action, they shame their guardians leading them to resort to violence to restore their honour. Traditionally marriage arrangements are delicate and seem to involve serious balancing acts and any disturbance of this balance by a woman refusing a father's choice are considered to affect the father's standing in society.

Sanctified Meaning and Magnitude

Honour crimes are the acts of violence, usually murder, committed either by male family members against female family members or who are held to have brought dishonour upon the family. They use the word of honour for such a dishonourable act while there is nothing honourable in such killings. In fact, they are nothing but the barbaric and shameful acts of murderers brutally committed by feudal minded persons. The loose term honour killing applies to killing of both males and females. In broader sense, an honour killing is the murder of a family (woman) or clan member by one or more fellow family members, where the murders (potentially the wider community, who are more or less related with victims) believe that the victim has brought dishonour upon the family, clan or community. Thus honour killing is murder of womenfolk by family members, generally male, who are compelled to remove stains on their family's honour. According to United Nation's report of special reporter in 2002, Concerning cultural practices in the families violent towards women (E/CN. 4/2002/83), indicated that honour killings had been reported in Egypt, Jordan, Lebanon, Morocco, Pakistan, the Syrian Arab Republic, Turkey, Yemen and other Mediterranean and Persian Gulf countries and that they had also taken place in western countries such as France, Germany and the UK within migrant communities.

Every year in the UK a dozen women becomes the victims of honour killing, occurring almost exclusively to date with Asian and Middle Eastern families and often cases are unresolved due to the unwillingness of family, relatives and community. In June 2008, report by Turkish Prime Ministry's Human Rights Directorate says that in Istanbul alone, there is one honour killing every week. The tradition of honour killing was first viewed in its most horrible form during the partition of country, i.e. in India between the year 1947 and 1950, when a large number of women were forcefully killed so that family honour could be preserved. During the partition, there were a lot of forced marriages, women from India to marry men from Pakistan and vice-versa. And the latest case of honour killing was when the two teenage girls were shot dead by a cousin in Noida for daring to run away to meet their boyfriends. Many such killings are happening regularly in Punjab, Haryana and western Uttar Pradesh. These are socially sanctioned by caste panchayats and carried out by mobs with or without the consent of family members.

Human Rights Issues on Honour Killing

Killing in the name of honour amounts to utter rejection of 'egalitarianism'– a corner stone of India's Constitution and testifies how the values of 'feudalism' and 'patriarchy' are rooted in our social systems and structures. Honour killings are rooted in anachronistic, antiquated attitudes and false promises. Articles 3 and 16 of Universal Declaration of Human Rights 1948 suggest that "Everyone has the right to life, liberty and security. In the same vein, right to love and live with a person of one's choice is enshrined as a fundamental right in the Constitution. Thus, honour killings constitute gravest disregard of universal human rights and massive violation of fundamental rights guaranteed by the Constitution.

A report by United Nations Population Fund (2000) estimated as many as five thousand women and girls being killed each year by relatives for dishonouring their family. Many of the cases involve the "dishonour" of having been raped.

Contributory Factors of Honour Killings

A woman can cause the stain on the family due to several reasons, including -

(a) Refusing to enter an arranged marriage or choosing to marry by own choice or

(b) Engaging in certain sexual acts considered immoral or

(c) Marrying within same gotra or

(d) Seeking divorce from an abusive husband etc.

Sometimes other women in the family also support the honour killing of female family member as they agree that family is the property and asset of only male members. Even the mother of the victim (women) may support an honour killing. In order to preserve the honour of other female family members, they agree to this heinous crime since many men in their society will refuse to marry the sister of a "shamed" female to whom the family has not chosen for punishment, thereby they purifying the family name by murdering the suspected female. Women are considered as the property of the males in their family, irrespective of their class, ethnic or religious groups. The owner of the property has the right to decide its fate. The perception that defines honour appears to be deeply immersed in patriarchic values and have been so widely interpreted to include male control which extends not only to the body of a woman, but all her behaviour including her movements, language and actions. In any of these areas, defiance by women translates into undermining male honour and ultimately damaging the family and community honour.

The sociologists are opined that the reason for increase in honour killing is the fear of losing their caste status through which they gain many benefits which makes them commit this heinous crime. The other reason is because the mentality of people has not changed and they just cannot accept that marriages can take place in the same gotra or outside one's caste. The numbers of honour killings is also increasing because government has not been able to awaire the public residing in rural areas. The shortcoming of our judicial system is also responsible for increase in cases of honour killings.

Khap Panchayat's Desperate Moves

Most of the honour killings are decided and ordered by the caste panchayats or khap panchayats or katta panchayats comprising of members of a particular caste. Very often, these panchayats encourage honour killings or other atrocities in an institutionalised way on boys and girls of different castes and religion, who wish to get married or have been married or interfere with the personal lives of people. These panchayats are organised through clans and gotras by which they uphold social norms in the community. Such assemblies gathered on caste lines assume themselves as the ultimate source of power and authority to declare on and deal with objectionable matrimonies and exhibit least regard for life and liberty. They are not deferred by the processes of administration of justice. The pernicious practice of khap panchayat is like taking law into their own hands and pronouncing on the invalidity and impropriety of sagotra and inter-caste marriages and handing over punishment to the couple and pressurising the family members to execute their verdict by any means amounts to flagrant violation of rule of law and invasion of personal liberty of the persons affected.

There are reports that drastic action including wrongful confinement, persistent harassment, mental torture, infliction of severe bodily harm, even death is resorted either by close relatives or through third party against the so called erring couple. Social boycotts and other illegal sanctions affecting the young couple, the families and even a section of local inhabitants are the common practices of khap panchayats. Khap elements zealously guard age old marital restrictions. They foster a culture of intolerance, making a family 'paraya' in village society if its members violate the khap marital norms. The family is subjected to repeated taunts, making its existence unbearable. This drives some of its members to commit murder of their family member to restore family honour. It is this social milieu spawned by khap elements which leads to honour crimes.

Enforcement Hazards and Betrayal

One of the major hurdles has been the way regarding the enforcement part, in which the public officials are reluctant to take on the system, accepting it as a custom – a way of life in the region, law-makers and enforcement officers condone the criminality of such actions, ignoring the violent and woman hating nature of the khap's dictum. Criminal intimidation is a punishable offence under the Indian Penal Code and those who provide it support can be booked for criminal conspiracy. To utter surprise, a former police chief of Haryana state, himself, a self-styled caste leader, went on record threatening khap critics. How can a former DGP publicly threaten law-abiding citizens, and yet continue to enjoy the hefty perks and pension out of the public exchequer? In fact, the worst betrayal is political as caste solidarity feeds into their vote banks. Usually real Panchayati raj institutions remain weak, because a khap panchayat is normally a collective of at least 12 or more village panchayat as compared to gram panchayat consists of single unit as 'gram' (villages). The Central government's Ministry of Home Affairs asked the Haryana government to send its views on the issue as the centre was contemplating suggesting strict legal measures to curb the menace of honour killings perpetrated in connivance with khap panchayats by amending the Indian Penal Code. The Haryana government opposed the proposal of banning khap panchayats arguing that such a 'rash step' would disturb law and order.

Legislative Sanction Proposed by Law Commission

Terming the practices of khap panchayats of handing down punishment to couples who go for 'sagotra' or inter-caste marriage as "flagrant violation" of the law, the Law Commission came up with draft of legislation. The draft known as Prohibition of Unlawful

Assembly (interference with the freedom of matrimonial alliances) Bill, 2011 utters that offences under the Act will be cognisable, non-bailable and non-compoundable. The Bill also proposes that no person or any group of persons shall gather with an intention to deliberate on, or condemn any marriage, not prohibited by law, on the basis that such marriage has dishonoured the caste or community tradition or brought disrepute to all or any of the persons forming part of the assembly or the family or the people of the locality concerned. Marriage, according to the draft law, includes a proposed or intended marriage. The Collector or the District Magistrate has been entrusted with the responsibility of ensuring the safety of the persons targeted in case any illegal decision is taken by the khap panchayat and he/she shall take all necessary steps to prohibit the convening of such illegal gatherings.

Any violation of the Bill will attract imprisonment up to three years and a fine of up to Rs 30,000. The cases will be tried in Special Courts presided over by a session's judge or additional sessions judge. The Supreme Court can also take suo motu cognizance of the cases. There has been a spurt in illegal intimidation by self-appointed bodies for bringing pressure against sagotra (same gotra) marriages and inter-caste, inter-community and inter-religious marriages between two consenting adults in the name of vindicating the honour of family, caste or community.

In number of cases, such bodies have resorted to incitement of violence and such newly married couples or couples desirous of getting married have been subjected to intimidation and violence which has also resulted into their being hounded out of their homes and sometimes even murdered. Although such intimidation or acts of violence constitute offences under the IPC, yet, it is necessary to prevent assemblies which take place to condemn such alliances. The proposed Bill says that adding it seeks to nip the evil in the bud and prevent spreading of hatred or incitement to violence through such gatherings. Criminal intimidation will have the same meaning as is given in Section 503 of the IPC. The Bill further says that any member of an unlawful assembly who alone or in association with other such members counsels, exhorts or brings pressure upon any person or persons so as to prevent, or disapprove the marriage which is objected to by the said members of the unlawful assembly, or creates an environment of hostility towards such couple shall be deemed to have acted in endangerment of their liberty.

It suggested that an entire assembly can be deemed to be unlawful and guilty if it sits deliberately on any matrimonial issue that is not prohibited by law. Guilt will also be assumed until the individuals who participate in such assemblies are proven to be innocent–what is called the "reverse onus" cause. Similar provisions about placing the burden of proof on the accused to prove their innocence are present in the new draft as well, but the latter extends to murders as well. While the Law Commission acknowledges that shifting the burden of providing his/her innocence to the accused in the case of murders or in their abetment would be against the cardinal principle of jurisprudence, it argues that a presumption of guilt in participation in unlawful assemblies is necessary because obtaining eyewitnesses for the presence of individuals in those assemblies is difficult. But why cannot such an assumption hold true in the case of an honour killing itself, difficult as it is to establish guilt because of the social sway that caste/clan panchayats hold over those involved in such crimes?

Dispensing Justice on Honour Killing

The judiciary does have a crucial role to play but has its limitations too. On June 23, 2006 Justice K. S. Ahluwalia of the Punjab and Haryana High Court made a revealing observation while simultaneous hearing of 10 cases pertaining to marriages between young couples aged 18-21. "The High Court is flooded with petitions where…judges of this Court have to answer for the right of life and liberty to married couples. The State is a mute spectator. When shall the State awake from its slumber and for how long can Courts provide solace and balm by disposing of such cases?"

In a recent landmark judgment by the Additional Sessions Court at Karnal in the Manoj-Babli "honour" killing case, in which five accused were given the death sentence, sent shock waves among caste panchayat leaders, as it reminded them that they were not above the Constitution.

The court took serious note of the fact that the policemen deployed for the security of Manoj and Babli actually facilitated the accused in perpetrating the crime. After the judgment in the Manoj - Babli case, however, a congregation of caste panchayats representing the Jat neighbourhoods from Haryana, Uttar Pradesh and Rajasthan was called at Kurukshetra. It was decided that panchayats would now fight for legal status to legitimately maintain the "social order." One of the main agendas of this Sarv-khap panchayat was to push for amendments to the Hindu Marriage Act, 1955 that would ban marriages within the same gotra (clan within which men and women are considered siblings and hence cannot marry). Under this Act, marriages between certain lineages from the paternal and maternal sides are already barred.

Misogynistic Approach

The regressive institution of the khap panchayats has come up with extremely misogynistic diktats from time to time, like ban on girls about wearing of jeans, going for a drive with a male friend or even use of mobile phones. These behaviours are considered perfectly normal for any young girl just a few miles away from the khap-dominated areas, can attract diabolical punishment here, in the khap governed areas. Justifying their diktat of prohibiting women from wearing jeans, khap leaders state that, "So many rapes happening nowadays, girls are teased only because they wear such clothes."

Rajinder Singh, vice president of Barah Birohar khap says, "We believe that a woman should be covered from head to toe in loose-fitting clothes that do not attract the male eyes. Our idea of beauty is a woman whose hands alone are visible. Even her eyes should preferably be under a veil." Women in various khap areas, below the age of 40 are not allowed to carry mobile phones with themselves. Another khap leader, Mr Dhankar says that, "This might seem drastic but we believe that this is the only way to stop honour killings in this region. Intermingling of girls and boys and influence of television has led to this situation. Even if the government will not do anything, we still have a duty to uphold the morals of the society."

In another bizarre suggestion issued by the khap panchayat of Haryana, it was stated by Sube Singh, a khap representative that,

"Boys and girls should be married by the time they turn 16 years old, so that they do not stray...this will decrease the incidents of rape."Another khap member said, "As soon as the children attain puberty, it is natural for them to have sexual desires but when these are not fulfilled, they stray...so there should not be any minimum age bare for marriage."

Fleeing away from the khap territory by the young couples spells doom to their kindred. There was a case in District Bijnor of Uttar Pradesh, where a woman was allegedly stripped and beaten up on the orders of the Madhi village khap, because she aided in the elopement of couples. Somewhat a similar happening took place in Bharatpur, Rajasthan when, following the orders of a khap, the kin of the boy were assaulted because he eloped with a girl of the same village.

Lately, a khap in District Jhajjar forbade a farmer from giving his daughter some money in return for withdrawing a case that she had filed to get her share of the family's ancestral land. The reason given was that it would embolden other girls to follow suit. Another horrifying incident attained nationwide acclaim when a khap panchayat in Bokaro allegedly ordered the rape of a 14 year old tribal girl by a married man. The village council gave such orders because the wife of the said man was allegedly misbehaved by the brother of the girl. The khap adjudicated that retaliation on behalf of the man for the wrong done to his wife would be to rape the assailant's sister. The justification of retribution rape given by khap panchayat is that it is used "as a way of settling scores" because the family's honour is tied to woman's 'purity'. So, if a woman is raped, that honour is lost.

A khap panchayat in Haryana recently imposed a ban on late night nuptial ceremonies stating that dancing on the DJ floors and inebriation that follows results in harassment of the females. In another irrational decision, a khap panchayat in Haryana has blamed that consumption of 'Chowmein' is behind the growing incidents of rapes stating that it leads to hormonal imbalance. To quote Jitender Chhatar, a president of Jind's Chhatar village and Thua khap panchayat leader, "To my understanding, consumption of fast-food contributes to such incidents. Chowmein leads to hormonal imbalance, invoking an urge to indulge in such acts."

Role of Judiciary and Politicians

The government, adhering to its astute vote-bank politics, tacitly gives its approval to these illicit activities. Haryana Chief Minister Bhupinder Singh Hooda perceives khap panchayats as 'NGOs' and a part of Indian culture. Somewhat similar is the opinion of the Chief Minister of Delhi Arvind Kejriwal who speaks about khap panchayats as a social instrument that serve a 'cultural purpose' to our country. In the process of upholding this anachronistic institution, women are being beaten, stripped, raped, murdered, publicly lynched and humiliated. How does this fill in the cultural gaps of the country? These retrograding strides should only be seen as crafty and cynical ones which politicians take to consolidate and ascertain their position. This only brings abysmal despair and hopelessness to the people of the nation.

Supreme Court of India termed the khap panchayats as 'kangaroo courts' and declared them illegal and which need to be ruthlessly weeded out. A bench of justices Markandey Katju and Gyan Sudha Mishra observed that atrocities with respect to personal lives of people, committed by brutal, feudal minded persons deserve harsh punishment. The apex court said "This is wholly illegal and has to be ruthlessly stamped out. There is nothing honourable in honour killing or other atrocities and, in fact, it is nothing but barbaric and shameful murder. Other atrocities in respect of the personal lives of people committed by brutal, feudal-minded persons deserve harsh punishment. Only this way can we stamp out such acts of barbarism and feudal mentality….." Supreme Court also intervened in the Birbhum rape case where 20-years old woman was raped by 13 men on orders of the khap panchayat and termed the case 'disturbing'. Karnal district court also awarded death sentence to Babli's brother, uncles and cousins for killing the couple. The leader of the Banwala khap was awarded life sentence for hatching the plot. But at the same time, despite the efforts and reforms brought forward by the Judiciary, the politicians of our country justify their Talibani dictates by putting a veil of cultural dictate on them and addressing khap panchayats as cultural institutions rooted in the past and give them a new lease of life. What was a dying institution a decade ago has been revived and given some legitimacy by vote-bank politics to enable it to emerge in a retrograde avatar?

In Lata Singh v. State of UP, the Supreme Court while speaking through Justice Markandey Katju observed: 'This case reveals a shocking state of affairs. There is no dispute that the petitioner is a major and was at all relevant times a major. Hence, she is free to marry anyone she likes or live with any one she likes. There is no bar to an inter-caste marriage under the Hindu Marriage Act or any other law. Hence, we cannot see what offence was committed by the petition, her husband or her husband's relatives.'

In a very recent case Arumugam Servai v. State of Tamil Nadu the Supreme Court strongly deprecated the practices of khap/katta panchayats taking law into their own hands and indulging in offensive activities which endanger the personal lives of the persons marrying according to their choice.

Justice Markandey Katju while delivering the judgment observed: In recent years we have heard of "Khap Panchayats" (known as "Katta Panchayats" in Tamil Nadu) which often decree or encourage honour killings or other atrocities in an institutionalised way on boys and girls of different castes and religion, who wish to get married or have been married, or interfere with the personal lives of people. We are of the opinion that this is wholly illegal and has to be ruthlessly stamped out. As already stated in Lata Singh case, there is nothing honourable in honour killing or other atrocities and, in fact, it is nothing but barbaric and shameful murder. Other atrocities in respect of personal lives of people committed by brutal, feudal minded persons deserve harsh punishment. Only in this way can we stamp out such acts of barbarism and feudal mentality. Moreover, these acts take the law into their own hands, and amount to kangaroo courts, which are wholly illegal.

Suggestions and Conclusion

A cursory glance at the demography of the states patronising khap panchayats makes clear how sex ratio is plunging to newer depths in khap governed areas. Haryana, home to the most number of peremptory khap panchayats in the nation, stands second in terms of per capita income in the country, has only 821 females for every 1000 male populations in the 0-6 age group. Female foeticide runs unhindered as parents are well aware of the fact that these places have a highly chauvinistic trend, and are not safe for their daughters to thrive and survive. Girls are generally deprived of their education and separate batches run for boys and girls. By raping dalit women, young Jat men authenticate their machismo and wear the 'achievement' as badges pinned on their chest. Khap panchayats do nothing about the matter; and instead shift the stigma to the victim and her family who are in many cases even ostracised or excommunicated from the community.

Khap panchayats further create the false impression that all marriages of choice between young couples are incestuous, thereby snatching away from them their basic right to choose a marriage partner. There have been myriad instances where khaps issued diktats in Jaundhi, Asanda, Hadaudi, and other villages whereby married couples were declared siblings and families had to face boycotts and excommunication from their native villages. Youth population of over a thousand are being killed annually owing to the diabolical diktats of khap panchayats issue in cases where marriages happen within the gotra, between people of neighbouring villages, or without the consent of family/clan/community members.

It is the responsibility of state and society to protect the human rights of its young citizens, to avoid honour killings, to create possibilities and opportunities for the people concerned to break free and to find protection, support and aid. It is suggested that social evil like honour killing cannot be just eliminated through law alone rather almost every substitution social, economic, political or cultural will have to be sensitised against this crime. No doubt law could be used as one of the important tools to fight this heinous practice. The usual remedies to fight such social onslaught are to require immediate sensitisation of police officials and other law enforcement agencies, setting up women police stations in the khap belts, counselling of women victims by civil administrations. It is to be suggested -

(1) It gives a wrong message that khap panchayats have their own law, in reality they don't follow any law. They adjudicate a procedure which they deem fit. They have scant regard to judicial institutions and courts.

(2) The steps shall be taken whosoever is involved in the crime and how so great he may be should immediately be brought under the law.

(3) Special clause should be added to Section 300 of the Penal Code to deal with the cases like honour killing.

(4) The onus should put on the accused persons (members of such groups/organisation/panchayats) thereby making them responsible to prove their innocence.

(5) The Special Marriage Act, 1954 needs to be amended for the removal of 30 days waiting period for registering a marriage provided there is a mutual consent and both are above the legally permissible age.

In the last these khap panchayats seem to keep themselves disparate from the existing rule of law and the Constitution. The instance where they bludgeoned a person to death in the presence of warrant officer and policemen is a clear assertion of their fearlessness and dichotomy with the law of the land. There should usher in an entirely new series of reforms at the national level which bring an end to the unjustifiable, regressive institution of khaps. These panchayats should in no way be deemed of serving a cultural purpose and an instant ban should be imposed to their existence and functioning. People should be taught that there is nothing honourable in killing one's own children. By placing demands and petitions to make amendments in the existing law so as to inhibit women from partaking their ancestral property shows that how incorrigibly misogynistic they are in their approach. Today men and women are walking with hand in hand in every field of life, the flourishing of such retrograding institutions and the dogma they imposes needs to be impeded. The country has seen ample blood spilling in the name of brotherhood and honour and is in no way ready to be a witness to more slaughter. The judiciary has already done its job. It is now the responsibility of the administration to give up its peevishness and cattle-like responsiveness and take up the dire situation that is in desperate need of proper attention and law enforcement.

References

- AIR 2006 S.C. 2522, 2524.
- Aishwarya Tiwari and Chintan Nirala, (2014), Khap Panchayats-Retrograding Avatar of the Moral Police, IJLP, Vol. 2, Issue, 4, December, 2014, p. 306.
- Anant Zanane, (2014), Marriages within clan cause dishonour killings, Supreme Court should not get into this mess, February 19, 2014 www.ndtv.com
- Article 3, 16 of the Universal Declaration of Human Rights, 1948.
- Arumugam Servai v. State of Tamil Nadu, (2011) 6 SCC 405, 411.
- Chaitra Arjunpuri, (2012), Female mobile phone bans. Al Jazeera 27 Dec, 2012, 11:59.
- Chander Suta Dogra, (2013), Jeans, mobiles and khap panchayats, The Hindu, October 19, 2013.
- Chander Suta Dogra, "Retrograde avatar of repressive traditions" The Hindu, dated 11th February 2014.
- Choudhury, D. R. (2011), Khaps shouldn't be allowed to have their Way, The Tribune, December 20, 2011 posted by NNLRJ India.
- Dr Satya Pal Ruhela (2006), Indian society; structure and change, Vol. 1 - first edition-2006, Shubhi Publications, Gurgaon, India.
- Economic and Political Weekly, Vol. XLIV No. 52, Dec 26, 2009.
- Five condemned to death for India honour killing, www.tribune.com.pk
- Half Steps against Honour Crimes, EPW, February 18, 2012 at 7.
- Janaki Fernandes, (2012), After Khaps, girls in Uttar Pradesh now say no to jeans, Asian Voice, July 28, 2012.
- Khaps says early marriage can curb rape cases, The Hindu, October 8, 2012.
- Lata Singh v. State of U.P. and Anr. (2006) 5 SCC 475.
- Lawz Bureau (1-2910), Analysis on Honour, Lawz Media (P) Ltd., New Delhi, Vol.10, No.8, Issue 108, pp.10-13.
- Manveer Saini, (2014), Haryana's biggest khap Panchayat scripts history, allows inter-caste marriages, The Times of India, dated April 21, 2014 www.timesofindia.indiatimes.com
- Manveer Saini, Haryana khap blames consumption of chowmein for rapes, The Times of India, October 16, 2012.
- Nupur Basu, Honour Killings – India's Crying Shame, reported on Nov 30, 2013 in Al Jazeera www.aljazeera.com
- Panchayat orders gouging lovers eyes (2012) Honour Killings/Crimes in India Deccan Herald; February 12, 2012 www.deccanherald.com

- Sangwan, Fagmati (2010), Khap Panchayat: Signs of Desperation? The Hindu, Visakhapatnam, May 8, 2010 at 10.
- Section 2(1), The Prohibition of Unlawful Assembly (Interference with the Freedom of matrimonial Alliances) Bill, 2011.
- Sharma, Divya (2009), Honour Killing: A Slur on Humanity, Lawyers update. 46, 47.
- Stamp out kangaroo courts. The Hindu, dated 25th January 2014.
- Sujoy Dhar. "West Bengal woman says gang-raped on orders of Panchayat, dated January 23, 2014" www.in.reuters.com
- The Home Department, Government of Haryana, vide its letter No.14/26/2010-31(C) dated 8.9.2010 to the centre and see also The Chief Minister of Haryana State vide its D.O. No.CMH-2010 PSC pi/3453 dt.30.9.2010.
- The Ministry of Home Affairs, Government of India, vide its D.O. No.12/24/2009 – Judl. Cell dated July 8, 2010.
- Universal's Criminal Manual 2009, Universal Law Publishing Co. Pvt. Ltd, Delhi.
- www.hindustantimes.com
- www.indlawnews.com
- www.supremecourtofindia.nic.in

Chapter - 15

Khap Panchayats and Honour Killings

—*Nutan Sharma*

Abstract

India is a democratic country and its citizens have various freedom and rights guaranteed under Indian constitution. The person residing in India have the right to peaceful assembly and right to form an association except not violating the rights of others, Article 21 of the Constitution guarantees life and personal liberty to its citizen. But today, across the globe honour crimes cut across racial, religious, cultural and regional divides. The culture of regulating and controlling their conduct and life and amputating, shattering the personalities marching against the accepted social and patriarchal traditions in the guise of protecting the family, caste, clan or tribe, honour is rapidly engulfing the entire ocean of mankind. Today violence involved in honour crimes and killings under the guise of protecting the honour of the family and the community varies in different forms but the use of force to uphold the worst forms of caste and cultural oppression is the most disturbing feature in all such cases. The role of khap panchayats needs to be analysed in a proper context so that the democratic choice of the people at large especially the women and weaker sections in particular, is not met with impunity and hostility by the retrogressive forces and mindsets. It has to be understood clearly that in any civilised society, the rule of the law must prevail. There can be one and only one source of authority - the State and no other institution customary, feudal or traditional should dare to take the law into its own hands. There is the need for decisive government interventions as there can be no excuse to allow senseless killings.

Key Words: *Rights, Traditions, Honour, Mindsets, Law.*

Introduction

The khap panchayats are the village councils usually comprising of 10-15 elderly men from a particular community that set the rules in an area comprising of one or more villages inhabited by the members of a single clan (caste). A number of khaps together form a 'Sarva khap' embracing a full province or state. Their elected leaders would decide which units would be represented at the khap level. Khap panchayats are one of the most mediaeval groups of elders in rural areas which have got handed down from pre-independence times. It always suited to the (British) colonisers; they wanted that the villages should handle their own matters rather than clogging the courts. In earlier times, all these khap panchayats have played a positive role in handling the various issues at village level.

These khaps are found in north-western India, primarily in Haryana, Eastern Rajasthan and Western Uttar Pradesh. Many put emphasis that khap panchayats use to perform in positive manner in past and judgments given by them were for a betterment of society. If one supports this constructive approach of the past, question naturally arises: why the same panchayats are giving such regressive opinion now? From where are they deriving so much of power? Why they are not scared of police and law? There should be an end to all this deliberate violation of the basic rights of the people sanctified by the law of the land. Despite of being illegal bodies they are functioning openly violating law and order of this country.

Honour Killing

The problem of honour killings is not a problem of morality or ensuring that women must maintain their own personal virtue; rather, it is a problem of domination, power and hatred against women who are viewed as nothing more than servants to the family, both physically and symbolically.

The sad consequence of this domination is that thousands of girls and women across the globe (although mostly centred in the Middle East) are murdered by male family members every year in the name of family honour. Honour killings are executed for instances of rape, infidelity, flirting or any other instance perceived as disgracing the family's honour, the woman is then killed by a male relative to restore the family's name in the community. Many women are killed due to only suspicion of family members and even not given the chance to defend themselves. The allegation alone is enough to defile a man's or family's honour and is enough to justify the killing of the woman. The men who commit the murder typically go unpunished or receive reduced sentences. Honour killings have been reported in Bangladesh, Brazil, Ecuador, Egypt, India, Israel, Italy, Jordan, Morocco, Pakistan, Sweden, Turkey, Uganda and the United Kingdom. Honour killings tend to be prevalent in countries with a majority Muslim population, but many Islamic leaders and scholars condemn that it is based on religious doctrine. Honour killing is actually a pre-Islamic, tribal custom stemming from the patriarchal and patriarchal society's interest in keeping strict control over power structures in family.

Honour killing is the murder of a person accused of bringing shame to their family. Victims have been killed for refusing to enter a marriage, committing adultery or being in a relationship that displeases their relatives. In many instances, the crimes are committed by family members against a female relative. In some parts of the world, women who have been raped have also been murdered for the victim of bringing disgrace or dishonour to family, caste and community. Honour killing is believed to have originated from tribal customs where an allegation against a woman can be enough to defile a family's reputation - 'a life without honour is not worth living.'

In other words, honour killing is, taking life for saving the honour. The crime of honour killings is usually committed by the family members against their blood relations on the ground saving or regaining the honour of the family or the society. These killings are usually committed because of the social pressure. Right to life which is nationally and internationally recognised as the cherished and most sacrosanct right gets infringed by honour killings.

In most of the honour killings, the verdict is given by the caste panchayats or khap panchayats, comprising members of a specific caste. These panchayats are the encouraging force behind these killings.

These panchayats people project themselves as upholder of traditional social norms creating their own laws. Khap panchayats allot severe punishment to such couple who marry in 'Sagotra' or outside their caste and religion. Sometimes, the couples are pressurised to become siblings even after their marriages. Unfortunately the government never takes any action against such atrocities. This action is not constrained to a particular geographical being. The number of events related to this practice have also increased in India in last two decades. Many such incidents have occurred in Haryana, Western Uttar Pradesh and the rural belt of Delhi. The number of love marriages might have increased in metropolitan cities but the reality remains different in the villages.

The khap panchayats have unwritten laws, and their decisions are clearly illegal and unconstitutional. As they are not elected bodies, their decisions are not supported by law, their terror will continue unless they are banned. There is nothing honourable in the killings or inflicting violence on the innocent people. The educated civil society in India is finding them repelling.

In Haryana, khap panchayats (known as katta panchayats in Tamil Nadu) have been in existence for centuries framing laws for the community. Over the years, khaps (social bodies) have emerged as an alternative dispute redressal mechanism in the villages. They opine that boys and girls in the same gotra are like brothers and sisters. These self-appointed courts issue dictates (fatwas) and act like kangaroo courts outside the judicial system. These panchayats harass those who dare to disobey them. They slap illegal fines, ostracize the kin of the bride and the bride groom, indulge in beatings and kill them, even hit with shoes, torture the young couples and urinate upon them. It has to be understood clearly that in any civilised society, the rule of the law must prevail and there can be one and only one source of authority - the State, no other institution whether customary, feudal or traditional must not be allowed to take the law into its own hands.

The evidence of injustice related to honour killing could be as brutal as murder of Manoj and Babli for the sake of 'honour' — a young couple from Karoda village in Kaithal district of Haryana who dared to challenge the archaic caste norms by tying the nuptial knot. Other victims were the scheduled caste couple belonging to same village who were forced to leave the village when they married on their own choice. Later the khap panhchayat gave a verdict of stoning the couple to death. In Ismaila village, district Rohtak, 2002, a Jat girl of the village was friendly with grown smith boy. The girl's family killed both of them. Similar case can be seen in Halva village of district Jhajjar and Miyandvala village of Fatehbad district in year 2002. Sonia Rampal a married couple of district Rohtak were declared 'brother and sister' by caste panchayat in Haryana but they refused to surrender. Evidence of khap panchayats opposing inter-religious marriage come into light when Muslim girl Afsana married to Hindu Boy Manoj in Meerut district in July, 2009. These all incidences indicated towards honour crimes which emerged as worst forms of caste and cultural oppression by some authoritative powers of society. Due to such type of institutions right of youth to life and choice is under tremendous threat.

The panchayat claimed that wearing of jeans has a bad effect on young women. According to them eve teasing incidents have increased due to their objectionable clothes. However, there is no logic behind the idea that wearing of jeans is hardly a reason for girls being harassed as girls wearing traditional Indian outfits have also complained about going through equal instances of harassment. It has been estimated that more than hundred men and women are murdered or forced to commit suicide every year due to fear of khap for not adhering to traditional norms. Hence, there is the need for decisive government interventions as there can be no excuse to senseless killings.

Either these khap panchayats should be legally recognised with control in hands of government or abolished. Public opinion should be recognised for making law in a democratic setup because state is the voice of the public. Jurist Salmond said "Law is not right alone or might alone but the perfect union of the two, it is just speaking to men by the voice of the state."

The main reason for commitment of an honour killing is belief that any member of family had brought dishonour to the family.

The dishonour can be of different types for different families. The perceived dishonour is normally the result of the following behaviours, or the suspicion of such behaviours, which are dress codes unacceptable to the family/community; or wanting to terminate or prevent an arranged marriage or desiring to marry by own choice; or engaging in certain sexual acts, including those with the opposite or same sex etc.

The most obvious reason for this practice to continue in India is because of the fact that the caste system continues to be at its rigid best and also because people from the rural areas refuse to change their attitude towards marriage. Men are expected to enforce such norms and traditions and protect family and male honour from shame. Women are expected to conduct themselves honourably. The understanding of this notion gives legitimacy to all forms of social regulation of women's behaviour and to violence committed against them.

So far, there is no specific law to deal with honour killings. The murders come under the general categories of homicide or manslaughter. Sometimes the honour killing is committed by a mob and in such cases it becomes difficult to pinpoint the culprit. The collection of evidence becomes impossible as eye witness never comes forward to help the police and judicial system.

Conclusion

Today the societal norms are constantly changing; there is always a tiff between the ancient practices being followed by older generation and the modern liberal opinion of the youth. India is a democratic country and its citizens have various freedom and rights guaranteed under Indian constitution. Decision through khap panchayats which are not legally recognised because violate the already established law of land related to the property and matrimonial matters. If the khap panchayat will adjudicate all the matters related to inheritance of property and marriages then what will be the function of court of justice and the competency of legislature in India. Honour killing is the direct violation of human rights of a person who by virtue of being a human have the basic birth right and in cases of honour killings, this right is violated by their own family member and in most cases by the father or by the real brother because they don't allow their daughter or female member to marry according to her will.

Honour killings have become common in many parts of the country, often young couples who fall in love have to seek shelter in the police lines or protection homes, to avoid the wrath of kangaroo courts. Honour killings come within the category of rarest of rare cases deserving death punishment. It is time to stamp out these barbaric, feudal practices which are a slur on our nation. This is necessary as a deterrent for such outrageous, uncivilised behaviour. For the sake of honour killings and other crime, a criminal is a criminal; he has no religion, caste, community, nationality. Therefore, the crime of honour killings should be severely punished as it violates the basic and inalienable human right that is right to life – and without this right, no other right have any meaning. The central government has to step in to ensure that the powerful and the retrogressive khap panchayats are dealt with firm determination and more strict laws. Both the state and central governments need to strengthen the observance of marriage and inheritance laws. Doing so will address the twin horrors of female foeticide and honour killings.

References

- Hansen, Kathryn. (1992). *Grounds for Play: The Nautanki Theatre of North India.* New Delhi: Manohar.
- Kachhwaha, Kavita. (2011). Khap Adjudication in India: Honoring the Culture with Crimes, *International Journal of Criminal Justice Sciences*, 6(1&2), 299.
- Rajalakshmi, T. K. (2004). Murder for Honour, *Frontline*, 21(3), January - February, 2004, web source: http:// www.frontline.in
- Sunita and Yudhvir. (2013). Khap Panchayats: Changing perspectives. *Asian Journal of Multidimensional Research*, 2(7), 14-20.
- Tanwar, Mukta. (2013). Threatening Khap Panchayats and Women. *International Indexed Refereed Research Journal*, 4(I).
- www.mainstreamweekly.net
- www.sciencepub.net
- www.scribd.com
- www.womenleadership.in
- www.boloji.com

Chapter – 16

Khap Panchayats as Agencies of Honour Crimes

—Sandesh Yadav and
Professor Haseena Hashia

Abstract

Khap panchayats are the self-proclaimed courts of caste lords in a village society. Though, khap panchayats are unconstitutional but still, this parallel system of justice enjoys full legitimacy and authority in a village society. In the present scenario, Khap panchayats are becoming agencies of honour crimes and perpetrating injustice in the name of sharia, Gotra and on the pretext of preserving tradition and culture. Khap panchayats get involved in honour killings for various reasons like refusal to enter into an arranged marriage, being victim of sexual assault, allegedly committing adultery or being involved with someone of another caste. Apart from this, honour crimes takes place in several other forms like chopping of nose and ear of accused person, holding of red hot iron rod in hands of victim, ex-communication from the village society etc. Khap panchayats have adopted the face of Indian Taliban and are spreading social terrorism. Khap panchayats usurps the power of elected panchayats and through honour crimes they violate fundamental rights of Indian citizens, human rights and several sections of Indian Penal Code (IPC). Khap panchayats need to be questioned in term of their legal status and the authority by which they punish people brutally or carry out killings in the name of honour.

The present chapter details the various aspects of khap panchayats and explores honour crime with special reference to honour killings along with broad understanding of modern trends followed by present generation as the main causes of honour crimes. The chapter also discusses the various provisions in Indian Penal Code, 1860 under which honour crimes are punishable offence and shows urgency to pass Indian Penal Code and Other Laws (Amendment) Bill, 2010.

Keywords: *Khap Panchayats, Gotra, Honour Crimes, Honour Killing, Fundamental Rights, Indian Penal Code (IPC).*

Introduction

Khap panchayats are great mysteries in a country having world's largest democracy. Question comes to mind that why khap panchayats are being addressed as "mysteries"? This question can be answered through the following facts:

- Their unconstitutional background.
- If they are unconstitutional in existence then how they are enjoying the full legitimacy and authority.
- What about the elected panchayats?

To understand the mysteries of khap panchayats in India we need to study in detail about definition, region of dominance, structure and composition, mode of operation etc. of Khap panchayats.

Khap panchayats totally stand against the literal meaning of panchayats and need not to be confused with panchayati raj institutions. Khap panchayats can be defined as the assemblies of some mighty and powerful persons which declare themselves as the "Caste Lords." These panchayats lack any constitutional or legal basis and are undemocratic in nature. These are also called as caste panchayats. Caste panchayats functions as a parallel judicial system and elected panchayats are either subordinated to or coopted by them." (Mullick and Raaj, 2007) These caste panchayats or khap panchayats derive their strength from the following -

- Concept of divergence evolution means superior caste has evolved from the common ancestors.
- Superior caste shows strong bonding against the low caste people.
- High degree of tolerance shown by the villagers.
- Weak nature of panchayati raj Institutions.
- High degree of politicisation and use of muscle power.

On the basis of territorial jurisdiction, khap panchayats are known by various names like Kheda, Patti, and Maha Panchayat. Presently, these khap panchayats exist in the State of Punjab, Haryana, western Uttar Pradesh, Bihar, Madhya Pradesh and Rajasthan.

Traditionally, these assemblies used to settle disputes between individuals in villages and judgements given by them were for the betterment of the society. But in the present scenario, these institutions are highly politicised and performing in highly inhuman, illegal and arbitrary manner and spreading the social terrorism. Presently, these are the agencies of honour crimes and their role is characterised by -

- Regressive Judgements
- Violation of law and order of the country.

Khap panchayats work as the custodian of honour and follow the rule of endogamy which means the rule restricting marriage to members of the same tribe, village, caste, sub-caste, or other social groups. Consequently, their existence has been justified in the name of preserving the honour and values of the community and to explode the sanctity of age-long customs and practices by regulating the conduct of people. These panchayats follows a certain code which is unwritten law for them, through which they serve and defend their honour, with the sanction of their whole community. Honour here revolves around the public perception of the individuals, more than their real behaviour. Honour as per khap panchayats can be described in terms of the following imposed restrictions on villagers -

- Marriage within the same gotra or sagotra is forbidden since in that case a boy and a girl are regarded as a brother and sister.
- Marriage in different gotras is also forbidden if a boy and girl belong to the same village or physically adjoining villages.
- Inter-caste marriages are strictly taboo.

They are perpetrating injustice in the name of sharia, gotra and on the pretext of preserving tradition and culture (Kumar, 2007). Atrocities inflicted by these killer machines are flagrant (Jalpark, 2010). Such intervention of khap panchayats deprives the person from his/her life and personal liberties granted under the Constitution of India. These institutions assume to themselves the power and authority to declare on and deal with objectionable matrimonies and exhibit least regard for the life and liberty and are not deterred by the process of administration of justice.

Honour Crimes with Special Reference to Honour Killings

Human Rights Watch (2004) describes that "honour crimes are acts of violence, usually murder, committed by male family members against female family members, who are perceived to have brought dishonour upon the family. A woman can be targeted by (individuals within) her family for a variety of reasons, including: refusing to enter into an arranged marriage, being the victim of a sexual assault, seeking a divorce even from an abusive husband or (allegedly) committing adultery. The mere perception that a woman has behaved in a specific way to dishonour her family is sufficient to trigger an attack.

The Oxford Dictionary of Law Enforcement defines Honour killing as "the purposeful pre-planned murder, generally of a woman, by or at the command of members of her family stimulated by a perception that she has brought shame on the family" (Oxford Dictionary of Law Enforcement, 2007).

Amnesty International observes that "honour killing of a woman by a male relative is not an individual act of violence, but one which is collective, planned, sociologically predictable, and socially approved by both men and women in the family and community concerned" (Amnesty International, 2011, p. 3).

Rout (2012), describes that honour killing is the homicide of the female member of a family or her paramour or both of them by the family members of the girl, due to the belief of the perpetrators that the deceased had brought dishonour upon the family or community. Honour killing are directed mostly against women and girls, but have been extended to men (Rout, 2012, p. 18).

Honour killing falls under the category of "Honour Based Violence" and it is the result of clash between tradition and modernity. In twenty first century the trends like western dressing, inter-caste marriages, self choice marriages, homosexual relationships etc. are prevalent among younger generation and a sort of challenges for traditional society and consequently gives rise to clash between the two. Further, the increasing empowerment of women is yet another aspect which makes honour killing as gender specific crime. Traditionally, women are considered as the property of community but in modern scenario, women are characterised by higher degree of independence or self-dependency and this is indigestible thing for traditional society.

The apparent shame and perceived honour is normally the result of the following modern trends:

- Western dressing sense.
- Self choice marriages.
- Sagotra marriages.
- Inter caste marriages.
- Extra marital affair.
- Homosexual relationship.

The other activities which comes under the category of honour crimes includes chopping of ear and nose, holding of red hot iron stick in hands, huge fines and penalties, ex-communication from village. Further, there are several ways of physical and mental harassment in the name of honour.

Khap Panchayats v/s. Law and Order

Honour crimes are acts of violence and shame and the involvement of khap panchayats in such heinous acts make them agencies of honour crimes and thus, violates the fundamental rights, various sections of Indian Penal Code (IPC) and Human Rights of Indian citizens.

The Khap Panchayats while carrying out or getting involved in honour crimes violate the Article 14, Article 15(1) and Article 21 of Indian Constitution.

Article 14 talks about equality before law. The khap panchayats or the caste panchayats believes in the concept of superior and the inferior caste and treat people according to their caste and consideration of women as secondary sex by the khap panchayats leads to the violation of Art.14 of Indian Constitution.

Article 15(1) says that the state shall not discriminate against any religion, race, caste, sex, place of birth or any of them. The discriminatory nature of khap panchayats or caste panchayats leads to the violation of Art.15 (1) of Indian Constitution. The suo-moto decisions related to ex-communication of families from the village, ban on the entry of lower caste people in temples etc. results in the violation of Art.15 (1) of Indian Constitution.

Article 21, talks about right to life says no person shall be deprived of his life or personal liberty except according to procedure established by law. The restrictions imposed by the khap panchayats in relation to sagotra marriages, inter-caste marriages, homo sexual relationships, wearing western clothes etc. leads to the violation of Art. 21 of Indian Constitution.

Honour Crimes and the Violation of Human Rights

The khap panchayats while imposing restrictions and committing atrocities against the villagers violate the Art. (3) and Art. (16) of Human Rights Declaration.

Article (3) says that everyone has the right to life, liberty and security of person. Honour crimes committed by the khap panchayats leads to the violation of Art. 3 of Human Rights Declaration.

Article (16) says that,

- Men and women of full age, without any limitation due to race, nationality or religion, have the right to marry and to found a family. They are entitled to equal rights as to marriage, during marriage and its dissolution.
- Marriage shall be entered into only with the free and full consent of the intending spouses.
- The family in the natural and fundamental group unit of society and in entitled to protection by society and the State.

The khap panchayats strictly oppose the sagotra marriages, inter-caste marriages, self-choice marriages and hence, violate the Art. (16) of Human Rights Declaration.

Inefficient Tools in Indian Penal Code, 1860 to Curb the Menace of Honour Crimes

Indian Penal Code, 1860 though lacks the specific provision related to honour crimes but still have following sections under which honour crimes are punishable offence:-

IPC Section 34 says that acts done by several persons in furtherance of common intention.

IPC Section 35 says that when such an act is criminal by reason of its being done with a criminal knowledge or intention.

IPC Section 102 says that commencement and continuance of the right of private defence of the body.

IPC Section 103 says that when the right of private defence of property extends to causing death.

IPC Section 104 says that when such right extends to causing any harm other than death.

IPC Section 105 says that commencement and continuance of the right of private defence of property.

IPC Section 106 says that right of private defence against deadly assault when there is risk of harm to innocent person.

IPC Section 107 says that Abetment of a thing.

IPC Section 108 says that Abettor.

IPC Section 108A says that Abetment in India of offences outside India.

IPC Section 109 says punishment of abetment if person abetted does act with different intention from that abettor.

IPC Section 110 says that punishment of abetment if person abetted does act with different intention from that of abettor.

IPC Section 111 says that liability of abettor when one act abetted and different act done.

IPC Section 112 says that abettor when liable to cumulative punishment for act abetted and for act done.

IPC Section 113 says that liability of abettor for an effect caused by the act abetted different from that intended by the abettor.

IPC Section 114 says that abettor present when offence is committed.

IPC Section 115 says that abetment of offence punishable with death or imprisonment for life if offence not committed.

IPC Section 116 says that abetment of offence punishable with imprisonment- if offence be not committed.

IPC Section 120A says that Definition of criminal conspiracy.

IPC Section 120B says that Punishment of criminal conspiracy.

IPC Section 299 says that culpable homicide and murder.

IPC Section 304 says that Punishment for culpable homicide not amounting to murder.

IPC Section 307 says that attempt to murder attempts by life convicts.

IPC Section 308 says that attempt to commit culpable homicide.

Honour killings are considered as brutal crimes of homicide under the IPC (Indian Penal Code). Section 299 and 301 of the IPC, deals with culpable homicide not amounting to murder while Section 300, deals with murder. Honour killing amounts to homicide and murder because the acts are done with the intention of murdering the victims as they have purportedly brought dishonour upon the family. The perpetrators can be punished as per Section 302 of the IPC. The members of the family as well as community can also be prosecuted under Section 302 of IPC for instigating suicide those who transgress the so called norms of the community.

Indian Penal Code and Other Laws (Amendment) Bill, 2010

Indian Penal Code and other laws (Amendment) Bill 2010 through which it is planning to bring amendments in Sec 300 (committing an intentional act which causes death) and 354 (assault or criminal force to woman with intent to outrage her modesty) of IPC and Section 105 (burden of proving that the case of accused comes within exceptions) of the Indian Evidence Act where the onus would be on the members of khap panchayats and family members to prove their innocence.

In Sec 300 of IPC, the government is planning to introduce honour killings as the fifth clause 18, which at present defines murder under the four categories. The proposed fifth clause says, "If it is done by any person or persons acting in concert with, or at the behest of, a member of the family or a member of a body or group of the caste or clan or community or caste panchayat (by whatever name called) in the belief that the victim has brought dishonour or perceived to have brought dishonour upon the family or caste or clan or community or caste panchayats."

In the explanations given for the clause, the proposal says that dishonours and perceived to have brought dishonour will include acts of any person adopting a dress code which is unacceptable to his or her family or caste or clan or community or caste panchayat.

The murders for choosing to marry within or outside the gotra (sub-caste) or caste or clan or community against the wishes of one's family or caste or clan or community will also come under the ambit of the honour killings. Killing somebody for engaging in sexual relations which are unacceptable to the community or caste panchayat or family will also fall under it.

Extermination of a person in the belief that he or she has brought dishonour will also be punished with imprisonment of either description for a term which may extend to two years or with fine or with both. On the point that who all come under the ambit of honour killings, the draft suggests that all members of a body or group of caste or clan or community or caste panchayat, ordering or abetting the commission of murder will be deemed guilty of having committed the murder and that would make it liable for the maximum penalty i.e. death sentence.

Apart from this, Union Government intends to bring a law on the matter in the current parliament session itself and has decided to amend the Special Marriage Act, 1950 to abolish "30 Days Notice Period" so as to protect the lives of the young couples who dare to go for inter-caste or inter-religious marriage against the wishes of their family members.

Conclusion

Today, khap panchayats have acquired the role of Indian Taliban which believes that villagers are supposed to live life according to their norms and conditions. These panchayats are agencies of honour crimes and spreading social terrorism. Extreme politicisation and use of muscle power have worsened the situation. Further, the following aspects are responsible for their existence:-

- Absence of specific provisions related to honour crimes in the Indian Penal Code.
- Limited powers of police personnel.
- Unawareness about own fundamental rights and human rights.
- Prevalence of narrow mindset.

People are to be made aware about their unconstitutional background, crimes committed by them in the name of honour and justice, caste politics. People need to understand the Hindu Marriage Act, 1946 and the Special Marriage Act, 1950 in order to realise the atrocities committed by the khap panchayats.

Acknowledgement

I would like to acknowledge Professor Rocket Ibrahim, Department of Geography, Jamia Millia Islamia, Delhi for his valuable guidance in understanding the scenario of khap panchayats in various states of India.

References

- Baxi, Pratiksha; Rai, Srinivas M. and Ali, Shaneem, Sardar (2006). Legacies of Common Law: Crimes of Honour in India and Pakistan. Taylor and Francis, Ltd. Vol. 27 (7), pp.1239-1253, 2006.

- Byreshwar, Pankaja (2014). 'Honour killing' The Menace. *International Journal of Applied Research (IJAR),* Vol. 4 (1), Jan. 2014.
- Deol, Satnam Singh (2014). Honour Killings in Haryana State, India: A Content Analysis. *International Journal Criminal Sciences* (IJCJS), Vol. 9 (2), pp. 192-208, July-Dec. 2014.
- Indian Penal Code (1860). Government of India, India.
- Kachhwala, Kavita (2011). Khap Adjudication in India: Honouring the Culture with Crimes. *International Journal of Criminal Justice Sciences (IJCJS),* Vol. 6 (1&2), pp. 297-308, Jan-Jun/July-Dec. 2011.
- Rana, Pranab Kumar and Mishra, Bhabani Prasad (2013). Honour Killings- A Gross Violation of Human Rights and Its Challenges. International Journal of *Humanities and Social Sciences Invention,* Vol. 2 (6), pp. 24-29, June-2013.
- Sunita and Yudhvir (2013). Khap Panchayats: Changing Perspectives. *Asian Journal of Multidimensional Research* (AJMR), Vol. 2 (7), July. 2013.
- Universal Declaration of Human Rights (1946), United Nations Organisation (UNO).
- Vishwanath, Jyoti and Palakonda, Srinivas C. (2001). Patriarchal Ideology of Honour and Honour Crimes in India. *International Journal of Criminal Justice Sciences (IJCJS)*, Vol. 6 (1&2):386-395, Jan-Dec. 2011.

Chapter – 17

Role of Khap Panchayat in Promoting Honour Killing

—*Ruchi Dhyani*

Abstract

The khap panchayats are the informal courts of a group of villages sharing the same caste or geography. A khap panchayat is usually a collective of at least 12 or more village panchayats. Khap panchayat works for protecting the honour of their community and its members, that's why inter-caste and inter-religious marriages are not approved by khap panchayat. Honour killing in India have been mostly reported in the northern regions of the country, especially in the states of Uttarakhand, Punjab, Haryana, Rajasthan, Uttar Pradesh and Bihar. Khap panchayat are the Taliban of India involving in shameful killing of young couple in the name of honour which is really unacceptable in civilised society.

Keywords: *Khap Panchayat, Honour killing, Gotra, Marriage.*

Introduction

The word panchayat is a derivative of Sanskrit root *panc*, means five, but in rural India, it is referred to as any community meeting of any number of men. It is the most commonly used as dispute processing forum in a village. The khap panchayats are the courts of a group of villages sharing the same caste or geography formed by the upper caste people to strengthen their power over the rest of the community. Khap panchayat is a pool of 84 villages or 12 Thambas (A thamba is a group of seven villages) created primarily by the Jats. The pradhan of each khap is elected in an informal meeting held by the elders of a particular khap, there is no formal election. There is one Sarv khap in the country which includes all the khap panchayats. The khaps are different from village panchayats, which are legally elected under the panchayati raj system. Technically, each village has two panchayats the legal panchayat and the other, an informal panchayat, whose members go on to represent the village in a khap panchayat. Khap panchayat is an exclusively male-dominated institution and the women have no share.

The khap panchayat are active in many states in India. They are called by different names at different places like khap in Haryana, Pal among Meos of Haryana and Rajasthan, Hatu panchayat and Parga panchayat among Munda Tribe of Jharkhand, Peddala panchayats (elders) in Visakhapatnam district, Kula caste panchayats in East and West Godavari districts of Andhra Pradesh respectively. Khap panchayat govern their own rules and laws for dealing with any situation in the concerning areas. They have set some rules which have to be followed by all the community members and if someone violates these rules then they are punished by khap panchayat. Khap panchayat have some principles that govern marriages and these principles have to be followed:

(i) Marriage within same gotra is prohibited because that makes a boy and girl siblings.

(ii) Marriage in different gotra is forbidden if boy and girl belong to the same village or physically adjoining village.

(iii) Inter-caste marriages are strictly barred.

(iv) Love marriages are considered a social taboo.

The sarv khap panchayat usually called for social boycott of individuals who raised their voice against the caste panchayats. Honour killing usually happens when someone dares to challenge the norms of the society and marry against the wishes of the family or community. Honour killing is a practice where male members kill a female relative who is perceived as having damaged the family honour. Her death restores the honour of the family. Honour killings originate in the ancient customs that have been incorporated into many cultures. According to such tribal custom the woman is the repository of her family honour and honour is closely related to respect and standing in society. (Ruane, 2000). Honour-based crimes are motivated by a desire to preserve family or community honour (Almosaed, 2004). Tahira Shahid Khan, a professor specialising in women's issues at the Aga Khan University in Pakistan, wrote in Chained to Custom, a review of honour killings published in 1999 "Women are considered the property of the males in their family irrespective of their class, ethnic, or religious group. The owner of the property has the right to decide its fate. The concept of ownership has turned women into a commodity which can be exchanged, bought and sold." Premeditated killings of family members, primarily women, who are thought to have brought shame or dishonour to their family by engaging in certain behaviours considered unacceptable (e.g. pre-marital or extra-marital sexual relationships, or relationships with boys not approved by the family), are often referred to in media reports as honour killings.

Most shocking incidence of honour killing happened in Kolkata where Mehtab Alam a 29 year old youth dragged his sister out on the street and cut off her head with one stroke of the sword in Ayub Nagar locality of Nadial. Mehtab Alam walked to a police station with the head in his left hand and the sword in his right. Mehtab put the sword and the head on table and told police officer that he is ready to be arrested for murdering his sister, 22 year old *Nilofar Bibi*. He told the duty officer to seize the head as evidence. Political leaders are also involved in honour killing as in Punjab, Bibi Jagir Kaur, the first woman President of the SGPC (Shiromani Gurdawara Prabandhak Committee), was a high profile minister in the then ministry of Prakash Singh Badal. Early in 2000, her pregnant daughter Harpreet, who married Kamaljeet, a *mona* (shaven) Sikh from a different caste, secretly and against her mother's wishes, was killed after a forced abortion.

These incidences proved that women are the vessel of family honour that's why they have to face domestic violence, but honour killings are distinct from domestic violence for three reasons:

(i) Planning: Honour killings are planned in advance, often at a family conference. The perpetrator's family may repeatedly threaten the victim with death if she dishonours her family.

(ii) **Family complicity:** Honour killings can involve multiple family members in the killing, such as parents, brothers and cousins.

(iii) **Stigma:** Perpetrators of honour killings often don't face negative stigma in their families or communities.

Oppression in the name of honour prevents girls and women from making choices about their own life. This restricts them in their everyday life, and is an act of serious discrimination and violation against human rights (Mansur *et. al,* 2009).

Talibani Rules of Khap Panchayat

Honour killing, much like genocide, is a crime with which only few would want to be associated with. It tarnishes the image of a people, nation, country, religion and culture which allows it to happen (Mojab, 2004). Honour killings are cases of homicide and murder which are brutal crimes under the Indian Penal Code (IPC). Section 299 and 301 of the IPC, deals with culpable homicide not amounting to murder while Section 300, deals with murder. The khap panchayats or family members can also be booked under Section 302 of IPC for instigating suicide, those who transgress the so called norms of the community. Such killings also violates Articles 14, 15 (1) & (3), 17, 18, 19 and 21 of the Constitution of India. Honour killing is a punishable crime in India even then such cases have been majorly reported in the northern regions of the country, especially in the states of Uttarakhand, Punjab, Haryana, Rajasthan, Uttar Pradesh and Bihar.

According to Delhi-based Indian population statistics survey (IPSS) in mid-2007, in India almost 655 homicidal cases have been registered as honour killings, while in Punjab and Delhi is 32 per cent and in Muzaffarnagar, the worst affected district of UP, 25 per cent honour killings have been registered so far. Around 700 females are killed every year in honour killings incidents. According to National Commission for Women, honour killings take place when young people challenge the accepted norms of marriage. The study conducted by National Commission for Women revealed that 326 cases of conflict surveyed so far nationwide, 72 per cent were because the couple crossed caste barriers and only three per cent were because the couple were from the same gotra. Love is awesome phenomena which can't be explained in words and to get true love, the lover don't care for society, community, honour of their family and even don't fear from the death. Indian history is full of true love stories. How we can forget ever charming and ever green love stories in our Indian history like Prithviraj Chauhan and Sanyogita, Akbar and Jodhaa, Salim and Anarkali, Shah Jahan and Mumtaz Mahal. These love stories are inspiration for the lovers who are searching for true love in their life. Society always put hurdles in the path of lovers. Some has to sacrifice their life when they failed to get their love. Many love stories have the tragic ending as khap panchayat never approve such daring acts of lovers. Ultimately young couple has to face the horrific consequence.

Khap panchayat applies Talibani rules to punish the lovers who oppose to follow their code of conduct which are forcefully applied on their community members. Many of the honour killings all over India are done by khap panchayat and they openly issue death warrant to those who bring dishonour or shame to their family and community through their actions. By giving horrible punishment to the offenders khap panchayat try to set an example for others so that no one try to violates khap rules. Many such incidences show the cruelty of khap panchayat and force us to think are they doing right?

Woman Gangraped on Orders of Kangaroo Court

A woman belonging to the Santhal tribal group and a non-tribal man from a nearby village in Birbhum district were in relationship for almost five years. Santhals have been known for living in peace in closely knit communities bound by ritualistic codes, with none of the caste-based hierarchies and conflicts which mark India's majority Hindus. When the man visited the woman's home with the proposal of marriage, villagers spotted him and organised a kangaroo court. During the proceedings, the couple were made to sit with hands tied, Birbhum police chief C. Sudhakar told the reporters. He said the headman of the woman's village fined the couple 25,000 rupees for the crime of falling in love. The man paid the fine but the woman's family was unable to pay so the headman, who was also a distant relative of the woman, allegedly ordered the rape the women. The family of the girl complained that the headman told the villagers that as family of girl failed to pay so enjoy the girl and have fun with her. Similar incident occurred in Bhawanipur village of Moradabad, Uttar Pradesh; the khap had ordered turn by turn rape of a mother whose 20 years old son eloped with a girl, daughter of an influential Yadav family. The diktat was passed in order to save the honour of Yadavs since her son had dishonoured the Yadavs. The boy belonged to the barber caste. Not only they gang raped her, they also burnt her alive to destroy the evidence.

Gundaraj of Khap Panchayat

Sometime khap panchayat does something which is really unethical and unacceptable in any civilised society. This reflects the cruelty and the ugly faces of the khap panchayat, as happened in the case of an 80 year old woman in Rajasthan was allegedly paraded naked on a donkey on the orders of the khap panchayat. The woman alleges she was first labeled a witch who would eat up the children of the village and then she was stripped, black paint was smeared on her face and she was then paraded naked on a donkey.

Many couples had tragic ending of their love story as khap panchayat didn't accept their decision. Ved Pal Moan, brutally beaten to death when he tried to secure his wife who was confined by her parents at Singhwal village in Jind district. He was escorted by a police party and a warrant officer of the High Court. Ved Pal had married neither within his gotra nor within the same village. In this case, another absurd code was invoked by the khap that the couple violated the custom of not marrying in the neighbouring village as it forms part of *bhaichara* (brotherhood). A khap congregation held in March 2009 publicly pronounced the death sentence for Ved Pal, and it succeeded in executing it in June.

Amreen and Lokesh also had a tragic ending of their love story. When lovers committed suicide after the local village council, ordered them to annul their marriage or face death. Amreen was Muslim and her husband, Lokesh, a Hindu. Their match was simply unacceptable to their communities. The couple poisoned themselves to suicide.

Vijander, a dalit boy, had eloped with his girlfriend, Roshni. She was a member of the higher-caste Jat community and from the same village, Mehrana, near the border with Haryana state. Vijander's cousin Ram Kishan, who had helped them elope. The couple returned to Mehrana a few days later thinking that anger would have subsided. The village people caught all the three. Village khap panchayat ordered to hang them with tree and burn them. In the morning the order of the so called panchayat was executed and all of the three were burnt alive to death in front of the whole village.

Manoj-Babli honour killing case in which the killing was ordered by a khap panchayat, a religious caste-based council among Jats, in their Karora village in Kaithal district of Haryana. The khap panchayat's ruling was based on the assumption that Manoj and Babli belonged to the Banwalagotra, a Jat community, and were therefore considered to be siblings despite not being directly related and any union between them would be invalid. Manoj and Babli were brutally murdered by Babli's relatives in June 2007, on the diktats of a khap panchayat for marrying in the same gotra. The verdict on Manoj and Babli case came on March 29th, 2010, Kaithal District Court found the accused guilty of murder, kidnapping, conspiracy, and destroying evidence under Sections 302, 364, 120 B and 210 of the IPC. Then, on March 30, 2010, in a first judgment of its kind the Harayna state, the court announced a death penalty verdict in the double murder case for five accused and life sentence to one for murdering a couple. All the accused were relatives of Babli, including her brother Suresh, cousins Gurdev and Satish, paternal uncle Rajender, and maternal uncle Baru Ram. Khap panchayat leader Ganga Ram (Ganga Raj) was given a life time imprisonment for conspiracy, while the driver, Manjeet Singh, held guilty of kidnapping, was given a jail term of seven years. The court also asked the Haryana government to provide a compensation of one lakh rupee to Manoj's family, as he was the only earning member.

Khap panchayat didn't learn any lesson from the court verdict and repeat the same story with Nidhi and Dharmendra who also became the victims of honour killing because both belonged to same gotra; the couple eloped to get married in Delhi. The couple was brutally killed in full public view at Gharnavathi in Rohtak; couple was in a relationship for almost three years. When both went missing, Nidhi's family got in touch with her and persuaded them to return home, with the promise that they would not be harmed. As they returned, Nidhi's family took them to their house and killed them. They broke the limbs of Dharmendra Barak before beheading him and dumping the body in front of his house. Family tried to cremate Nidhi body but police reached on the spot and recovered her half burnt body.

These are heartbreaking love stories through which khap panchayat wants to create a terror in the minds of lovers. Khap panchayat issues unnecessary circulars which are not relevant as done by khap panchayat in Shoram village in Uttar Pradesh's Muzaffarnagar district a bizarre diktat, which bans girls from wearing jeans, using mobile phones and the internet. The ban will have an effect on 46 villages in Muzaffarnagar district of Uttar Pradesh. Panchayat leader Chaudhary Naresh said jeans are a part of western culture and therefore, should not be allowed in India as they spoil the society.

Khap panchayats are not legal and they don't have right to justifying their honour killing and other wired acts on any grounds as Bench of Justices Markandey Katju and Gyan Sudha Misra said, "This is wholly illegal and has to be ruthlessly stamped out. There is nothing honourable in honour killing or other atrocities and, in fact, it is nothing but barbaric and shameful murder. Other atrocities in respect of the personal lives of people committed by brutal, feudal-minded persons deserve harsh punishment. Only this way can we stamp out such acts of barbarism and feudal mentality. Moreover, these acts take the law into their own hands, and amount to kangaroo courts, which are wholly illegal."

Conclusion

Khap panchayat is male-dominated council always acting as the protector of honour and if any person tries to harm the honour of their community they will pass the judgment to kill that person which leads to honour killing. But in reality khap panchayat are illegal and just involved in barbaric and shameful murder. There are so many incidents and judgments passed by them showing their insensitivity toward humanity. There are so many young couples who lost their lives in the name of honour of their family and community. Union Finance Minister P. Chidambaram commented on khap panchayat by saying that India does not need these anymore as these are very conservative organisations.

References

- Almosaed, N. (2004). Violence against women: a cross-cultural perspective, *Journal of Muslim Minority Affairs,* 24(1), 167-188.
- Baxi, Pratiksha, *et al*., (2006). Legacies of Common Law: Crimes of Honour in India and Pakistan, *Third World Quarterly,* 27(7), 1241.
- J. Venkatesan (20 April 2011). "Stamp out khap panchayats: court." *The Hindu - Issue New Delhi, April 20, 2011* (Chennai, India).
- "Khap panchayats Taliban? When will barbarism 'in the name of honour' end" available at http://daily.bhaskar.com
- Mansur, Y., Shteiwi, M. Moch Murad, N. (2009). *The Economic Underspinnings of Honour Crimes in Jordan.* Research report. Jordan, Mathlouma. Available: http://mathlouma.com
- Mojab, S. (2004). The particularity of 'honour' and the universality of 'killing': from early warning signs to feminist pedagogy. In S. Mojab and N. Abdo (Eds.), Violence in the name of honour: Theoretical and political challenges. Istanbul: Istanbul Bilgi University Yayinlari.
- Ruane, R. A, (2000). 'Murder in the name of honour: violence against women in Jordan and Pakistan, Available at:http://www.abo.fi
- Vasanth Kannabiran and Kannabiran Kalpana.(1991). Caste and Gender, Understanding Dynamics of Power and Violence, *Economic and Political Weekly*, XXVI (37), 35-37.
- http://www.anti-caste.org
- http://www.deccanchronicle.com
- http://www.justice.gov
- http://www.legalservicesindia.com
- http://www.ndtv.com
- http:/www.icdeolhpu.org
- http://timesofindia.indiatimes.com

Section–D

Khap Panchayats and other Non-State Agencies

Chapter – 18

Media Standing Tall Against Feudal Khap Panchayats

—*Dr Deepa Awasthi*

Abstract

Although khap panchayat and such type of other institutions working on the same ideology of patriarchy and male dominance existed in all the parts of country from centuries but they came in lime light when media attracted the attention of public not only in country alone but at global level exposing their undemocratic way of working, their unconstitutional and illegal dictates and inhuman ways of implementing those dictates. Media not only exposed their barbaric acts but also criticised them with full strength and created an unfavourable environment against them in society. Beside this media has compelled the judiciary, parliament, police and civil society to stand with the victims of khap panchayat who were negligent towards this social evil till now. This Chapter focuses on the role of formal and informal media to encounter the evil of khap and issues related to them. Chapter also discusses about the steps media must initiate to minimise the ill impacts of khap panchayats on society.

Key Words: *Attention, Public, Patriarchy, Inhuman, Strategies.*

Introduction

Initially it was considered that any democracy stands on three pillars – Executive bodies, Legislative bodies and Judiciary but with advent of society, media as fourth pillar of democracy, has not only played a vital role in providing direction to society but also have drastic impact on all the three pillars of democracy. A society without media is just like body without soul. Somebody has rightly said that a pen can do what even sword can't do. In last century media has gained unlimited strength, it emerged as most powerful tool to regulate the society. Hardly an issue or field has left which has not attracted the attention of media; it may be social, political, economical etc. Media has even affected the personal life of individuals. People listen what media wants, people watch what media wants and even people think what media wants. It has emerged as ideal canvas for the common man to express their views and ideas.

Media and society are the two faces of same coin. Media is always considered as the mirror image of society. It has always provided the best possible solutions to various socio-political and socio-economic problems, mankind have ever faced. Just like all other issues it has always helped the civil society to continue its war against feudal khap panchayats and its centuries old ideologies. They published and broadcasted their unconstitutional and inhuman dictates and their barbaric ways of implementing those dictates. It made the society to think that is there any need of khap panchayat and such type of institutions in country like India which claims to be world's one of the largest democracy and most ancient civilisation. Through publishing and broadcasting the views and interviews of famous personalities including politicians, film actors and actresses, social workers, law experts, businessmen and other dignitaries it had created an environment against khap panchayats not only in the region where they are active but also all over country and abroad too.

For the sake of understanding media can be categorised in to two types – formal and informal media. Formal media is again of two types – Print and Electronic media. Print media includes Newspaper, magazines, journals etc. Electronic media include radio, television etc. Informal media include social media, internet, cinema etc.

Role of Formal Media

Newspaper and magazines which are popular among literate people of country plays a decisive role in developing a public debate among intellectual class of country. News related to khap panchayat has always become the headlines of newspaper and magazines. Not only news but the articles, features and cartoons published against khap panchayats have exposed their feudal thinking on priority basis. Supporters of khap panchayats are aware of the impact and credibility of print media in society that is why several times khap panchayat have threatened to attack newspaper offices and journalists, but media and media personnel always continued their hard work in public interest, putting their life and property at risk.

Newspapers and magazines are most reliable source of information as they have a large readership. Some of the national level newspapers even have their readership in crores but they have their limitations. As per census data 2011, the overall literacy percentage of India is still only 74 per cent (82.1 per cent among men while 65.5 per cent among women). It means for 17.9 per cent men and 34.5 per cent women, the content published in print media are meaningless. Here starts the role of Radio and Television. They are popular among all people in India whether literate or illiterate, poor or rich and belonging to any age category. They are being listened and watched even in rural and most remote part of country. Electronic media provides big canvas for public discussion as compared to print media.

Interviews and statements of dignitaries on news channel provides energy and courage to youth and women which are worst affected by dictates of khap panchayat and such type of other institutions functioning on same ideology. This courage comes from the belief that they are not alone but whole country is standing behind them.

Khap panchayat works on the ideology of restricting the liberty of women especially young girls and boys. Media has always criticised the elements which are responsible for discriminating and marginalising women. It always made them aware about their rights and procedure to achieve these rights. Sometimes formal media is criticised for deforming the news by making and presenting them in sensational and spicy way to increase their TRP and readership but due to this only, the positive role of media in handling the social issues like khap panchayats cannot be ignored.

Role of Informal Media

Similar to formal media, informal media has always criticised the khap panchayats. In year 2015 bollywood cinema has made enormous efforts and released a number of movies against khaps and their unconstitutional acts giving social message to its viewers. These movies have gained a lot of popularity.

Film titled 'Heropanti' released in year 2015 was a super hit in which hero started his fight against the khap leaders by helping his friend who fell in love with the daughter of a khap leader. As story continued he himself fall in love with another daughter of same khap leader. Ultimately hero succeeded in making them understand that ideology of khap is always not right.

Next film in this series is 'Guddu Rangeela' released in same year which was based on the true story of Manoj – Babli case. In this film popular actor Arshad Varsi played the role of victim Manoj. Film successfully portrayed the barbaric acts of khap panchayats.

Source: www.financialexpress.com

Fig. 18.1: A scene from movie "Guddu Rangeela".

Another national award winning film released in same year on 26th June, 2015 was "Miss Tanakpur hajir ho" mocking at the meaningless decision of khap panchayat in which the hero of the film was held accused for the crime of raping a buffalo – winner of miss Tanakpur award. In the panchayat meeting khap ridiculously decides that accused has to marry the rape victim. Annoyed from the movie a khap in district Muzafarnagar of Uttar Pradesh issued an order against Vinod Kapri – the director of the movie that the person who will kill the director of the film will be awarded with 51 buffaloes. Khap also threatened the cinema hall owners not to show the film in their cinema theatre, otherwise they have to face the consequences.

Source: www.indianexpress.com

Fog. 18.2: Poster of movie 'Miss Tanakpur Hajir Ho'.

Before this revolution in bollywood in 2015, a film titled 'Khap' was released in year 2011. Story of the film revolves around the two couples Ria-Kush and Veer-Surili. As movie starts Veer and Surili were killed in the Omkar Chaudhary's village. Ria was not known to Omkar Chaudhary who was her grandfather, as her father Madhur left the native village due to his differences with his father on the issue of tradition of honour killing. Madhur was appointed to investigate the incident of killing of couple Veer and Surili. In the last khap leader Omkar Chaudhary entangled in the love of his son and his strong belief in custom of honour killing promises his son that he will put an end this shameless tradition. Film also portrays the psychology of Veer's father Daulat Ram who remains unmoved to his son's death as he himself was a strong supporter of honour killing and Surili's father Sukhi Ram who was completely broken by her daughter's death was unable to decide whether to approach to Human Right Commission or not.

Source: www.blog.wsj.com

Fig. 18.3: Poster of movie 'Khap'.

Bollywood and khap panchayat again stood against each other face to face when a participant of show *'Satyamev Jayate'* hosted by popular bollywood actor Amir Khan, broadcasted an episode on 3rd June, 2012 against the khap panchayats and honour killing in which a couple Abdul Hakim and Mehwish who came forward saying that they eloped from their village in Merrut in 2010, and roaming here and there hiding their identity, they cannot go back to their village as they fear to get killed by their own family members or the supporters of khap. Unfortunately show revealed their true identity and

Source: www.bollywoodlife.com

Fig. 18.4: Film Actor Amir Khan at Press Conference on case of Abdul Hakim's Murder.

Abdul Hakim was shot dead in district Bulandashar of Uttar Pradesh on 22nd November, 2012 almost after five months of that episode was aired. While talking to media person Abdul's brother revealed that his brother was assassinated at public place but none of the eye witness came forward to help the aggrieved party. As always Police moulded the story and held that Abdul Hakim was murdered due to some personal feud.

When Amir Khan, host of the show came to know about the incidence he talked to government officials of Uttar Pradesh who promised for justice to Abdul Hakim's family and police protection to his wife Mehwish and other family members. Case is still lying in court for justice.

Role of Social Media

In recent few years twitter, whats app, facebook, linkedin etc. have emerged as strong medium to communicate and disseminate information especially among youths. With the increasing popularity of smartphones and tablets young generation of India remain online for 24 hours. A number of jokes, cartoons, posters, videos mocking and criticising the decisions and acts of khap panchayat have been viral on social media. The best advantage of communicating through social media is that here message flows from one individual to another but it reaches to mass making a chain from one to another.

Khap leaders have also recognises the popularity of social media among youths as a result number of times they have issued the dictates restricting the use of social media among youths especially girls. According to them using facebook, whats app by youths is misuse of technology and reason for reducing moral values in society.

Along with advantages social media has certain disadvantage that they are equally accessible to khap supporters also. Khap leaders have used this medium to promote the implementation of their rules, regulations and orders and gathering mob and support for them. There is no control of government on social media about what purpose it is being used. Number of times unsocial elements have used it as platform to create social nuisance or clash between group of people on the basis of caste, religion or ideology. Government of India has recognised the challenges posed by social media and decided to have controlled check on these media.

What Better Media can do to Minimise the Impact of Khaps

Although media has done their best to find solutions of various social problems from time to time including issue of khap panchayat but still there is group of people who criticise the media for not investigating properly before printing or broadcasting the news related to khaps. For increasing the readership of newspapers and magazines and increasing the TRP of news channels the news of khap panchayat is presented after making them spicy and sensational. According to them media has created a complete negative image of khap panchayat as they are the one and only one organisation responsible for the vulnerable condition of women in country but that is not the complete true picture, khap panchayat are different and much better than the image people have in their minds.

Khap supporters view that media has portrayed the khaps as killing machines. They never cover the news when khap has given decisions to resolve the various social issues in positive way. It is the tendency among journalists to become first to report the incidence. It is the lack of knowledge and too much commercialisation, due to which media has always questioned the existence of khap panchayats. They further ask the society that if media can demand to ban the khaps for few misdirected judgements then why media should not be banned first for yellow journalism of media persons misguiding the society through hiding the truth from public. Everybody knows that most of the media houses are being run by big business tycoons who use their newspaper or electronic channel for lobbying in their favour or creating environment in somebody's favour in return of money. Question arises what better media can do to encounter the impact of khaps on innocent public?

Each type of media whether formal or informal has four roles to play – to inform, to advertise, to entertain, and to educate.

As time has passed focus of media remained limited to three functions only - informing, advertising and entertaining. All these three functions earn money for them directly or indirectly. Media has presented the news of khaps on priority basis but hardly one would have read an article or story educating the public or bringing awareness among them against khap. Most of the time khap leaders have used the media to disseminate their message to large number of people, but media always lagged behind in performing their responsibility of educating the public.

It is responsibility of media persons to take extra precautions in reporting the news on various social issues. They should first estimate the impact of their news on society. Journalists must think that besides being a media person he has certain other responsibilities as citizen of India. Just imagine a journalist, one who cover a story of khap panchayat which has passed a dictate against women and print it word by word in their newspaper or broadcast it live on their news channel, while the other one who help the police and administration to stop the meeting of khap panchayat which was called with the intention to pass the dictates against women. Next day he publishes the news how police positively acted and stopped the khap panchayat which was called with the intention of passing an order restricting the liberty of women. Media personnel must understand that truth can be presented in other way also.

Conclusion

Media always stood tall against the khap and such type of other self-originated social institutions but the war of media against khap panchayat will remain incomplete till they do not bear the responsibility of educating the public especially in rural India. Khap panchayat and such type of other institutions gain their strength from public. Till the day public will keep on listening them they will be able to represent them as self-born social leaders. Just imagine the day when people will leave going to khap meetings, the same day they will lose their relevance. There will be no need to ban them. But this is only possible when media will educate the public not only to common man but also to the supporters of khaps. Apart from this media must take extra precautions while covering the news related to khap and such type of other social issues.

References

- Amir Khan Seeks Action Against Khap Panchayat, www.bollywoodlife.com (retrieved on 28th August, 2015).
- Bhardwaj, A. (2014), Are Khap Panchayat as Vile as Media Portrays Them? www.dna.com (retrieved on 24th August, 2015).
- Good Khap V/s Bad Khap, www.indiapositive.com (retrieved on 21th August, 2015).
- Guddu Rangeela – Entertaining Look at Dark Reality of Khap Panchayat, (2015). www.financialexpress.com (Published on 3rd July, 2015).
- Khap Panchayat against Movies That Mocks Them, www.eastcoastdaily.in (retrieved on 24th August, 2015).
- Khap Threats for Miss Tanakpur, (2015). www.freepressjournal.in (Published on 25th June, 2015).
- Khap, (2011). www.indb.com, www.bollymeaning.com
- Social Media and Khap – Curious Indian (2014). www.curiouindian.com (retrieved on 21th August, 2015).

Chapter – 19

Khap Panchayat as Parallel Judicial System

—Manvi Manisha Tigga

Abstract

Way before the foundation of modern judiciary was set up, panchayats were use to impart justice to the people in the villages. The members of panchayats were raised to a pedestal and called panch parmeshwar. Generally, these panch were the elders of the village who looked into the social matters of the village and impart justice. This system was metamorphosized into khap panchayats. The members of khap panchayats are not elected by the people, their influence and power made them the custodian of justice. Khap panchayats continued to exist even after the judiciary was set up and panchayati raj came into being. The methods of khaps are obsolete and, though the ordeals given by them are not suited for contemporary India because of the orthodox mentality of the members of the khaps but people still have faith in this parallel Judicial system. The laws made by the khaps and punishment meted out by them violates the laws made by our parliament and formal judicial system. These rulings of khaps encourage violence, crimes and killings. These laws are regressive and inclined to make India a backward nation. Women and couples are the main target of these khap panchayats. Strict measures are taken to save women from male gaze, and any kind of interaction between men and women of different communities is banned by these khaps. Inter-caste marriage results in murder and sometimes families are eliminated from the village for the same. The laws implemented by them are absurd and more absurd are the punishments decided by them. It is surprising that even after 68 years of independence such a parallel system prevails and is also given impetus to assert its presence. The Courts have pronounced these khaps to be illegal but they still exist and continue working. There are no strict actions taken to stop the functioning of these khaps. People are used to it and may be so is the Judiciary and government also.

Key Words: *Khap Panchayats, Judicial system, Violence, Killings, Panchayti Raj.*

The essence of a Federal Constitution, like ours, is the division of powers between a Central and the State Governments and this division is expressed in written words. Since language is ambiguous, its meaning may not be taken as the same at all times. So, some people do not obey the law passed by the Parliament. They defy the law because they consider it unjust, improper and harsh; some people also violate law because they are criminal minded and some others violate law as they are ignorant. Whatever may be the reason, the person violating a law should be punished after their guilt is established. The organ of the State which discharges this duty termed as judiciary. Thus, the task of a judicial system is to impart justice to the people. For this purpose the British rulers in modern India set up a well organised system of law courts.

Long before the judiciary system was set up, in India, the khap panchayats came into existence, on similar lines, around the fourteenth century. These khap panchayats were primarily called upon by the affluent and upper caste people who desired to consolidate their power and position. The term p*anchayat* literally means assembly (*yat*) of five (*panch*) prudent and respected elders who were chosen and accepted by the village community. Usually, some of the mighty and powerful people, with the coerced public consensus and without any election, group together and declare themselves as 'the king of the caste', thereby constituting the caste panchayats. Traditionally, these assemblies used to settle disputes between individuals in villages though, they lacked any constitutional or legal basis, these caste panchayats functions as a parallel system as it was the need of that hour. When the panchayati raj system was introduced by constitutional amendments in 1992, it was based upon the traditional panchayat system of South Asia. When panchayats were elected, these elected panchayats became either subordinated to or coopted by the caste panchayat. This happened because khap panchayats had already established themselves as the custodians of honour and they enjoyed full legitimacy and authority. After independence, the authority of these khap panchayats has been challenged by modern institutions of justice such as courts, which functions on the principle of rule of law.

The khap panchayat, like the caste system and joint family system, is a traditional institution engaged primarily in dispute resolution and in regulating the behaviour of individuals or group in rural areas of north India. While the smaller issues are taken up by village panchayat and khap panchayat resolve the disputes of wider concern within their operative territory, sometimes active in political sphere but mainly confined to social issues. The khap panchayat attracted the attention of scholars when electronic media highlighted some of their decisions which violated the human rights of individuals. These decisions were mainly related to marriages which violates the traditional code of conduct, especially the concept of village *bhaichara* (brotherhood), gotra *bhaichara* (clan brotherhood) or khap *bhaichara* (brotherhood among persons belonging to same khap) which forms the basis of community harmony in Indian villages, especially in northern India. Time changed but no change has been noticed in the modus oprandi of the khap panchayats.

The khap panchayats have been successful in dividing people along caste, class and gotra lines. This is similar to the divide and rule policy of the Britishers. It is surprising that even after 68 years of independence such type of mindset prevails in Indian society. People cannot marry whom they want, due to the limitations of caste, class and gotra. These caste, class and gotras are not God made but people made. So the members of the khap panchayats have become the "Demi-Gods" ruling the people. They do not let the people forget the old caste, class and gotra matra. People are continuously memorised to protect their honour based on these class, caste and gotra. In the name of preserving Indian culture, they are perpetrating crimes and thereby nurturing a culture of crimes for descendants. Members of this unconstitutional, parallel system of justice often summon an all male get together that crouches around a *chabutara* in the village (smoking *hookah* sometimes to symbolise brotherhood) aspiring of taking quick, unilateral and incontestable decisions on multiple issues like social transgressions, marriage, offences, property rights, inheritance, or regarding any situation threatening tranquility in the village.

Source: www.thehindu.com

Fig. 19.1: Khap Panchayats being organised at Village Level.

Khap panchayats are prevalent, primarily, in the states of Uttar Pradesh, Haryana, Rajasthan and West Bengal. The people accept the decisions of the khap panchayats due to fear, illiteracy and their herd mentality. Over the years, it has become more of herd mentality to follow the orders of khap panchayat than a choice. People have the choice of walking out of the clutches of the system of Khap Panchayat and going to courts or formally elected panchayats under panchayati raj system to solve their problems but they refrain from doing so.

In the name of honour girl child is incessantly sacrificed, in the name of honour people are killed, in the name of honour women and widows are brutally beaten and murdered. All these anti-social activities are for the sake of honour. It is surprising that in this era of "selfie with daughters", daughters are being killed, and daughters as mothers and sisters are beaten and severely punished. Worst of all, there is no judicial system for their help. The self proclaimed khap panchayats are the be all and end all for the women who live in these villages. In the name of saving the honour of the village and her family, girls are forced to marry their rapists, they are forced into child marriage, forced to cover their faces, forced to give up studies, perhaps, forced to give up the right to live. All this is being done parallel to the actual judicial system. There is no human right just the right of the khaps.

The law treats honour killing as "homicide" and murder (Justice Mazida Rizvi: Treat honour killing as homicide). The honour crime also violates Article 14, 15 (1) & (3) 19, 21 and 39 (f) of the Constitution of India. It is against various international commitments of India. It is against the spirit of the UDHR and ICCPR. It is a matter of great shame that even today there is no legal definition of honour crime in India. In the Indian Penal Code, penalties for such crime find ground in sections 299-304, 307, 308, 120A and B, 107-116, 34 and 35. However, this huge number of penal provisions has proved inefficient to deal with this social evil. The perpetrators more often get away with murder, torture and violation of laws.

Their ways of punishing the guilty, as proclaimed by them, are disturbing. Sometimes, ear or nose of the accused is chopped off, sometimes there hair are cut, face is polished black and he/she is made to ride over donkey in the whole village or is forced to run naked and bare footed. If a woman is declared to be a witch she is beaten to death, sometimes her family too meets the same fate. According to khap panchayats, couples cannot have inter-caste marriage or sagotra marriage. Although the rulings of khap panchayats have no legal validity, there is a long list of uncivilised punishments meted out by khap panchayats to those couples that offended the khap traditions. A couple of examples are:

- In June 2009, Anita and Sonu, who had violated the khap propriety, were tricked to return to their village only to be stabbed to death in public.
- In April 2010, the khaps imposed such a heavy financial penalty on a family of Rajasthan that there was no other alternative for them than to commit suicide. Five members of the family jumped before a running train and took their lives.

This is against the Supreme Court who expressed concern over the growing opposition to, intimidation of, and violence against inter-caste couples. A Bench consisting of Justices Ashok Bhan and Markandey Katju directed the administration and the police throughout the country to extend protection to such couples against harassment and initiate action against those who resorted to or instigated violence.

But a person in these villages has no democratic right to go to courts; instead they are dragged to khap panchayats. Furthermore, such punishments are inhuman and prohibited by law. The khaps, on the other hand, want an amendment in the Hindu Marriage Act, 1955, to ban marriages within the same gotra (sub-caste) including mother's gotra and within the same village because local customs dictate that a boy and a girl belonging to the same gotra are brother and sister. Ironically enough, Haryana and Punjab khap leaders who violently prohibit same gotra marriages are from areas in which there is a shortage of girls to marry their sons and they are therefore secretly sourcing brides from Jharkhand and other areas.

As if these atrocities were not enough, if a person has to prove that he/she is not guilty, no evidence is needed. Instead self-proclaimed Judges (khaps) put oil in a pot and boil it. A coin is placed into it. The accused is asked to take out the coin from the boiling oil. He/she is considered innocent if managed to do so. Another way to prove innocence is by the iron stick. An iron stick is heated red hot. The palms of the accused are smeared with turmeric and seven leaves of *Peepal* are tied on them by a weak thread. The red hot stick is kept on it and the accused is asked to walk seven steps carrying the stick in his hands. If the palms do not burn or no red sensations appear on them, he/she is presumed innocent. This practice is usually followed where the character of the accused is questioned. There are numerous other such atrocious ways to prove innocence. But no evidence is required. Any proper judicial system requires evidence to pronounce a person guilty or innocent but khap panchayats do not come under any jurisdiction. They are parallel judiciary, doing what they like and the way in which they like. Their jurisdiction does not end in killing or punishing or deciding marriages. It extends to deciding who should be born and who should not to be born. In the urban areas and some rural areas as well, women are treated at par with men. They have made a place for themselves but in the areas ruled by khaps giving birth to a girl is a taboo.

The political and judicial power that the khaps have established, affects the life of many to a great extent. In order to act according to the rules older khap members try to keep the young people apart. Some schools are also forced to have separate timings for the boys and girls; or girls are not allowed to go to school at all. Fearing their daughters would go astray, many parents marry them off at an early age. People have unquestionable faith in the justice of khap. The question of rights for women does not exist anywhere in the territories ruled by khap panchayats. That girls are seldom sent to schools is especially harmful because education can empower various sections of society, and women in particular, more than anything else. As a result of the power of the khap panchayat, some states remains completely feudal and patriarchal in terms of attitudes to labour, marriage, inheritance, caste and gender relations.

To curb interaction between girls and boys the khap panchayat, in 2013, prohibited girls from using mobile phones. They were also asked to follow a dress code. On this issue the Supreme Court said it was an offence to order women not to use mobile phones or to dress in a particular manner. A bench of Justices Aftab Alam and Ranjana P Desai asked "Imposing a dress code on women and asking them not to use mobile phones, are such orders not socially retrograde? But these are also against the law. How can anyone ask women not to carry a mobile phone." The bench said this after taking note of the presence of many elders, sporting colourful turbans and belonging to different khaps of UP and Haryana, in the court's visitors' gallery. A large number of khap members were also present in the court room in response to the

KHAPS DRAW THE LINE

- **A khap panchayat in Rohtak feels banning same-gotra marriages will end honour killings**
- The resolution also proposes a dress code for girls that bans jeans, tops and all 'gaudy' clothes
- **They have also resolved to introduce a ban on porn sites**
- Another khap panchayat in Jhajjar banned jeans and tops and mobile phones for female college students
- **The Jhajjar khap has also banned drinking in public places**

Source: www.dailymail.uk

Fig. 19.2: Khaps Draw the Line.

bench's desire to hear their views on socially retrograde diktats and honour killings.

In 2011, The Supreme Court of India declared these khap panchayats illegal as they often encourage honour killings and other atrocities against boys and girls of different castes and religions who wish to get married or are already married. Khap panchayats are also referred to as kangaroo courts. They are undemocratic in origin. Without application of law and acting on their whims and wishes, they impose self-created norms backed by the sanction in the name of preserving morals and values of the society.

Source: www.indiatvnews.com

Fig. 19.3: Khap Panchayat.

So many unlawful laws have been passed by the khap panchayats, so many people have been killed as per the order of the khap panchayat, so many women and girls living in the shame and fearing their lives. The prevailing judicial system is not treated at par with the khap panchayats. Still, people prefer to go to the khaps rather than going to courts. Perhaps, it is because of the high fees charged by the lawyers, or distance one has to travel to get to the courts, or the time taken to get a date for the hearing. Whatever might be the reason or reasons we together as a country have to fight against the khap panchayats. The orthodox mindset of the khap panchayat has to be changed. They have to include educated, modern people in their councils who can pronounce proper judgements. Even if the khap panchayats do not have any legal sanction, they have a positive role to play by being more transparent, political and fair in their judgment. This way, they can help poor and native villagers from injustices. The khap panchayats which are social entities and not legal entities should be taught a serious lesson of strong and severe government action and prosecution if they play with the lives of young people.

Beside this politicians should also help khap panchayats to remain socially relevant, and they should not use them as vote banks. If the Judiciary is not able to save and preserve justice, how can it be expected to ensure rule of law in country. Instead of solving problems, now khaps create more and more problems. India resides in its villages and if these villagers are not meted out justice, it's not just the failure of the Judiciary but our country as a whole.

References

- Avasthi, P. A. (2011). Indian Government and Politics, Lakshmi Narayan Agarwal Publications Co., Agra.
- Kavita Kachhwahal, Khap Adjudication in India: Honouring the Culture with Crimes, Dr. Ram Manohar Lohiya National Law University, Lucknow, India. https://www.facebook.com
- Sharma, R. S. (1994). Panchayati Raj and Education in India, Mittal Publications, New Delhi.

Chapter – 20

Khap Panchayat, Inter-caste and Inter-religious Love Marriages

—*Preeti*

Abstract

Khap panchayats are the social organisations, which are united by caste and geography. These panchayats are dominant especially in Jat communities of Haryana, Uttar Pradesh, Rajasthan and rural belt of Delhi. These traditional institutions resolve the disputes and regulate the behaviour of individuals or groups of that particular area, which belongs to that Khap. These panchayats are patriarchal in nature and works on the concept of 'bhaichara' and 'hukka-pani'. These panchayats does not have any legal authority to govern their own rules and regulations for the maintenance of old traditions and customs on the basis of their power and position. In present time khap is attracting the attention of media because of controversial decisions on some issues, in which major decisions are regarding marriages. Marriage with own choice is barred in the khap governed areas. According to these panchayats, marriage from outside the caste or religion is a social crime and it is against the laws and rules of khap panchayats. If anybody dare to do inter-caste/religious love marriage in khap governed area than khap impose heavy fines on their families, boycott them from community and sometimes even kill the couples on the name of honour or impel them for committing suicide. This chapter discusses about the khap panchayats and their role in inter-caste/religious love marriages. Chapter also expresses that in spite of modernisation and increasing development in all fields still some societies are trapped into old traditions and customs. The Supreme Court of India had declared these panchayats illegal and passed the orders for state governments to take criminal actions against those persons, who violets the rights of individual or go against the laws of the country. But despite these laws still people of some community or society gave the preference of khap panchayats rules.

Key Words: *Khap, Inter-caste/Religious Love Marriage, Society, Traditions, Customs.*

Introduction

The origin of the word khap is derived from 'faank', which means an offshoot or fraction. Historically the khap word was used first time in Rajasthan during the medieval period. This word has come into existence in the census report of the year 1890-91, the first census report based on religion and caste and was prepared in Jodhpur (Sadiq and Khan, 2015) khap is a social organisation, which is particularly dominant in the Jat community of Haryana, Rajasthan, Uttar Pradesh and the rural belt of Delhi. It is a system of administration peculiar engaged in resolution of disputes and regulating the behaviour of individuals or group according to the traditional and cultural norms of the area to which that khap belongs. Its domain of functioning is a particular cluster of villages, which is united by caste and geography. The concept of khap is based on patriarchal society, which has the principal of '*bhaichara*' (brotherhood) and '*hukka pani*' (community living and eating together). The marriages of boys and girls, belonging to the same khap or carrying same gotra is not allowed. According to khap rules people belonging to same gotra are considered as siblings. Apart from this the two persons belonging to different gotra and falling under the same khap also cannot get married. These patriarchal bodies are not only undemocratic but also anti-women in nature because it always opposed the right of inheritance of property for women. These panchayats not only limits a women's right to choose her partner for matrimonial purpose but also puts restraints on her personal liberty like what kind of cloths is allowed or not allowed to wear and in which geographical area she can move or not.

Presently more than hundred khap panchayat are active in Haryana (Singh, 2014). The head of the khap, who has known as 'pradhan', regulate the special agenda to work according to social and cultural norms of the khap related area. The pradhan of the khap is chosen by the agreeable response of people living in that village, which came under the domain of that particular khap. Women participation in the khap panchayats administration is negligible. Women are considered inferior to man and they are not allowed to become representative of khap panchayats (Sangwan, 2008).

According to the information given by people associated with the khap and written references about the khap exist since historical times. Its origin can be traced back to the Vedic period but it was found highly active in medieval period. The factors, which are responsible for the long period survival of khap panchayats because these panchayats do not involve any money, less time consuming, they directly negotiate the settlement between both parties and they act as an important agency of social control (Sangwan, 2008). In recent time khap panchayat has become a burning and popular issue in media because of the some extremely controversial decisions, which violated the human rights of individuals.

Hence it is interesting to study that inspite of increasing development, level of education, modernisation; still the society is trapped in old traditions and customs of caste and religion. Despite the existence of unbiased judicial system, some societies of the country still follows the rules of traditional caste based panchayats.

Objective of the Study

On the basis of existing literature, the following objectives have been framed for the study:

- To discuss about the khap panchayat and their role in inter-caste/inter Religion love marriage in India.
- To highlights some of the issues related to inter-caste/inter-religion love marriage and how the laws of khap related to these issues are different from the laws of Indian government.

Judicial Status of Khap Panchayats

Khap panchayat has no legal authority, their decisions are not executed by law but still they implement the rules very strictly for maintenance the old traditions and customs. These unconstitutional bodies are basically responsible for administering social justice for its people and it takes unilateral and indisputable decisions on multiple issues like social transgressions, marriage, offence, property rights etc. These khap panchayats in Northern India works as a self-proclaimed courts of caste lords, in a village with full lawfulness and authority among the sections of their caste. These illegal assemblies are gathered on the basis of caste lines and considers themselves powerful with authority, they deal with objectionable matrimonies issues and give the decisions against personal liberty. Some illogical statements are also been given by these panchayats about marriage, which does not have any relevance in present time. According to Sube Singh, a khap representative "boys and girls should be married by the time they turn 16 year old, so that they do not stray. This will decrease the incidents of rape." Another khap member also gave the statement that "as soon as the children attain the age of puberty, it is natural for them to have sexual desires but when these are not fulfilled, they stray, so there should not be any minimum age limit for marriage" (NDTV, October 7, 2012).

The Supreme Court of India had declared these unconstitutional panchayats 'illegal' on April 19, 2011 and the court also demanded a strict criminal action against those people, who are doing barbaric activities like honour killing in the shade of these panchayats. The Supreme Court of India also compared khap panchayats with 'Kangaroo courts' where justice is meted out without any regard to judicial process of the country (The Indian Express, April 20, 2011). Despite these things, the terror of these illegal bodies are continue in the life of people living under the areas of khap panchayats.

Khap Panchayat and Inter-caste/Inter-religious Love Marriage

Caste system and religious discrimination is a barrier in the progress or development of India. In the Indian society it is the deep-rooted problem from centuries. Caste and religion also plays a major role in the selection of mates in marriage. Marriage is considered as a most important social custom and socially supported union, which involves two or more individuals. Inter-caste/religion marriage refers to, when two people from different castes/regions or social groups get married. In many societies, this type of marriage is considered against the social traditions and customs. Indian orthodox mindset could not imagine marriage beyond the same caste, community or religion. According to their conception, marriage is only possible in the same community and caste (Das *et al.* 2011). According to National Family Health Survey round three, in India total 9.9 per cent inter-caste and 2.1 inter-religion marriage happened, in which the proportion of inter caste marriage is 11.6, 17.3, 8.6, 2.3 per cent and the proportion of inter-religious marriages is 2.2, 1.9, 1.3 and 0.7 per cent in khap dominated states Delhi, Haryana, Uttar Pradesh and Rajasthan (IIPS, 2007).

There are many factors such as urban residence, education level, employment in modern occupation etc. The other factors, which contribute to the changing trends in the marriage pattern, are urbanisation, modernisation and globalisation.

Inter-caste/inter-religious love marriage and marriage in same gotra are against the laws of khap panchayat. In khap related community love is considered as a social crime. From the khap panchayat perspective, getting married in other caste or religion is a shameful activity for the couple's family and for their community from which they belong. If any couple goes for inter-cate/inter-religion love marriage, then the khap may impose heavy fine on their families and may close their *hukka-pani* in village (boycott them from society in which they live). Sometimes khap also kills the couple on the name of honour, who goes against the khap panchayat's rules of marriage, this is called honour killing. Honour killing refers to the murder committed by family members and the people belonging to the concerned caste/religion of family members. (Sadiq and Khan, 2015). A study conducted by National Commission for Women (NCW) has suggested that around 600 people may have fallen victim to honour killing between 2005 to 2010. The study by NCW also shows that out of the 326 cases of conflict surveyed so far nationwide,**72 per cent were because the couple crossed caste barriers and only three per cent were because the couple were from the same gotra (Times of India, July 07, 2010).**

The khap panchayats pursue the people of their area that how their children can humiliate to their families by their act and what they have to do to protect the honour of their family. So in most of the cases family members themselves kill their children on the name of honour. The first major case, which attracted attentions towards the khap panchayat decision on inter-caste marriage was Mahrana killing in 1991. Marana is a village of northern Indian state Uttar Pradesh, where a middle class girl belonging to jat community named Roshni run away to get married with a boy named Vijendra, who belongs to former untouchable caste. The village people caught both of them and one of their friend, who helped them to run away. The panchayat ordered to hang them with tree and burn alive, in the next morning all of the three were burnt alive to death in front of whole village. The khap panchayats also harass couples and also their families for getting married in other caste. One of the case of harassment reported by couples in Rajasthan in 2012 after doing inter-caste marriage. According to the couples, the members of the caste council in their village force them to vacate the shop that they were running, rendering them completely jobless (Times of India, July 1, 2012).

The rules and regulations of khap panchayat violate the human rights of individuals. In India constitution guarantees right to life and personal liberty of its citizens in Article 21, according to this, every person of the country has the rights to life, dignity, liberty, choice etc.

In case of marriage, according to Indian law, every person who has attained the age of 18 years in case of female and 21years in case of males has the right to marry according to their will. Even the Hindu Marriage Act, 1955 also does not prohibit the inter-caste/inter-religious marriage.

Reasons for Khap Involvement in Marriages

The decision of the khap panchayats about any issue depends upon the type of issue, the nature of fault, community feeling and unity between different khaps. There could be many reasons, responsible for khap being so strict on the marriage issues. Some of these reasons are discussed below -

- The first reason is the strong deep-rooted caste and religion system in society, which make them stick to the tradition of not marring outside the caste and religion.

- The second reason is the mindset of the people living in that particular society, who are still against the right of choice in marriage. These people are trapped in old traditions and customs and they are not ready to accept the marriage outside from caste or religion.
- Third reason is the lack of governance. In Indian society, in spite of the strict laws against inhuman decisions of these panchayats still they are functioning openly and violating laws and orders of the country. Indirectly a number of politicians also support these khap panchayats and silently approve to their illicit activities because they consider that these khap panchayats are their vote-bank.

Here are some views of politicians about khap panchayats, which shows that how they indirect support these illegal bodies. The former Chief Minister of Haryana Bhupinder Singh Hooda feels that khap panchayats are as 'NGOs' and a part of Indian culture (Times of India, February 7, 2014). According to the Chief Minister of Delhi Arvind Kejriwal - khap panchayats are the social instruments that serve 'cultural purpose' to our country. The present Chief Minister of Haryana Manohar Lal Khattar had said that khap rulings are justified as they are only trying to maintain Indian traditions and culture in the state (One India, October 23, 2014).

- The other factors are traditional value system, community feeling, cooperation and the feeling of *bhaichara*, which gives the strength to this unconstitutional body (Sangwan, 2008).

Conclusion

The views of khap panchayats on marriage issues are strongly binding from old traditions and customs. When any person takes decision of getting married against the khap panchayats rules then the reaction of panchayat changes in to violence. These unconstitutional bodies not limiting the choice of youth in getting married to the person of their choice under moral pressures but also are creating the fear in them and their families (Gupta, 2014). Although the Government of India as well as Supreme Court has issued certain guidelines and made strict laws against those, who violets the rights of individuals but despite all these judicial laws, these panchayats are functioning fearlessly and the terror of their rules exist in the mind of the people, those who are living in khap governing areas. The main reason of the increasing power of khaps is the support of politicians, which promote it in a positive sense. With the change of time, advancement of technology, urbanisation, education, modernisation and globalisation there is need of bringing changes to khap panchayats also. This problem could not be solved, till the caste and religion discrimination remains deep-rooted in the mindset of people. For stopping the feudal and barbaric practices of khaps, strong legal provisions are needed and there is also a need of changing mindset of people about caste and religion then only all the peoples of khap governed areas could live with dignity and could enjoy their liberty.

References

- Das, K., Das, K. C., Roy, T. K., and Tripathy, P. K. (2011). Dynamics of inter-religious and inter-caste marriages in India. Washington DC: Population Association of America.
- Gupta, J. (2014, July). Caste, Culture and Khap: No Honour, Only Killings. *International Journal of Research in Humanities, Arts and Literature, 2*(7), 39-48.
- International Institute of Population Studies (2007). *National Family Health Survey (NFHS-3)* Mumbai.
- Kachhwaha, K. (2011, December). Khap Adjudication in India: Honouring the Culture with Crimes. *International Journal of Criminal Justice Sciences, 6*(1), 297-308.
- Kumar, A. (2012, January). Khap Panchayats: A Socio-Historical Overview. *Economic and Political Weekly, XLVII*(4), 59-64.
- Madsen, S. T. (1991). Clan, Kinship, and Panchayat Justice among the Jats of Western Uttar Pradesh. *Anthropos*, 351-365.
- NDTV. (2012, October 7). Haryana Khap panchayats says marry them young to avoid rape cases.
- One India. (23 october, 2014). Haryana's new CM supports Khap; had blamed women for rising number of rapes in India.
- Rana, P. K., and Mishra, B. P. (2013, June). Honour Killings-A gross violation of Human rights and Its Challenges. *International Journal of Humanities and Social Science Invention, 2*(6), 24-29.

- Sadiq, S., and Khan, A. (2015, January). Khap panchayats in india: precepts and practices. *International Journal of Current Research, 7*(1), 11753-11757.
- Sangwan, K. S. (2008). Khap Panchayats in Haryana: Sites of Legal Pluralism. In K. Kannabiran, and R. Singh, *Challenging The Rules(s) of Law: Colonialism, Criminology and Human Rights in India*. SAGE Publications India Pvt Ltd.
- Singh, M. (2014, November). Harmonious Coexistence of Khap Panchayat and a Gram Panchayat- A Case Study of Village Danoda Kalan. *Indian Streams Research Journal, 4*(10), 1-8.
- Singh, R. (2009, August). Feudal roots. *Frontline, 26*(17).
- Singhal, A. K., Malik, I., and Malik, A. K. (2013). Khap Panchayat and Personal Laws in India. *Researcher, 5*(2), 39-43.
- Sunita, and Yudhvir. (2013, July). Khap Panchayatas : Changing Perspectives. *Asian Journal of Multidimensional Research, 2*(7), 14-20.
- The Indian Experss. (2011, April 20). Inter-caste marriages in national interest: SC.
- *Times of India. (2012, July 01)*. 'Couple Harassed for Inter caste Marriage'
- Times of India. (2010, July 07). Now, honour killing rocks TN: Father attacks daughter.
- Times of India (2014, February 07). Bhupinder Singh Hooda equates khap panchayats with NGOs.
- Tiwari, A., and Nirala, C. (2014, December). Khap Panchayats-Retrograding Avatar of the Moral Police. *Indian Journal of Legal Philosophy, 2*(4), 303-312.
- Vishwanath, J., and Palakonda, S. C. (2011, December). Patriarchal Ideology of Honour and Honour Crimes in India. *International Journal of Criminal Justice Sciences, 6*(1), 386-395.
- Yadav, B. (2010). Khap Panchayats: Stealing Freedom? *Economic and Political Weekly, 44*(52), 16-19.
- Yakkaldevi, A. (2014, Feb). Inter-religion and Inter Caste Marriages in India. *Research Direction, 1*(8), 1-8.

Index

N

O

P

Q

R